Bernardino de Sahagún

Portrait of Bernardino de Sahagún, by Cecil O'Gorman, courtesy Dionisio Pérez Jácome.

Bernardino de Sahagún
First Anthropologist

MIGUEL LEÓN-PORTILLA
TRANSLATION BY MAURICIO J. MIXCO

UNIVERSITY OF OKLAHOMA PRESS : NORMAN

OTHER UNIVERSITY OF OKLAHOMA PRESS BOOKS
BY MIGUEL LEÓN-PORTILLA

Aztec Thought and Culture: A Study of the Ancient Nahuatl Mind
Fifteen Poets of the Aztec World
Pre-Columbian Literatures of Mexico
Time and Reality in the Thought of the Maya

Publication of this book is made possible through the generosity of Edith Kinney Gaylord.

LIBRARY OF CONGRESS CATALOGING-IN-PUBLICATION DATA

León Portilla, Miguel.
  [Bernardino de Sahagún, pionero de la antropología. English]
  Bernardino de Sahagun, first anthropologist / Miguel León-Portilla ;
translation by Mauricio J. Mixco.
    p. cm.
  Translation of: Bernardino de Sahagún, pionero de la antropología.
  Includes bibliographical references and index.
  ISBN 978-0-8061-3364-5 (cloth)
  ISBN 978-0-8061-4271-5 (paper)
    1. Sahagân, Bernardino de, d. 1590. 2. Aztecs—History—16th century. 3. Franciscans—Mexico—Biography. 4. Missionaries—Mexico—Biography. 5. Ethnologists—Mexico—Biography. I. Title.

F1231.S33 L4613 2002
972'.02'092—dc21
[B]
                                                            2001053465

Originally published as *Bernardino de Sahagún: Pionero de la Antropología,* © 1999 Universidad Nacional Autónoma de México.

CONTENTS

ILLUSTRATIONS

Illustrations are from the author's collection unless otherwise noted.

EDITORIAL NOTE

To enhance readability in the quotations and extracts from the works of Bernardino de Sahagún and other authors, we have modified the punctuation to reflect modern usage. In other stylistic matters (e.g., capitalization), we have retained the style used in the original manuscript.

The translation of the main portion of the manuscript follows modern American conventions regarding punctuation, capitalization, note and reference format, and other stylistic matters. Inadvertent typographical and factual errors that appeared in the original Spanish version of this book have been corrected wherever possible.

BERNARDINO DE SAHAGÚN

INTRODUCTION

Bernardino de Sahagún lived nearly ninety-one years, from 1499 to 1590. He spent one-third of those years in Spain and two-thirds in Mexico. The years in Spain were formative. Those in Mexico he dedicated basically to the tasks of evangelization because, above all else, he was a Franciscan missionary.

Nonetheless, in his work among the people of Nahua stock, he did not limit himself to teaching the Christian message, preaching, administering the sacraments, and celebrating the divine services. He held two other tasks to be indispensable. One was to write works in Nahuatl for the instruction of converts. The other, the one that has brought him the greatest celebrity, consisted of undertaking research on those who were being proselytized by him and his brothers in religion.

In his research, he proceeded with a methodology considered to be the precursor of modern anthropological field technique. Assisted by his former native students who were fluent in Nahuatl, Spanish, and Latin, he conferred with elders and other learned men, who, by sharing their books of paintings and pictorial representations, provided him with a vast collection of testimonies on the most varied aspects of their culture. These testimonies, which were obtained in several locations, transcribed by his students, and subsequently compared among themselves, were the object of Fray (Brother, Friar) Bernardino's protracted attention. After gathering a corpus of linguistic information and pondering the content of the various collections of testimonies, he set himself to organizing them into several categories, focusing on three basic themes: those concerned with the gods, religious beliefs, and religious practices; those dealing with "human things"; and those concerned with facts of nature. This work was an entrée for his linguistic interest, which was directed to "bring to light the vocabulary of this language [Nahuatl] with its proper and metaphoric meanings" as well as the various ways in which the "phrasis" is constructed in this tongue.[1] Finally, after having devoted several years to this enterprise, he divided the greater portion of what he called his "writings," which is to say his texts, into twelve books, with chapters and paragraphs in keeping with European practice. In this manner, he produced a work in which he brought together pictures and testimonies in Nahuatl, supplemented by a paraphrased, that is nonliteral, version in Spanish, augmented on occasion by his own thoughts. This bilingual opus is known today as the *Historia general de las cosas de la Nueva España* (General history of the things of New Spain; also called the *Florentine Codex*), now preserved at the Medicean-Laurentian Library in Florence, Italy.

Bernardino de Sahagún's contribution has been an object of study for many scholars, but it has not been studied in its entirety. One example of what has not been accomplished is a detailed comparison of the Nahuatl texts, gathered at various times and places, with the version that he prepared in Spanish. This would reveal the procedures he adopted to present the results of his investigations to potential European readers.

CRITICAL ASSESSMENTS

There have been different assessments of Sahagún's work from several points of view, in particular, the Nahuatl texts he had

had transcribed on the basis of their oral versions and the native codices. The assessments address both the purposes that guided his research and the critical value of the testimonies he collected. While the friar's merits and the significance of those testimonies have been pondered, his contribution has been judged in other ways. Although for many his work is that of a pioneer of anthropological research, for others his work is vitiated at its root. The argument is adduced that his investigations were directed toward the goal of identifying what he characterized as the idolatrous ideas and practices of the Nahuas in order to eradicate them. In that light, one recalls what he expressed about his approach as a physician who is incapable of

> effectively prescribing the medications for the patient without first knowing from which humor or from which cause the illness stems. . . . Preachers and confessors are the physicians of the soul; in order for them to cure spiritual illnesses, it behooves them to have experience with spiritual remedies and diseases. . . . Nor is it wise for the ministers of this conversion to carelessly state that among these people there are no other sins than drunkenness, theft, and carnality. . . . The sins of idolatry and of idolatrous rites and superstitions have not disappeared altogether. In order to preach against such things, and even to be aware that they exist, it is necessary to know how they were practiced in the time of their idolatry. Thus, in order for the ministers of the Gospel who will succeed those who arrived first . . . not to find occasion to complain about the former, for having left in the dark the things pertaining to these natives of New Spain, I, Fray Bernardino de Sahagún . . . , have written twelve books about the divine things, or rather idolatrous, human and natural things of this New Spain.[2]

Several of his writings included in the Spanish version of his *Historia general,* such as the one entitled "Refutation" and another entitled "The Author's Exclamation," bespeak his zeal to eradicate

idolatry. In the former, he forcefully attacks the principal deities
of the Nahua pantheon with expressions such as this:

> We are also aware, from your own testimony, that your
> ancestors worshipped and held the Devil to be a god, whom
> they called *Tlaloc* or *Tlaloc Tlamacazqui*. . . . In honor of this
> Devil and of his cohorts, they held a great feast . . . in which
> they killed children on the hilltops.[3]

As though upon being confronted with such practices, he
wished to exculpate the natives, he turns, as do other religious,
to the idea of satanic intervention: "The horrendous cruelty they
committed . . . deceived by the demons, enemies of humankind,
and having persuaded themselves that it was they who brought
the rains."[4] The reference to the devil also appears in the "The
Author's Exclamation" that Sahagún included after the text about
the first feast called *Atlcahualo*:

> It is a lamentable and a horrible thing to see that our human
> nature should have come to such a low and opprobrious
> state, that the parents, at the behest of the Devil, should kill
> and devour their children. . . . The fault of such cruel blind-
> ness . . . should not be imputed as much to the cruelty of the
> parents, who did so shedding copious tears and with great
> pain in their hearts, as to the most cruel hatred of our most
> ancient enemy, Satan. . . . Deprive him, Oh Lord, of all his
> power to injure![5]

And yet (as has been noted by some students of Bernardino's
works), he was to lament many years later, around the year 1585,
the fact that, despite his arduous labors to expose the idolatries of
the Indians in order to more easily identify and extirpate them,
many had survived. The reason for this was that the first friars to
arrive in Mexico had stated that in a few years "this people had
come to the Catholic faith of the Roman Church, that there was
no need at all to preach against idolatries because they had truly
left them behind."[6] Such a deception was due, according to Saha-

gún, to the fact that these friars and others who had followed them had not been concerned with acquainting themselves with the beliefs and idolatries of the Indians. For that reason he states,

> For this matter to be rectified, it is necessary for the confessors to be acquainted with the idolatrous rites that the latter [the Indians] formerly practiced in their sacraments as well as in their sacrifices and superstitions.[7]

After enumerating the many idolatrous beliefs and practices that, in his opinion, had survived until then (1585), he adds,

> Many still hold to the aforementioned errors, that is to say, all those who still have the idolatrous faith stuck in their craw. And in the book that follows [*Art of Divination*], there are many idolatrous errors contained therein, to which they still adhere and believe in, those who still have faith in the gods of old and in the ancient ceremonies. . . . For this very reason, I shall avail myself of this book for those who are once again setting out to convert the idolaters.[8]

Is it possible to imagine, in light of all this, that Sahagún considered at his advanced age (he was nearly eighty-six years old when he wrote the above) that his work had been of little advantage and entirely futile? Furthermore, what is one to think of all that he collected in his research? Was it invalidated by his stance on exposing the idolatries, which he considered to be inspired by the devil? Sahagún was a man of his time. Although he was educated in the Renaissance atmosphere of the University of Salamanca, in his own mentality there persisted medieval vestiges that were difficult to eradicate.

CONTRARY JUDGMENTS

It must have seemed a grave matter to Bernardino that, whereas many friars showed little appreciation for his work, some came to express contrary judgments among themselves against it. Many declared (as have some recent scholars and nonscholars) that all that he collected was too far from being a testimony of the ancient culture to be accepted as authentic. Sahagún, who was familiar with this type of criticism, answered them in the prologue to Book IV of his *Historia general:*

> It will be seen very clearly in this book that what has been affirmed by some detractors that everything written in these books, preceding and following this one, are fictions and lies, they speak ruled by passion and are liars, because what is written in this book cannot fit into the mortal understanding of a human being to fabricate, nor can any living man invent the language that is in it.
>
> And any knowledgeable Indian, if asked, would affirm that the language is their ancestors' own and proper to the works they produced.[9]

In a paradoxical contrast with this, although many friars had ignored Bernardino's contribution, there were others who considered it dangerous, believing that it preserved idolatrous beliefs and descriptions of the ancient rites. They felt obliged to denounce it before the Council of the Indies. The consequence of this was that Philip II, by royal order in 1577, commanded Sahagún's papers to be confiscated and remitted to Spain to be scrutinized. In compliance with that order, Sahagún forwarded a portion of his papers but held on to the rest.

The outrage of his opponents would have been even greater had they read some of the headings that Sahagún had affixed to several chapters in Book VI, which his "detractors" held to be fictions and lies. Regarding several prayers in honor of Tezcatlipoca, which he transcribed there, he declared, "It is a prayer in which they make use of beautiful metaphors and turns of phrase."[10] In a similar vein he remarked of another, "It contains very delicate imagery."[11]

Had they occasion to read it, what Sahagún wrote concerning the advice of Nahua parents to their daughters would have provided even greater affront to his opponents: "These two talks, because of the language and style in which they are expressed (*mutatis mutandis*), would be of greater profit spoken from the pulpit than many a sermon preached to the boys and girls."[12]

As can be seen, in his zeal to penetrate the culture of the Nahuas, Bernardino came to be interested in it and to appreciate it, in and of itself. Without intending it at first (because his intention was to uncover idolatries in order to eradicate them), he came to perceive in the culture he was studying human values that he deemed worthy of admiration. Furthermore, in cases such as the speeches and the traditional form of education among the natives (to give just two examples), he held those values to be morally superior to their European analogues.

Sahagún's life was replete with paradoxes: this I wish to make clear from the outset. Curiously, as I have already hinted, the varied and even contradictory valuations made of his life and work in his day have continued up to the present. These stem, above all, from a lack of knowledge of his goals as a Franciscan missionary, but also from ignorance concerning the changes he underwent in his assessment of extremely important facets of the native culture, a consequence of his protracted contact with it. To these valuations may be added the critical stances that question the authenticity of at least some of the testimonies collected by Sahagún. There has been no lack of those who have written books to prove that the narratives he gathered from the lips of the native elders, witnesses to the Conquest, were his own invention derived from his reading of biblical and medieval texts.

A new book by Walden Browne, titled *Sahagún and the Transition to Modernity*, was published while my book was being translated into English. Equipped with what is offered as an arsenal of epistemological weapons, Browne, in an extremely critical attitude, asserts that

> after Sahagún's brief concession to using the lifewordly experiences of Nahua informants to gather his material, he

retreated into what is a decidedly unmodern systematization of his newfound knowledge. The original information was no longer tested against the world, but rather tested against itself in an attempt to smooth over internal discrepancies.[13]

Browne's assertion, however, is negated by Sahagún himself in his prologue to Book II of the *Historia general*. Sahagún declares that he had checked the original information about the Nahua world with three different groups of knowledgeable Nahuas, a procedure that differs from testing the original information against itself:

> Thus the first sieve through which my works were sifted was the people of Tepepulco; the second, the people of Tlatelolco; and the third, the people of Mexico [City].[14]

Browne ends his book with an ambivalent statement:

> Sahagún stands in the threshold of knowledge because his experience with the Nahuas tested the limits of a knowledge that was primarily defined through *memoria*. It is misleading, however, to interpret Sahagún as a foundational figure of modern knowledge.[15]

Explaining what he means by "a foundational figure," Browne adds,

> The notion of a foundational figure assumes a complete or near-complete rupture with the past, but this kind of rupture with the past was the last thing that Sahagún intended.[16]

At the very beginning of the present book I have emphasized that Sahagún was "above all a Franciscan missionary." At the end of this book, however, I present facts that support the assertion that Sahagún was a pioneer of anthropological research, even though "he did not break with his own past" as a Franciscan missionary. In this respect I believe that my book challenges the claims that Walden Browne makes in his book.

In writing here about Sahagún's life and work, I have striven, to the extent that I have been able, to remain objective. I have taken into account the works and opinions of several Mexican, Spanish, German, North American, French, Italian, Dutch, and other scholars, who for many decades now have turned their attention to the topic that occupies us here, though they have not managed to encompass in an exhaustive manner Sahagún's truly complex work, nor have they managed to translate everything from the Nahuatl language that he includes in it.

THE COPIOUS CONTRIBUTIONS ON SAHAGÚN AND HIS WORK

Sahagún's works, though they were the rather transitory object of a few studies and scholarly advances in the sixteenth century and at the beginning of the seventeenth, subsequently fell into oblivion for a very long time. His principal writings ended up scattered in many places, mostly in Spain and Italy. In Mexico, only a single part has been preserved. These main works were used by such figures as Philip II's court physician, Dr. Francisco Hernández, who visited Mexico between 1571 and 1577. An examination of his several works reveals that in some places he copied what Sahagún had said and in others he took it freely into account. This is obvious in his *Antigüedades de la Nueva España* (Antiquities of New Spain).

The very first notice on Bernardino and his work was left to us by the Franciscan chronicler, Jerónimo de Mendieta, in his *Historia eclesiastica indiana* (Ecclesiastic history of the Indies), which was completed toward the end of the sixteenth century but remained unpublished until 1870. Bernardino's work was also mentioned by Juan de Torquemada in his chronicle of chronicles, *Monarquía indiana* (Monarchy of the Indies), which appeared in

1615; beyond copying what Mendieta had written, he included numerous fragments from what Sahagún had gathered. Worthy of special mention is what he used from these when writing on the Conquest. In a parallel manner, though without mentioning Sahagún, the royal chronicler Antonio de Herrera, in his *Decadas del Nuevo Mundo* (Decades of the New World), took into account his testimonies about that confrontation.

I shall make mention of another three authors who also profited from Sahagún's writings. These were the chronicler of Chalco-Amecameca, Chimalpahin Cuauhtlehuanitzin, who eulogized Sahagún's work; the Creole Juan Suárez de Peralta, who wrote on the history of New Spain; and the Jesuit Horacio Carochi and his *Arte de la lengua mexicana* (Grammar of the Mexican language; 1645), in which he adduces as examples some Nahuatl texts from Bernardino.

After that limited use, Sahagún's work was to be remembered only by people such as the Franciscans Nicolás Antonio in his *Biblioteca Hispana Nova* (New Hispanic library; 1672) and Agustin de Vetancourt, who in his *Teatro mexicano* (Mexican theater; 1698) noted that he had in his possession Sahagún's *Vocabulario en tres lenguas* (Trilingual dictionary; Nahuatl, Latin, and Spanish). In the eighteenth century, Juan José de Eguiara, in the *Biblioteca mexicana* (Mexican library), and a native of Veracruz, Francisco Xavier Clavijero, in his *Historia antigua de México*, only mention Sahagún and his writings.

It was a happy occasion when in 1783 the royal chronicler Juan Bautista Muñoz rediscovered in the Franciscan monastery of Tolosa (Navarre) a copy of the Spanish text by Bernardino entitled *Historia universal de las cosas de la Nueva España* (Universal history of the things of New Spain), the existence of which had been mentioned in 1733 by Fray Juan de San Antonio in his *Biblioteca universal franciscana* (Franciscan universal library). Based on that copy, which subsequently was passed on to the Royal Academy for History in Madrid, the first two editions of Sahagún's *Historia general* (originally titled *Historia universal*) were published in the nineteenth century. Although the two figures who brought these editions to light were cognizant of the hisotriographic significance of the work, they nevertheless had other interests in their respective efforts. One editor, the Oaxacan Carlos María de Bustamante, had ardently participated in the movement that culminated in the independence of Mexico. When he published his edition of the extant copy of Sahagún's *Historia general* in 1829 and 1830 (as he had done with the works of other chroniclers), he offered it as a valuable testimonial of the ancient indigenous culture. He intended to set it up as a priceless legacy, in contrast to what was Spanish in origin, with which Mexico should sunder all ties.

The other early editor of the *Historia general* was the Englishman Edward King, Lord Kingsborough, who had undertaken the great enterprise of publishing, in nine large volumes, a series of native codices and testimonies under the title *Antiquities of Mexico*. His life, which resembles a tragic novel, took a turn for the worse with regard to this undertaking when he landed in prison because of his inability to pay the cost of its publication. The English lord was motivated by the desire to publish the most authentic testimonies of Mexico's Indian past but was also compelled by a belief that others before and after him shared. Kingsborough, who was of Jewish ancestry, was inclined to believe that the American Indians, and in particular those of Mexico, descended from the Lost Tribes of ancient Israel. What Sahagún had written, it seemed to him, supported that thesis; consequently, it must be made known.

If Bernardino's work is complex in its many aspects, so is the story of its rediscovery, study, and publication. There were several distinguished scholars at the end of the nineteenth century and in the first decades of the twentieth century who contributed greatly to lauding the significance of his contributions. The first to call attention to the figure and work of Sahagún was Alfredo Chavero, who in 1877 wrote a relatively brief biography about him and, with it, indicated at the same time the testimonial riches of his work. Somewhat later, in 1880, the Frenchmen Edouard Jourdanet and Rémi Siméon translated into French and published in Paris the first version of the *Historia general* to appear in a European language other than Spanish. Interest grew, and in 1885 José Fernando Ramírez, meritorious historian and ill-fated politician, demonstrated in an article that the Franciscan's work encompassed much more than the *Historia general* published by Carlos María de Bustamante. It is fitting to recall as well that several years before (1858), an Italian, Bernardino Biondelli, had published in Milan an *Evangelarium* and an *Epistolarium* (collections of the Gospels and Epistles from the New Testament) for the Sundays of the year in Nahuatl, with a parallel text in Latin, which he attributed to Sahagún.

Even more revealing were the contributions of Joaquín García Icazbalceta, Francisco del Paso y Troncoso, Daniel G. Brinton, and Eduard Seler. Thanks to them, one can ascertain much more clearly the substance of Sahagún's contribution. García Icazbalceta, in collaboration with Paso y Troncoso, wrote about Sahagún in his *Bibliografía mexicana del siglo XVI* (Mexican bibliography of the sixteenth century), which first appeared in 1886. Aside from describing the sole work that Sahagún was able to publish (*Psalmodia christiana* [Christian psalmody] in 1583), García Icazbalceta was the first to reveal accurately the genesis and breadth of the Franciscan's work. Daniel G. Brinton gave early evidence of its riches with his edition and English rendition of the twenty sacred hymns collected by Sahagún. As if to highlight the value of these texts, Brinton brought them to light in Philadelphia in 1890 under the rather extravagant title *Rig Veda Americanus: Sacred Songs of the Ancient Mexicans*.

At about the same time (1890), the German scholar Eduard Seler began his series of contributions on Sahagún in an influential work in which he presented Nahuatl texts, with their translations, on the "regalia and attributes of the gods." With this publication, Fray Bernardino's work became an object of attention for other non-Spanish Europeans, as had occurred shortly before with the French edition of the *Historia general*. Seler continued publication of other texts collected by Sahagún (1892, 1899, 1904, 1927, . . .); in addition, he profited from them in his commentaries on the codices as well as in other works.

Francisco del Paso y Troncoso carried out a great salvage operation with far-reaching implications. He had been of great help to García Icazbalceta, as can be ascertained by referring to two quite lengthy communiqués that Paso y Troncoso addressed to him in 1884 (published for the first time in 1982 and 1983). Paso y Troncoso, who was interested in making available to scholars the oldest documents that preserved Sahagún's Nahuatl texts, undertook the task of reproducing them in facsimile. His efforts bore fruit with the appearance in the capital of Spain (1905–1908) of four large volumes, including the ones known to us today as the *Códices matritenses* (Madrid codices) of the Royal Palace and the Library of the Royal Academy for History. With this edition, it became easier to approach the oldest documentation, the major portion of which was in Nahuatl and on which Bernardino had relied to write his *Historia general*. The latter, in Nahuatl and Spanish, had been included in the so-called *Florentine Codex* because of its having been found in the Medicean-Laurentian Library in Florence after many different avatars. The works of García Icazbalceta, Siméon, Jourdanet, Brinton, Seler, and Paso y Troncoso cleared the way for the task, as yet unfinished, of completely appreciating and taking advantage of all that was achieved by Bernardino.

Given the abundance of works that have been produced up to the present, it is neither possible nor pertinent to offer here even a summary index of these. For that reason, we shall deal only with the most relevant ones.

It is of some interest to highlight the pursuit of these studies in Germany. We owe to Walter Lehmann (1949), Leonhard Schultze-Jena (1950–1952), and Eike Hinz (1978) editions of several texts from the *Códices matritenses* and others. Several monographs may also be mentioned, among them one (1978) dealing with the forms of thought as the object of epistemological analysis in the Nahuatl texts from Books IV and VI of the *Historia general.*

In Mexico research on Sahagún was reinitiated in the work of Alfonso Toro (1924) and Wigberto Jiménez Moreno (1938 and 1974). To the latter we owe a penetrating analysis of the successive orderings with which Sahagún progressively structured the totality of the materials in his *Historia general.* This analysis was included in a new (1938) edition of the *Historia general* prepared by Joaquín Ramírez Cabañas. In the same manner, Jiménez Moreno published (1974) a translation of the texts treating the cycle of feasts of the twenty-day periods of the Nahua calendar. Another edition of the *Historia general,* still in keeping with the Tolosa manuscript, is owed to the Venezuelan Miguel Acosta Saignes (1946), who enriched it with extensive analytic indexes and pertinent bibliographic references.

Thanks to Angel María Garibay K., Fray Bernardino's person and work attracted new forms of attention. In his *Historia de la literatura náhuatl* (1953–1954), he reserved a rather prominent place for them.[17] Somewhat later (1956) he published another edition of the *Historia general,* in which he included the Nahuatl version of Book XII, *The Conquest,* along with other texts. He also provided openings in two volumes for Sahagún's testimonies regarding the *pochtecas,* or itinerant merchants (1961), and for the *Twenty Sacred Hymns* (1958).

The students of Garibay—Miguel León-Portilla, Alfredo López Austin, and Thelma D. Sullivan—proceeded further with the study and translation of other Nahuatl texts included in the *Códices matritenses* (1958, 1969, 1971, 1972, . . .). For the first of these, the book of the *Coloquios* and the *Doctrina christiana* (1986), León-Portilla edited a facsimile and included a paleography and a Spanish version. Furthermore, his exploitation of the testimonies collected by Sahagún may be seen as an innovation because he described Nahua culture in a series of monographs of a historical nature. There is ample evidence for this in *La filosofía náhuatl* (Nahuatl philosophy; 1956), *Antiguos mexicanos* (1961), and other books by León-Portilla, as well as in works by Alfredo López Austin, Víctor Manuel Castillo, and others. López Austin's studies have dealt with Sahagún's research methodology and his contributions on medical and educational matters (1974, 1975, and 1985). It is also of interest to mention the bringing together by Ascensión Hernández de León-Portilla of ten significant studies on Sahagún and his work (1990 and 1997). Luis Villoro (1999) reveals a subtle insight from the perspective of a philosopher in his demonstration of the manner in which Sahagún penetrated the culture of the "*Other*," as far as was compatible with his faith as a Christian missionary.

The excellent facsimile edition of the three volumes of the *Florentine Codex*, realized under the patronage of the *Archivo General de la Nación*, occupies a prominent position among the works on Sahagún. With it, scholars have ready access to this precious manuscript. We owe a description of the contents of this codex to José Luis Martínez (1982). Another facsimile is one of the *Brief Compendium of Idolatrous Rites*, forwarded by Sahagún to Pope Pius V. This edition was prepared by María Guadalupe Bosch de Souza (1990). Pilar Máynez Vidal's contribution dealing with the linguistic aspects of the *Historia general* is worthy of mention here (1989).

Another stride forward has been the publication of the Spanish text of the *Historia general*, no longer based on the belated manuscript of Tolosa but on the *Florentine Codex*, just as Sahagún had it copied. We owe this feat (in three editions: 1982, 1988, and 1989) to Alfredo López Austin and Josefina García Quintana. A parallel work was brought out in print in Spain by Juan Carlos Temprano (1990). It can be affirmed, thanks to the above and to the several facsimiles I have mentioned, that it is now relatively easy to access the most significant portions of Bernardino's work.

In the United States, there was also a growing interest in Sahagún's works. In 1932 Fanny R. Bandelier translated into English the first four books of the *Historia general*. A place of distinction is due to the *magnum opus* by Arthur J. O. Anderson and

Charles E. Dibble, editors, paleographers, and English translators of the *Florentine Codex*, the final presentation of the *Historia general* in Nahuatl and Spanish. The work of these scholars, which appeared in twelve volumes between 1950 and 1982, constitutes a milestone in this field. Anderson and Dibble have also published numerous articles dealing with Sahagún. To Anderson especially, we owe the edition of the previously unedited text of Sahagún's *Adiciones y apéndice a la postilla y ejercicio cotidiano* (Additions and appendix to the commentary and daily exercise; 1993), along with an English version of the only work Sahagún ever saw in print, the *Psalmodia christiana* (1993). Among other North American Sahagún scholars, the following deserve mention at the very least: Howard F. Cline (1971 and 1973), Henry B. Nicholson (1973, 1974, and 1988), John B. Glass (1978), and J. Jorge Klor de Alva (1980, 1982, and 1988). Thanks to these works, it may be said that in their country "Sahagún has come into vogue." The posthumous contribution of a former student of Garibay and León-Portilla is also important: I refer to Thelma D. Sullivan and her paleography and English translation of the Nahuatl text of what Paso y Troncoso referred to as the *Primeros memoriales*, which is to say the oldest texts collected by Sahagún. This work, which appeared in 1997, followed the facsimile reproduction of the same manuscript in 1993. With the publication of both editions, these valuable testimonies became accessible.

Sahagún and his work have not been absent from Spain. Manuel Ballesteros Gaibrois offered a description, folio by folio, of the contents of the *Códices matritenses* (1962) and later a biography of Bernardino (1973), with which we shall deal shortly. Likewise, Jesús Bustamante García, in addition to several other studies, published in 1990 *Fray Bernardino de Sahagún: Una revisión crítica de los manuscritos y de su proceso de composición* (Fray Bernardino de Sahagún: A critical review of the manuscripts and the process of their composition), which sheds new light on the matter announced by its title.

The list of contributions dealing with Sahagún as a topic is impressive indeed. Despite the few invidious "detractors" whom Bernardino had while alive and subsequently in modern times (let us recall that there is no valuable person or thing that has not been attacked), works of appreciation and utilization of what he achieved continue to be extremely numerous. I mention only a few produced elsewhere. The results of the research carried out by the Frenchman Georges Baudot on previously slighted aspects of the biography and works of our friar are amply acknowledged (1969, 1974, 1982, . . .). From the Italian Giovanni Marchetti, we have a pertinent study entitled "Toward a Critical Edition of Sahagún's Manuscripts" (1983). Furthermore, the Netherlander Rudolf van Zantwijk, who had taken account of several of Sahagún's testimonies in his works (1982, . . .), has published a version of Book XII of the *Florentine Codex* in Dutch (1991).

There are also many anthologies of studies on the Franciscan and his complex and rich body of contributions. One such anthology was prepared and published by Munro Edmonson (1974), who gathered together the conference papers delivered by specialists from many countries at a colloquium on Sahagún, which convened in Santa Fe, New Mexico. Another anthology was prepared by J. Jorge Klor de Alva, Henry Nicholson, and Eloise Quiñones Keber (1988), containing work mostly by North Americans. The anthology edited by Ascensión Hernández de León- Portilla (1990 and 1997) has already been mentioned. It is clear that Bernardino still has the power to bring scholars together many years after his death.

THE SAHAGÚN BIOGRAPHIES

It can be affirmed that in many of the works that I have cited, it is not only the achievement but also the person of Fray Bernardino that is the object of appreciation. This is especially the case in what Joaquín García Icazbalceta wrote about the friar in his already cited *Bibliografía mexicana del siglo XVI*. Aside from studying with great acumen the process of preparation of Sahagún's *Historia general*, he has left us, in a concise synthesis, what can be considered the first modern biography of the Franciscan, whom we acknowledge today as the great pioneer of anthropology.

Well into the twentieth century, there have been four biographies, properly called, on Sahagún. The first of these, imbued with affection toward the scholarly friar, we owe to the expatriate Spaniard residing in Mexico, Luis Nicolau D'Olwer. It appeared in 1952, was translated into English by Mauricio J. Mixco, and was published in 1987 with a foreword by Miguel León-Portilla. Its title is quite unassuming: *Fray Bernardino de* Sahagún *(1499–1590)*. Nicolau D'Olwer wished to make it clear from the outset that he wrote about him because

> "Sahagún stands out [as the] creator of anthropological research methodology and [the] prime authority on the Aztec culture and religion."[18]

He organized his biography into eleven chapters. The first nine, written with great concision and quite readable, present the course of Fray Bernardino's life from his childhood up to his last days in Mexico. Nicolau D.Olwer joins the literary style of one writing a biographical narrative with a historian's scholarly technique.

The last two chapters depart from the biographical focus and deal with the analysis of Sahagún's methodology, the ideological foundation of his work, and his stance toward the realities of New Spain, in which context he worked. The book concludes by reconstructing the long process of exhuming (rediscovering and studying) the *Historia general* and what is implicated by it, that is to say, tracing the several manuscripts in Nahuatl as they are being transformed into the Spanish version. Nicolau D'Olwer notes, without yet being familiar with Nahuatl,

> It is not a literal translation, rather it is an abbreviated interpretation of the Nahuatl text. . . . At times, Sahagún inter-

rupts the translation, departs from the "letter," as he calls the original text; we might say that he confronts it and, carried away by his religious zeal, he execrates idolatry and its rites. In such moments, as well as in certain digressions and in the prologues, in sum, whenever Sahagún speaks for himself, we recognize his personal style: calm, unencumbered, sober.[19]

It is the first extensive biography of Sahagún. Even though its author obviously could not take into account some quite significant contributions (those which I have already mentioned that appeared after 1952), it maintains a prominent position among Sahagún studies. It was also an opportune indication of what remained to be studied if the great contribution of this Franciscan was to be fully realized. Today, a half century after its publication, we see that some of the goals insightfully set by Nicolau D'Olwer have been achieved.

Conceived for a different purpose, *Vida y obra de fray Bernardino de* Sahagún (Life and work of Fray Bernardino de Sahagún), by Manuel Ballesteros Gaibrois, appeared in 1973. The author reasoned that "after [Nicolau] D'Olwer's book, no one should attempt a new biography of the Franciscan; rather, they should quite simply reproduce it, re-edit it."[20]

Ballesteros Graibrois explains the motivation for his work: "to make known one of the high points of Spanish science, unknown . . . to almost everyone, especially in Spain."[21] In other words, his intention was to publicize, for the purposes of both knowledge and acknowledgment, the contribution by one who, in his opinion (one shared by many), should be considered as the founder of anthropological learning in the New World.

Ballesteros Gaibrois uses as his point of departure a summary of the cultural and social realities of the "Old and New Worlds at the moment of contact." Like Nicolau D'Olwer before him, he divides his exposition in two. The first part treats the life of Sahagún himself, though it also makes mention of his research into the Nahuatl world. The second limits itself to what he refers to as "Bernardino de Sahagún's science and work." Briefly it can be said that this study is a work of popularization, though by someone who had first approached the figure of this friar and the rich trove of Nahuatl testimonies collected by him as they related to work on his doctoral thesis. His study compares favorably with Nicolau D'Olwer's work in that the latter, because he had no knowledge of the indigenous language, could not directly approach the Franciscan's "writings."

Bernardino de Sahagún, *primer antropólogo en Nueva España (siglo XVI)* (Bernardino de Sahagún, first anthropologist in New Spain [sixteenth century]) is the title of a biography published in 1986 by Florencio Vicente Castro and J. Luis Rodríguez Molinero.[22] Greatly influenced by the two works described above, it also establishes a division between the course of Bernardino's life and the gestation and culmination of his *Historia general* in Nahuatl and Spanish.

It is a clearly estimable work and a new form of celebrity for Bernardino and his work. Though the authors have no knowledge of Nahuatl nor of the wealth of codices and other sources, with their work they have contributed to sparking interest in Spain in the significance and even the mention of Bernardino de Sahagún.

THE BIOGRAPHY I OFFER HERE

Bearing in mind all of these contributions, it behooves us to inquire about what the present biography contributes. Though it maintains a link to the one I published in Madrid (1987),[23] I can affirm that it is a different work. In the former, I provided a more detailed description of the settings (Spain and Mexico) in which Sahagún lived as well as certain little-known aspects of his work. Beyond this, I aimed to highlight his active role in research regarding the ancient culture of the indigenous peoples of New Spain.

The present new biography of Bernardino (I reiterate that it is in many ways very different from its predecessor) has been enriched in two ways. First, I take into account the contributions made by scholars who have attended to Sahagún and his work in the last decade. Second, I describe in greater detail the settings in which Bernardino's life unfolded in Spain and Mexico. In contrast to the aforementioned biographies, in this one I establish no separation between an approach to the life of Bernardino and the long process of gestation of his works, in particular of the *Historia general*. In this biography I include testimonies, some originally in Nahuatl or Latin, that have previously been either neglected or discounted entirely. I should add that I also consider and evaluate critical assessments that have been made of Sahagún's research methods and of the value of the texts he gathered. I present these assessments not exactly in an apologetic manner but rather in an objective search in the light of a critical review.

Despite the extensive research that has been done on Sahagún and his work, one is obliged to reiterate that the latter has by no means been explored or made public in its entirety. To a certain degree, Bernardino himself is responsible for this. His writings are complex, not only because of the diversity of their subject matter—linguistics, Christian doctrine, and pre-Hispanic culture—but also because of the essence of their complexity—the fact that, for various reasons, he was obliged to redo virtually all of his writings, at times redesigning his original conceptualization and plans, and at others, editing them, enriching them, and in final accounts, modifying them.

Bernardino himself gives us an account of these changes and purposes in the reflections and diverse annotations he weaves in here and there throughout the *Historia general*. Thanks to this, and to a lesser degree to other chronicler friars and to documents that mention the *Historia general*, I shall attempt to dig more deeply into his thoughts and feelings, into his zeal to come to grips intellectually with the indigenous culture. A certain ambivalence arose in his sentiments through his confrontation with the latter.

He stated that he proposed to investigate the "human, natural, and divine things" of ancient Mexico, but, immediately correcting himself, he emended "or better said, the idolatrous things."[24]

As he penetrated more deeply in his search for and identification of the "sickness of idolatry," he began to feel himself captivated, not just by the mysteries and richness of the native language, but also by the very culture of those Mexicans "among whom wise men, rhetoricians, virtuous and courageous people were regarded highly . . . , most devout before their gods, most zealous regarding civic matters, and most urbane among themselves."[25]

He set out as a missionary friar to detect the sickness of idolatry. Enthralled by the object of his studies, he progressed until he had developed his own research methodology, which in modern times has earned him the title of "first anthropologist."

In his own time, however, his pursuits were to call down upon him incomprehension, envy, and open hostility. His was a long life, fruitful, if not to say most fruitful, with regard to his contributions, yet not exempt from peril and even anguish. It should suffice to state that, in his latter years, he would be excommunicated by a Father Commissioner acting in a manner that was as lacking in brotherly love as it was juridically absurd.

I shall deal with his spiritual biography and his magnum opus in this book. What has been revealed up to this point allows us to glimpse the interest in drawing close to his person and his affairs. As for myself, I can state that, for more than forty years, I have dedicated much time to his works. Among other things, I have translated into Spanish some of the texts he collected in Nahuatl.

As a first step, we shall concern ourselves with what his life and education consisted of in the atmosphere of cultural ferment that was Renaissance Spain. Subsequently, we shall address what his encounter with the New World signified for Sahagún, along with the manner in which he first behaved in Mexico in the midst of the major clashes between groups of Spaniards, including the friars of his own order. A major portion of the book will then focus on his principal project, which included linguistic research as well as the conceptual decanting of the Christian gospel and doctrine into Mexican vessels, with the embellishments of a Renaissance perspective in conjunction with millenarian influences. As an essential component of his contribution with respect to those purposes mentioned above, we turn to his rescue of the ancient texts and other native testimonies. Several pages will be devoted to the latter, given that it constitutes the heart of his superlative contribution. With a critical focus, we shall inquire there as to the origin and authenticity of the narratives, oratory, sacred hymns, descriptions of feasts, and other manifestations of the Nahuatl speech forms, responding to modern critiques of what Sahagún had seen transcribed as the fruit of his research.

The latter years of his long life, with its labors, upheavals, and hopes, shall receive the attention they deserve. This study will conclude with an assessment of Sahagún's legacy: his work in the light of what it represented in his time and in our own.

CHAPTER ONE

ROOTS AND EDUCATION IN RENAISSANCE SPAIN (1499–1529)

A truly unusual event occurred in Sanlúcar de Barrameda toward the end of August in 1529. It is a well-known fact that for many years galleons from Seville and Sanlúcar (at the mouth of the Guadalquivir River) had weighed anchor sailing for the so-called West Indies, which is to say, the New World. From there, several ships had departed for the Antilles: Hispaniola, Puerto Rico, and Cuba. Only recently, in the years following the Conquest of Mexico in 1521, had some galleons set sail with a final destination known as New Spain; it lay beyond the islands, on *terra firma*, the mainland of the new continent, a fabulous land with cities and many marvels recently conquered by Hernán Cortés.

Thanks to documents preserved at the Archivo General de Indias (General Archive of the Indies) at Seville, and at the same time by the testimony of the royal chronicler Antonio de Herrera and the Mexican native Chimalpahin Cuauhtlehuanitzin, a report of this event, which took place that year, has come down to us. It occurred just before the fleet departed for Veracruz in the freshly conquered Mexico. As on other occasions, a group of friars was on board, in this instance twenty young Franciscans recruited, we might say, to evangelize the Indians of New Spain. They were led by another older, more experienced friar, Antonio de Ciudad Rodrigo, who, having lived in Mexico since 1524, had returned to Spain toward the end of 1527 with a dual purpose. One was to secure from Charles V the lifting from the Indians of the burden of the many travails and vexations with which they were afflicted. The other consisted of gathering together this very group of missionaries.

Having accomplished both purposes, Fray Antonio was hastening to return with his twenty youthful friars when he was charged with a command by the same emperor. The royal chronicler Antonio de Herrera, in referring to the agreements that the monarch had reached with Hernán Cortés, relates what occurred then:

> And for those Indians whom [Cortés] had brought with him, the Emperor ordered that they be provided with clothes and a few gifts . . . so that they might cheerfully return to their nature [their land]; and he charged Fray Antonio de Ciudad Rodrigo to see to it that they be well treated on route, and who were given monies with which they might purchase holy images and objects of devotion that they might take to their country.[1]

In compliance with that royal order, the necessary funds and whatever might be required for the voyage of those Indians were provided to Fray Antonio de Ciudad Rodrigo. The names of the Indians are to be found in the Archivo General de Indias and in Chimalpahin's account. Among them were those who had already been baptized with Spanish names: Don Martín Cortés Nezahualcóyotl, the son of Motecuhzoma Xocoyotzin with María, the Lady of Copolco, in the *barrio* (city ward) of Atzacualco; Juan Tecayatl; Diego Yacamecatl; Santiago Pilteuhtli; along with eighteen others from Tlatelolco, Tacuba, Tetzcoco, Tlaxcala, Culhuacan, and various locations in the Central Plateau.

The same documentation informs us that the young Nahuas were given shirts, jerkins, capes, breeches, and handsome and colorful hats as well as fine cloth.[2] Fray Antonio himself, with all the funds he received, also paid the ship's master, Pero Díaz, for his own passage and his accommodations on the good ship *Santa*

María. For his part, Chimalpahin corroborates the information on the earlier departure of these natives for Spain with Hernán Cortés. Most of the natives were of the nobility, and Fray Ciudad Rodrigo, in obedience to Charles V's orders, saw to it that they "were well treated" on their return voyage to Mexico. He speaks of this at some length with several addenda in the translation he did of the *Historia de la conquista de México* (History of the Conquest of Mexico) by Francisco López de Gómara.[3]

It was in this manner that they sailed a month later from Sanlúcar on the 28th of August, 1529, with the Indians and friars having first gathered together in Seville toward the end of July. Although it may not have been all that extraordinary an event, it is plausible that the departure of the friars might have aroused the attention of several Andalusians. What would have struck them indeed was the fact that in their company was another group consisting of natives from the remote New Spain. It was said (and it was indeed so) that they had been brought to the peninsula a year before by the conquistador Hernán Cortés.

In so many ways—by their apparel and, in particular, by their demeanor—the presence of those natives, all of them speakers of Nahuatl, would have been an unexpected reality. It is worth repeating that, with the exception of a few Indians who were expert in the ball game and in other forms of entertainment, the majority were members of different branches of the native nobility of Mexico. Among others sailing home, after having been presented at court by Cortés to Charles V and after having visited places such as the royal monastery of Guadalupe in Extremadura, were the aforementioned son of Motecuhzoma and a close relative of his, Gaspar Tultequitzin, as well as Pedro Castañeda Colomochcatl, later to become lord of Chalco and assistant to Viceroy Don Antonio de Mendoza.

Just as we are acquainted with the names of the Mexican natives en route to their homeland in August 1529, we also have some information about members of the group of Franciscans. We shall focus here on one in particular. His name was Bernardino de Sahagún. According to another friar chronicler who knew him, Bernardino would also have aroused the attention, if not of the men of Andalusia, then indeed of the ladies of that land, for "he was a religious gentleman of good presence and face, for which reason, when he was a youth, the older religious would conceal him from the common gaze of women."[4]

Of course, upon sailing with the other friars and the group of Indians, it would have been impossible for those older religious to "conceal him from the common gaze of women." We owe to Juan de Torquemada, who knew him well, a comment that would have pleased those older religious: Bernardino "was so virtuous that nothing perturbed his spirit because, from a very tender age, he had consecrated it to God."[5]

Fray Bernardino, then around thirty years of age, in the full bloom of his life and vigor, must have experienced at that time a profound thrill of anticipation. He was about to set sail for the New World and with him traveled, in addition to his Franciscan brothers, all those natives, who were also young men. After a year's residence in Spain, of necessity their mastery of the language of Castile would have improved somewhat; it was a language they had heard in Mexico on the lips of conquistadors and of other friars. For Sahagún, drawing close to those whose mother tongue was Nahuatl would be the beginning of his long and fruitful American venture.

He was leaving behind forever all that had constituted his life in Spain. Behind him lay his roots and his family; there his body had grown and his spirit matured. In his baggage, he had no trinkets with him that he might trade with the Indians, nor did he bring along any other trace of earthly ambition. His best possession was what he bore in his soul: what he had been endowed with at birth and by his upbringing in the Spain that was experiencing its Renaissance.

THE TOWN IN WHICH SAHAGÚN WAS BORN IN 1499

The man about whom we are speaking left us clear testimony about the town in which he was born in the prologue to what would be his principal work, his *General History of the Things of New Spain*. In it he writes, "I, Bernardino de Sahagún, professed friar of the Order of our Seraphic Father, Saint Francis, of the Observance, native of the town of Sahagún, in Campos."[6] The reference, as can be seen, is to a town, which was never very large but did have considerable importance. The friar alludes to its geographic disposition in noting that it is to be found in Campos, which is to say in the region known as *Tierra de Campos* (Land of Campos), an area of Spain that comprises adjacent districts of the modern provinces of Palencia, Valladolid, and León, between the rivers Carrión and Cea and the hills of Torozos, a region devoted to traditional crops of grain. The Tierra de Campos was a region that had been settled by diverse peoples from time immemorial, as the archeological remains, which are ubiquitous in the area, demonstrate. A more recent testimony of its past is the fact that it was also known as *Campos Góticos* (Gothic Fields) in the kingdom of León.

With regard to the year in which Bernardino was born in the town of Sahagún in Tierra de Campos, he himself made it known when in 1572, upon presenting a denunciation before the Inquisition, he declared himself to be 73 years old.[7] His birth had therefore occurred in 1499. This concurs with what Fray Jerónimo de Mendieta asserted upon Sahagún's death in 1590, when he wrote that "he ended his days at a venerable old age, being over ninety years of age".[8]

Having established both place and date of birth, as must be done in any tightly woven biographical account, it behooves us to uncover as much as we can about the life of Bernardino. This is to be achieved, not as an isolated occurrence, but rather first and foremost within the context of the times and places in which his childhood and youth unfolded in Spain. Of the town of Sahagún in Tierra de Campos, where he was born, it is fitting to mention above all that it had had a long history and no small significance. A settlement named *Camala* had existed there since Roman times. In the vicinity of this town, Brothers Facundus and

Methodius had given their lives as martyrs for their Christian faith. They were later held to be saints, and a Roman settlement was named after the former. Thus, *Sanctus Facundus* was transformed into *Sanfacundo*, and this into *Sanfagún*, until it became *Sahagún*.

Already by the Middle Ages the town of Sahagún enjoyed considerable fame. In *The Guide for the Pilgrim to Santiago de Compostela*, written in the twelfth century, one reads,

> Inde est Sanctus Facundus, omnibus felicitatibus affluens, ubi est pratum in quo hastae fulgurantes victorum pugnatorum ad Dominum laudem infixae, olim fronduisse referetur.

> [From there, one proceeds on to Sahagún, wherein reigns all prosperity and where there is a meadow, in which the resplendent lances of the victorious warriors for the glory of God, planted there, as it is said, had sprouted long ago.][9]

The same *Guide* continues with another fact of considerable interest with regard to this town:

> Item, visitanda sunt corpora beatorum martirum Facundi scilitet et Primitivi, quorum basilicam Karolus fecit.

> [Furthermore, the bodies of Facundus and Primitivus must be visited, whose basilica was constructed by Charlemagne.][10]

The town, as it was when Bernardino spent his childhood and early youth there, exhibited (and to a point still preserves) architectural attestations that recall the passage and settlement of peoples of quite diverse origins. To the archeological remains from Roman times can be added others from the Gothic era that justify the name of this land as *Gothic Fields*. Some elements of *mudéjar* (Islamic) art have also survived there, and some Romanesque traces are also visible, especially at the church dedicated to Saint Tirsus. The churches of San Juan (Saint John) and La Santísima Trinidad (the Most Holy Trinity) also deserve mention, as well as the latter's tall steeple erected in the sixteenth century. Also worthy of attention is what remains today of the monastery of Saints Facundus and Methodius. Its church was built in a style reminiscent of the naves of San Isidoro (Saint Isidore) in León.

In the time of Alphonse VI (1080–1109), who had inherited the kingdom of León from his father and after a clash with Don Sancho, his brother, the king of Castile, went on to become the sovereign of León and Castile, the town and monastery of Sahagún achieved a great blossoming. Benedictine monks from the celebrated French abbey of Cluny established themselves there. The monastery and those living in it achieved for it prominence not only in religious and cultural affairs but also economically and as a center of political power, which, in the feudal manner, exercised total authority in the region. This, as is to be expected, gave rise in many cases to conflicts not only with nobles and burghers but also with the peasantry, who were obliged to pay tribute and provide services to the monastery.

Given the close ties that Bernardino de Sahagún came to have with the Franciscan Order, it is worth mentioning that among the religious structures to be found in Sahagún is the monastery of the followers of Saint Francis, founded in 1257, with its adjoining church known as the *Santuario de la Peregrina* (Our Lady the Pilgrim's Sanctuary). This is in reference to the Virgin Mary as the patroness of those who passed through on their way to Santiago de Compostela. We owe to Fray Francisco Gonzaga, who came to be the minister general of the order, some interesting information on how the monastery was founded:

> When the most devout Abbot of the monastery of the Benedictine Fathers of Sahagún, in view of the great esteem in which he held the Franciscan family, with the approval of his own monks, granted the space requisite for the building of a monastery to a few of its members in the year 1257, these same priests saw to it that the first stone laid down was blessed by the Pontiff, Alexander IV, who reigned in Rome. The latter showed such piety to said brothers that,

aside from this benefice, he sent apostolic letters to the Most Reverend Martín, Bishop of León, so that the first stone blessed by him be placed as a foundation for the entire construction of the church and monastery and that he [the bishop] should also bless it. . . .

Thanks to the aid of the Supreme Pontiff, the monastery that exists today is occupied comfortably by thirty brothers and, with the alms from the diverse faithful, it was completed and its church consecrated in honor of Saint Francis by Bishop Martín. No less significant for its construction was the donation provided by the noble heroine María, legal spouse of that courageous and heroic Spanish military leader, Don Rodrigo de Cisneros, celebrated throughout Castile. For this reason, as much for herself as for her daughter, Juana Rodríguez, noble and pious heroine, she secured their burial there.[11]

From this beginning, the chronicler Francisco Gonzaga reminds us, stems the considerable importance that continued to be bestowed in his own time (the second half of the sixteenth century) on the monastery of San Francisco, founded in 1257 in the town of Sahagún. As we have seen, the town was located on what is known as the Road of Saint James, that is to say, it was a place through which thousands of pilgrims from all parts of Spain and Europe were obliged to travel on their way to where they believed the tomb of the apostle to be, Santiago de Compostela. Such a situation augmented, as is natural, the wealth, along with the religious and cultural influence, of the Benedictine monastery. This accounts for the fact that other ethnic groups also prospered in Sahagún, as is confirmed by the existence of sections of the town known as *la morería* and *la judería* (the Moslem and Jewish quarters, respectively).

A point of interest is that in 1348 in the selfsame Sahagún, under the authority of the Benedictines, who had begun to be regarded as members of the Order of Saint Facundus, a center for general university studies was established. With the passage of time, nevertheless, the predominance of the Benedictines declined. In 1496, three years before the birth of Bernardino, the monastery had lost its full independence and, with such deep Benedictine roots, came under the sway of the monastery of Saint Benedict in Valladolid, with no small loss of its economic and political power. This does not signify that it was dispossessed of its role as an important cultural focus.

It is fitting to recall a single fact in support of the latter. A few years after Bernardino sailed for Mexico, a printing press was set up at the monastery. The result of this was the early and splendid publication of an all-encompassing opus in two volumes, the first consisting of 259 folios printed on both sides; the second contained 104 folios, also on both sides. The work, the fruit of a long-term familiarity with the texts of Aristotle, was prepared by Fray Francisco Ruiz of Valladolid, abbot of the monastery at Sahagún. Written in Latin, its title is *Index Locupletissimus, Duobus Tomis Digestus, in Totius Aristotelis Stagiritae Operae* (Most richly endowed index, in two tomes, on the works of Aristotle of Stagira).[12] This great contribution, the elaboration of which must have required several years (from the time Bernardino was still in Spain), is worthy of being consulted and pondered up to the present day. In fact, it constitutes a model of research, in which not only the authors cited by Aristotle (along with their respective philosophical conceptualizations) but also the ideas of the Master of Stagira are the object of elucidation and cross-referencing in the manner of a modern analytic index of far-reaching proportions.

The historian of philosophy in Spain, Marcial Solana, has commented, by way of an evaluation, on the transcendental significance of this work:

> Not with the great deal that we have advanced in the study of the doctrines of the Philosopher [Aristotle], nor with the most scrupulous editions that have been published on the works of the Stagirite, nor with the multitude of tables and references with which these contemporary editions have

been provided, has any of the value that the monumental *Index* by the abbot of Sahagún had in the sixteenth century been lost; the fact is that Fray Francisco Ruiz managed to compose a truly everlasting work.[13]

This work, a convincing proof of the flowering of Renaissance learning at the monastery of Sahagún, and the elaboration of which required a lengthy process of scholarship on the part of Abbot Francisco Ruiz, was the first edition (*princeps*) published in 1540 by the press installed there.

BERNARDINO'S FAMILY

Such was the town in which Bernardino spent his childhood and early youth. No documentary evidence has been preserved about his family or about its social or economic standing. Only through inference can it be surmised that his parents enjoyed, although not exactly a noble rank, at the very least, comfortable means. Had it not been so, it would be difficult to explain how (before entering the Franciscan Order) Bernardino could have gone to Salamanca for his university studies. Even more unlikely would be the possibility that the son of illiterate peasants would ever think of becoming a man of learning.

Some modern scholars of the work and person of Bernardino have maintained that he came from a family of Jewish converts to Christianity. I cite in this regard what Angel María Garibay K. wrote in his introduction to the *Historia general*:

> Bernardino de Ribeira, his family name, of Sahagún, after his profession of vows in the Franciscan Order, came from a town which he made famous by adding its name to his Christian name. There are vehement suspicions that he came from a family of Jewish converts. It is one of the points that must be cleared up.[14]

It is relevant to note that this issue has not been cleared up to this day. In support of Garibay's hypothesis of a Sephardic origin for Sahagún, one might adduce his citations from the Old

Testament, in which at times he compares the Indians to the Jews, almost always revealing admiration and sympathy for the latter. Without intending either to contradict or to accept the hypothesis of Bernardino's Sephardic origin, we should recall that in the Spain he lived in, it was not uncommon for a multitude of families to have ties with people of Jewish ancestry.

What does seem to call for comment is the attribution to him of the surname Ribeira. This name was first proposed by Jules-César Beltrami, author of a book for a popular public titled *Le Méxique*, which appeared in Paris in 1830. Around 1850 Beltrami had the good fortune of locating an ancient manuscript with a Nahuatl version of the Sunday Gospels and Epistles. His acquaintance with the Italian scholar Bernardino Biondelli made it possible for the latter to publish the manuscript in a splendid edition. In it he attributes to Bernardino de Sahagún the Nahuatl version of these Gospels and Epistles.[15]

In his introduction to the Latin-Nahuatl text, Biondelli accepts what Beltrami had affirmed previously and presents Sahagún as Bernardino de Ribeira. Since Biondelli's edition, other scholars of the work and person of Sahagún have accepted uncritically that his surname was Ribeira. Such was the case with his biographers, Alfredo Chavero (1877), Luis Nicolau D'Olwer (1952), and Angel María Garibay K. (1953–1954).

With keen perspicacity, Arthur J. O. Anderson planted the seed of doubt with regard to this attribution. After many years of intense labor in collaboration with Charles E. Dibble, he had published the English translation of the *Florentine Codex*. Anderson understood that Beltrami's claim about the surname Ribeira (Judeo-Portuguese?) had been introduced without any substantiation. Nevertheless, the same Anderson brought the issue back to life. He confirmed that Wayne Ruwet at the library of the University of California at Los Angeles had communicated to him that he knew of a document in which is registered the name of a certain Bernardino Ribeira, student at the University of Salamanca in 1516.[16]

Because this document has yet to be published, and because it would also be necessary to demonstrate in what context this student was mentioned and whether he could be identified with Bernardino de Sahagún, the issue remains far from resolved. The only thing that can be asserted with any degree of certainty is that Bernardino was born in Sahagún, Tierra de Campos, in 1499 in an environment in which culture thrived within a deeply rooted tradition. People from the many far-flung directions of Europe passed through the town as pilgrims following the road to Santiago de Compostela. There, in the Benedictine abbey of Saints Facundus and Methodius, despite its economic and political decline, works of high culture were pursued, such as the studies carried out on Aristotle by Abbot Francisco Ruiz.

This is the environment from which Bernardino sallied forth to attend the University of Salamanca as a student. We have no precise date for this event. The previously cited Jerónimo de Mendieta states sketchily that, "being a student at Salamanca, he took the religious habit at the Monastery of San Francisco of that city."[17] There, a much broader world of culture than had flourished in his home town would open up for him. If he had already heard anything about the marvels that were being propagated about the New World, he would now have access to more numerous and better-founded reports. Bernardino was proceeding to one of the great centers in which the Spanish Renaissance was truly alive.

BERNARDINO DE SAHAGÚN AT SALAMANCA

The University of Salamanca, founded toward the beginning of the thirteenth century during the reign of Alphonse IX, had become by the second decade of the sixteenth century, when Sahagún registered there as a student, one of the principal centers of culture in western Europe. Among other subjects taught there was philosophy, with practitioners of such renown that one came to speak of a "*Salamanca School*." Among these celebrated teachers were Fernán Pérez de Oliva, who, while still quite young, was named rector of the university, and Fray Alonso de la Veracruz, who years later was to become a professor at the university founded in Mexico in 1551. In theology and jurisprudence, there shown such luminaries as Francisco de Vitoria, Domingo de Soto, Melchor Cano, and Juan López de Palacios Rubio. In the study of grammar and foreign languages, there was none other than Elio Antonio de Nebrija, author of the first *Grammar* and of a *Diccionario latino-español* (Dictionary of the Latin and Spanish languages). There were also specialists in Hebrew, Greek, and Arabic. Those immersed in such studies came to be known as *trilinguals*, a designation that Bernardino de Sahagún was to apply in years to come to his native students at an important college founded near Mexico City. Sahagún's trilinguals were experts in Latin, Spanish, and Nahuatl.

Without wishing to offer here a complete list of all the classes taught at Salamanca during Sahagún's stay, I will at least add that the following subjects stood out: medicine, mathematics, astronomy, music, moral theology, canon law, and history. Bernardino almost certainly attended courses taught by professors in grammar, history, canon law, moral theology, and theology.

In fact, later on in some of his writings, there is evidence of some of the learning he had acquired in these subjects. He would have occasion to allude to history, beginning with the Romans and Greeks. He would evince a strong attraction to the study of languages, above all Nahuatl or Aztec, and would write a grammar and trilingual dictionary, including references to Spanish and Latin. Furthermore, he introduced in many of his manuscripts the morphological analysis of numerous words. As a moralist and theologian, he would issue many judgments and would be consulted in difficult cases. As a philosopher and theologian, he would express his opinions on how to proceed in transmitting the Christian message to the natives, occasionally insisting, on the specific manner in which words should be employed and on the coining of vocabulary for the expression of subtle theological and philosophical concepts.

At the University of Salamanca, as in other famous institutions such as Alcalá de Henares, Valladolid, Barcelona, Valencia, and Seville, one breathed an invigorating air. In particular, the influence emanating from Italy could be felt; it was personified by the presence in Spain of scholars such as Lucio Marineo of Sicily and Peter Martyr of Anghiera. We are familiar with the former's *Epistles* and *De Rebus Hispaniae Memorabilibus* (Of the memorable things of Spain); from quite early on, works by the latter, such as *De Orbe Novo Decadas* (Decades of the New World), began to circulate widely. Thanks to Italian humanists such as these, reports about important recent events were widely disseminated and assessed in the light of day, with an open perspective in search of objectivity.

In their works or in other chronicles and histories, Bernardino de Sahagún, as a student at Salamanca, was able to learn about the taking of Granada in 1492 and its significance. With the consummation of the *Reconquista* (Reconquest) of Spain, the expulsion of the Jews took place, an event that was to shake the entire nation to it roots. In many instances, members of the same family were obliged to separate, the converts remaining behind while the others were marched off into exile, one of several that Spaniards have suffered during their history. About the Catholic monarchs, he also learned much. In particular, he learned of the reforms introduced by Cardinal Francisco Ximénez de Cisneros. Emperor Charles V's ascent to the throne, the monarch born one year after Sahagún in 1500 (to which the latter would later allude several times), must have also left an indelible impression on him.

He must have followed very closely the series of events at the beginning of young King Charles's reign (then as young as Bernardino himself); these would lead to open rebellion, the one associated with the *comunidades de Castilla* (communes of Castile). Those who had taken part in the *Cortes* (parliament), which was convened in Valladolid in 1518, were outraged at the dismissive attitude of the Flemish lords who were present. As a harbinger of a reaction that was already gestating, it was demanded that non-Spaniards be excluded from any civil or ecclesiastic appointments. This rejection was directed in particular at the covey of Flemings, especially at William of Croy, Lord of Chièvres, a member of the clique that surrounded Charles, who soon thereafter, in 1519, was elected emperor.

To the above confrontation was added, on the one hand, the demand that Charles always speak Spanish, and on the other, the denial of the subsidy that the sovereign had requested from the members of parliament convened at Santiago. With the emperor away in Germany, where he was to be anointed "King of the Romans" at Aachen, his decision to leave the Spanish kingdoms in the hands of persons not at all to the liking of the nobility and populace gave rise to a serious outbreak of violence. In 1520, while Bernardino was already at Salamanca, the *Junta Santa* (Holy Junta or League) was organized: Toledo, Segovia, and Valladolid, followed by Salamanca, Zamora, and other cities and towns that joined the movement.

The *comuneros* of the Junta Santa, the insurgents led by Juan de Padilla, seized Tordesillas and Valladolid. The uprising spread like a wild forest fire. Charles V, now emperor, ordered the repression and total defeat of the rebels. This came to pass at the Battle of Villalar on the 23rd of April, 1521. Juan de Padilla, Juan Bravo, and Francisco Maldonado—the latter a representative for Salamanca—fell prisoner and were executed. Five years later, as a consequence of related actions, the bishop of Zamora was also condemned to death.

All of these events, which seemed to cast a pall over the figure of Charles V at the very beginning of his reign, were to become palpable to Bernardino upon his arrival in Mexico, when he was confronted with a violent situation comparable in a certain manner to the one in Spain. This one was provoked by Nuño Beltrán de Guzmán, president of the first *Audiencia* (the Justice Tribunal, which, in the absence of a viceroy, governed New Spain), and affected the old conquistadors, Indians, and friars. With a different perspective after the passage of time and conscious of Charles V's favorable predisposition toward the Franciscans in New Spain, Bernardino would express gratitude toward the emperor and even come to praise him.

It is to be supposed that, as a student at Salamanca, Bernardino remained mindful of events in Spain and had occasion to keep informed about what was happening in more remote environments. From the manner in which he alludes to them in his writings it is plausible that, with respect to the New World, he was already attracted by reports that were spreading about encounters with exotic lands and peoples having different ways of living. Among others who appear in his writings are Christopher Columbus and Hernán Cortés. What he had read about the Conquest of Mexico (more than likely in the letters of Cortés) and what he himself was to witness led him to express some judgmental conclusions about it, such as the following, in which the fate of the Indians is compared to that of the Jews:

> For the curse had befallen them that Jeremiah had fulminated about and called down on Judea and Jerusalem, speaking for God, saying in the fifth chapter, I shall have a people come against you I shall bring them down upon you from afar, a strong people and fierce, an ancient people skilled in war, a people whose tongue you shall not comprehend, nor shall you have ever heard the manner of their speech; in all, a strong and spirited people, lusting for the slaughter. This people shall destroy you, your wives and children, and all that you possess, and they shall destroy all your towns and edifices. This has happened to the letter to these Indians at the hands of the Spaniards; such was their ruin and destruction and of all they possessed, that nothing is left of what they once were.[18]

What Sahagún refers to as "the curse . . . that Jeremiah had fulminated about," seen as a paradigm within which to assess what had "happened to the letter to these Indians," evokes the thought that, probably since his days as a student at Salamanca, he was acquainted with the denunciations of some of the friars who had returned from the New World. Some were vehement indeed, such as those by Antón de Montesinos and Bartolomé de las Casas, who had spoken so strongly before the sovereign about the injuries and destruction of which the Indians were victims.

It is impossible to ascertain precisely which reports from the New World were the ones that most impressed the young Bernardino. It is no vain hypothesis, however, to suppose that because he had been profoundly influenced by the Renaissance atmosphere at Salamanca, his spirit must have resonated upon learning about the positive and negative realities of those immense lands and peoples, which were until recently beyond his ken. He was to express this himself later:

> In the fullness of time ordained by Our Lord, around one thousand five hundred years, to reveal and bring into the embrace of the Church that multitude of peoples, kingdoms, and nations, He moved the heart of the Spanish people to traverse the Ocean Sea to make discoveries toward the West.[19]

Finding himself in the ebullient cultural environment described above, redolent with news of the New World, Bernardino decided to become a Franciscan, as is sketchily alluded to by the chronicler Jerónimo de Mendieta. Though we do not know the exact year in which this occurred, two circumstances may help us to establish with some degree of latitude the moment in which he became a follower of Saint Francis. On the one hand we know, as indicated by Mendieta, that "being a student at Salamanca, he took the religious habit at the Monastery of San Francisco of that city."[20] On the other hand, we know that this would have had to occur some years before his departure for Mexico in 1529 because by then, not only was he a professed friar, but he also had been ordained a priest. It is conceivable, consequently, that his entry into the Franciscan Order took place toward the beginning of the twenties. It was then he concluded his novitiate, taking his vows as a friar and continuing his studies of canon law and theology at the university until his ordination into the priesthood.

If the Renaissance atmosphere at Salamanca and the reports from the New World affected the young Franciscan, which they did, then the circumstances and transformations experienced by the religious order that he had joined would also leave an indelible mark on him. The whole of Christendom was being convulsed at that time by various reform movements, in particular the one led by Martin Luther. In Spain especially, the diverse currents of theological and moral thought, which were also reformist, made themselves felt. It is important to recall the efforts of Cardinal Francisco Ximénez de Cisneros, who, until his death in 1517, struggled mightily to imbue the Spanish church with a new spirit. Also the presence of humanists who were followers of Erasmus of Rotterdam should be noted. With regard to the Franciscans, little or nothing will be understood of their attitudes if we do not consider the transformations that, at least among many of them, were gestating and bearing fruit precisely before Sahagún joined the order. Given that such transformations (reforms and new ideas, some with ancient roots) would mark forever the thought and destiny of the future missionary in Mexico, we shall turn to them.

ERASMIST INFLUENCE AND REFORMIST MOVEMENTS AMONG THE FRANCISCANS

In the last years of the fifteenth century, shortly before Bernardino was born, the winds of religious transformation could be felt. Since 1495 a growing interest in biblical studies was due to Elio Antonio de Nebrija. He who had bestowed on the language of Castile its first grammar was already at work at the beginning of the sixteenth century on what he called the *Grammar of Sacred Letters*. On the 25th of November, 1504, Nebrija assumed the Chair of Grammar at Salamanca upon the death of Isabel the Catholic, who had granted him her protection. Pressing on with his method, which today we would refer to as linguistic-philological as applied to the biblical texts, he attracted to himself the adverse gaze of the Grand Inquisitor Diego de Deza. Nebrija turned to Cardinal Cisneros, who sought the renovation of the church by other paths, including that of biblical scholarship.

Under the protection of the cardinal, Nebrija came to participate, albeit for a short period, in the great edition of what is referred to as the *Biblia políglota* (Polyglot Bible). The cardinal, for his part, kept in view a reform that would need to be carried out in Spain to prevent another radically heterodox one that was developing in the northern lands, particularly in Germany.

At the University of Salamanca, where Bernardino was studying, along with other realities of the Spanish Renaissance, the memory of Nebrija's contributions would leave a lasting impression, in particular his efforts to approach the Sacred Scriptures with the new linguistic philological method. It is also quite natural that in the same environment at Salamanca, reports arrived that in northern Europe, in this case Belgium, Holland, and Germany, similar efforts were being made to draw more closely to the biblical texts in pursuit of a renewal of the Christian life, bringing about purer and more authentic forms.

The works of Erasmus of Rotterdam began to be known in Spain; in fact, Cardinal Cisneros had invited him to visit in order to foster enterprises of mutual intellectual and religious interest. Despite Erasmus's decline of this invitation, his close contact with the Valencian humanist Luis Vives, and above all the spread of his works throughout Spain (one of these, the *Enchiridion*, was translated and published in Spanish in 1524), ensured that his ideas would enjoy great influence in Spanish intellectual circles. Erasmus, like Nebrija, proclaimed the need to enliven a new form of biblical humanism. He concurred with his contemporary, Martin Luther, in granting a fundamental importance to the Sacred Scriptures as a light that would guide Christians, freeing them from falsehoods and corruptions.

For this reason, since 1519, when Luther's rebellious stance became manifest, suspicions and accusations had arisen against Erasmus. The mood in Spain was heated as never before in matters of faith and religious practice. To the persecution of crypto- Jews were soon added the condemnations of those who appeared to be or were suspected of being heretics or laboring under Lutheran influence.

Some time before all of this occurred, other movements of a popular origin had arisen in Spain; these were also directed to transforming the lives of Christians. Such was the case of the *iluminados* (illuminated ones), a tendency that prospered among certain groups of Franciscans. Proclaiming the gift of prophecy, they advocated an array of transformations, such as putting an end to the power of princes and the pope and looking toward the true Jerusalem, where the primitive church had been born. Numerous *beatas* (pious or devout women) appeared in various parts of Spain, announcing their supernatural visions. While all of this was on the rise (the influence of Erasmus and of those acquainted with the doctrines of Luther), the Inquisition was on the prowl, ready at a moment's notice to pounce and punish severely.

It is important to mention here another type of reformist movement that would influence Bernardino de Sahagún after he had become a Franciscan and had been transferred to Mexico. This movement can be adequately evaluated only as it relates to the currents and persons that have already been mentioned. Among these persons was his fellow Franciscan Juan de Guadalupe, whose ideas and actions would come to have a decisive influence on the departure of a group of twelve Franciscans sailing for Mexico in 1524, five years before Bernardino's voyage. He, along with other members of his order since the time of Saint Francis, was motivated by the thought of Gioacchino di Fiore, the Italian mystic and Cistercian monk (1130–1202), and, in a general way, by those who insisted on the capital importance of the Sacred Scriptures, which needed to be harmonized by taking into account both Old and New Testaments. They shared in the belief that absolute poverty, charity, and a certain form of millenarianism with an apocalyptic hue should be used to confront the false and corrupt realities of civil and religious society. Already in the fourteenth century, the so-called Spirituals among the Franciscans had brought new life to the doctrines of Gioacchino di Fiore. Now, at a time when it was known, among other things, that the old world had come into contact with a new one, the Franciscan Juan de Guadalupe was returning to the heart of the ancient message in his own thinking, in a context in which everything seemed in need of transformation. As we shall see, the twelve friars he would send to Mexico would always base their preaching on the book par excellence, that is the Sacred Scriptures. These needed to be made known to the natives, and for that purpose it would be necessary to translate the Scriptures into their languages. This way of thinking would be preserved among the Franciscans in Mexico until, as a result of the Council of Trent, such translations would be prohibited along with generalized access to the Bible.

Fray Juan de Guadalupe secured Pope Alexander VI's authorization to found houses and hermitages in order to live there in pure observance of the Rule of Saint Francis; in poverty, study, and meditation on the Bible; and with eyes open to their own destiny in a Christianity that had to be sublimated. Fray Juan thus built his first hermitage in Granada. However, because of the hostile attitude of the bishop of that city, Juan de Guadalupe's disciples moved to Extremadura. There, armed with new papal bulls, they established four centers in Alconchel, Salvaleón, Trujillo, and Villanueva del Fresno, as well as another in Villaviciosa, Portugal.

Among the Franciscans who, with great ardor, followed in Fray Juan de Guadalupe's footsteps was Fray Martín de Valencia, who would later lead the group of twelve that traveled to Mexico in 1524. Years before, Fray Martín, who had wished to found a monastery with similar purposes, obtained the juridical permission from the Franciscan province of Santiago. He thus managed to build a monastery and chapel, which he named for Our Lady of Berrocal, in the town of Belvís de Monroy in Extremadura. He attracted there several of those who would eventually travel with him to Mexico. According to the testimony of Fray Toribio de Benavente Motolinía, Fray Martín

> built a house near Belvís [of Monroy], where he established a monastery that is called Santa María del Berrocal, where he lived for some years setting such a good example and doctrine that, in that region, they held him for an apostle and everyone loved and obeyed him like a father.[21]

Fray Martín de Valencia, faithful to his ideals, along with the followers of Fray Juan de Guadalupe with their respective monasteries and others who joined them, made up a *custodia*, or consortium of monasteries that were not numerous enough to form a province. This custodia bore the name *Santo Evangelio* (Holy Gospel) in Extremadura. In time, when the custodia had expanded, it was converted into the Franciscan province of San Gabriel of Extremadura.

Fray Martín was its second provincial. Three years later, just months before Cortés launched the final assault on Mexico-Tenochtitlan in 1521, two other Franciscans, Fray Francisco de los Angeles and Fray Juan Clapion (the latter of whom had traveled to Spain with Charles V and three Flemish Franciscans and had known of those lands inhabited by so many people in the New World), obtained from Leo X a bull that permitted a move to Mexico. Because Juan Clapion had died upon his arrival in Spain and Francisco de los Angeles had been elected minister general of the order, Fray Martín decided that he himself would select other friars for the proposed mission to Mexico. Fray Toribio de Benavente Motolinía tells how this came about:

> When the Most Reverend Fray Francisco de los Angeles had become Minister General, who later became Cardinal of Santa Cruz, and he arrived for a visit to the Province of San Gabriel, he convened a chapter meeting at the monastery of

Belvís in the year 1523 on the day of Saint Francis, when it
had been two years that this land had been conquered by
Hernando Cortés and his companions; as they were gathered in the chapter one day, the General called Fray Martín de
Valencia and presented very good reasoning, as he described
to him how the land of New Spain had recently been dis-
covered and conquered, where because of the multitudes of
peoples and their quality, he believed and hoped that great
spiritual fruits would be reaped with such laborers as he,
and that he himself had determined to come personally at
the time he had been elected General, which election had
hindered his passage thither that he had so desired; consequently, he beseeched him to travel with his twelve companions, for if he were to do so, he had great trust in Divine
Bounty that the harvest of conversions of peoples that he
expected from his voyage would be great.

[As for] the man of God who had waited so long for the
Lord to fulfill his desire, anyone can imagine the joy and
cheer that his soul experienced by him with such longed-for
news and how many thanks he owed to Our Lord; he had
accepted the arrival as a son of obedience.[22]

Both Toribio de Benavente Motolinía and Francisco Ximénez
de Cisneros wrote about what happened subsequently in their
Life of Fray Martín de Valencia. According to Cisneros the very
general of the order, Fray Francisco de los Angeles, traveled to
Seville to bid farewell to the twelve who, with Fray Martín, were
about to sail for New Spain. Motolinía, for his own part and as a
witness to all of this, wrote,

And having received the blessing of their elder and Minister General, they departed the Port of Sanlúcar de Barrameda on the day of the conversion of Saint Paul, which that
year fell on a Tuesday. They arrived at La Gomera [Canary
Islands] on the 4th of February, and celebrated Mass in the

Church of Santa María del Paso, and received the body of
Our Redeemer very devoutly, and then set sail again. They
arrived at the Island of San Juan and disembarked in Puerto
Rico after twenty-seven days at sea, which was on the third
day of March, which fell at the midpoint of Lent that year.
They were on the Island of San Juan for ten days, departing on Passion Sunday to arrive on Wednesday in Santo
Domingo. They remained six weeks on the Island of Hispaniola, from which they departed for the Island of Cuba,
where they landed the next day in April. They only stayed
three days on Trinidad. Setting sail once more, they arrived
at San Juan [U]lúa on the 12th of May, which that year was
the Eve of Pentecost; and they stayed in Medellín ten days.
And there, having given thanks to God for a safe voyage,
they came to Mexico and then dispersed throughout the
principal provinces.[23]

It was in this manner that some of those who had founded the
custodia of the Holy Gospel, with monasteries in several places
in Extremadura and Portugal, along with other members of the
same Franciscan Order, had reached Mexico on the 12th of May,
1524. There they caught up with three Flemish friars—among
them, Peter of Ghent—who had preceded them by less than
a year. It fell on them to begin the process of evangelization of
the recently conquered land. As did those who would soon follow them, including Fray Bernardino, who arrived in 1529, they
encountered a living reality that was totally different from the one
that existed in Spain. Little by little they came to know it: some
only in its most superficial aspects; others, like Sahagún, more
deeply after dedicating many years to penetrating research on it.

BERNARDINO, NOW A FRANCISCAN, AND OTHER
MEMBERS OF THE PROVINCE OF SAN GABRIEL

In 1519, at about the same time that the custodia of the Holy
Gospel was being converted into a Franciscan province, Juan de

Church of San Tirso (twelfth century) in the town of Sahagún. Built of ashlar stone and finished in brick. It is in the Romanesque style with Moorish influence and has been referred to as "sahagunino" (Sahagunine).

Church of San Lorenzo (thirteenth century) in the Moorish style.

Franciscan convent and the church known as the *Santuario de la Peregrina* (Our Lady the Pilgrim's Sanctuary), founded in 1257.

Remains of the original south entrance of the Benedictine monastery church of Saints Facundus and Methodius. Today it is an archway under which a road passes.

Monstrance, an extraordinary example of goldsmithery in the former Benedictine monastery in the town of Sahagún.

Façade of the University of Salamanca.

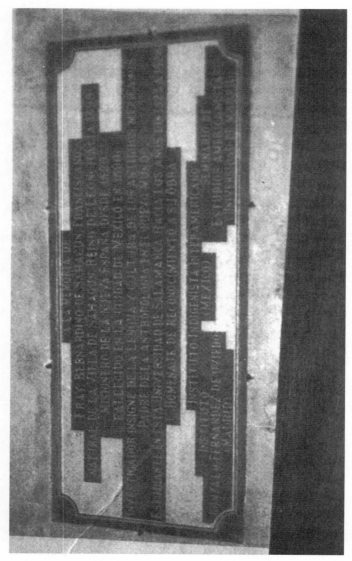

Commemorative stone for Fray Bernardino, set in place on 12 January 1966 in the cloister of the University of Salamanca.

Ruins of the open chapel of Tlalmanalco, state of Mexico.

Plateresque retable of the church of Huexotzinco, state of Puebla.

Mural with figures of the twelve Franciscans who arrived in Mexico in 1524. Cloister of the Franciscan convent of Huexotzinco.

Grijalva, weighing anchor off of Cuba, was exploring a part of the coast of what would come to be known as the Gulf of Mexico. A year later Cortés would land at *Chalchiuhcueyecan*, "the Place of She-Who-Wears-Jade-Skirts," that is, on the shore where the *Villa Rica de la Veracruz* (the Rich Town of the True Cross) would be erected and where until that time, as evidenced by the Nahuatl toponym, the Mother Goddess, patroness of the Nahua peoples, had been worshipped.

The Conquest of Mexico by Cortés was concluded on the 13th of August, 1521. Less than three years later, on the same shores where the Mother Goddess, "She-of-the-Jade-Skirts," had been worshipped, Fray Martín de Valencia landed in the company of eleven other Franciscans, all from the province of San Gabriel in Extremadura.

As has been mentioned above, three Flemish friars had preceded them; sent by Charles V, one of them, so it was alleged, was a relative of his. This lay brother, Peter of Ghent, would come to distinguish himself greatly as an educator of the Indians.

An interpretation of this event provided by Diego Valadés, a friar born in Tlaxcala, is a reflection of Franciscan spiritualism: if one Martin Luther could through heresy separate from the church many thousands of people at that time, another Martin, that is, Father Valencia, would have as his mission to compensate for the loss by attracting thousands of Indians to the true Christianity.[24]

We owe to Bernardino de Sahagún, from circa 1564, a reconstruction of the arrival in Mexico of Martín de Valencia and his companions. He accomplished this by writing down in Nahuatl and Spanish a prototypical reconstruction of *Coloquios* (Colloquies) and dialogues that the recently arrived Franciscans had sustained on religious topics with the surviving learned men and native priests in 1524. The text, charged with drama, provides an example of the confrontation of ideas in the clash between two worlds on Mexican soil. The reconstruction of what very plausibly was said then was made possible for Bernardino by his consultation with other friars, as well as by availing himself

of his own experiences in dealing with the Indians and, as he
indicates, by having before him "old papers and notes" in which
were preserved the memory of such encounters.

Some fragments of the text that Sahagún reconstructed allow
us to experience the drama that he read into the words plausibly
exchanged between the friars and the Indians:

> Thus [the friars] gathered together, convoked
> all the lords and rulers
> who lived there in Mexico.
> "Please you, listen well, beloved of ours,
> those of you who have come here to inform yourselves,
> those of you who have come out together,
> you Mexicas, you Tenochcas,
> you lords, you rulers,
> do us the favor of considering here,
> place within your hearts
> what we are about to expound, to proclaim,
> the word, the message. . . .
>
> "Listen, beloved of ours,
> in truth we know,
> we have seen, and we have heard
> that you,
> not just one but many,
> so numerous are they
> whom you hold to be gods,
> whom you honor,
> whom you serve,
> The sculptures are innumerable
> in stone, in wood,
> that you have fashioned.
> Yet if they were true gods,
> if they were in truth the Giver of Life,
> Why do they so mock the people?
> Why do they ridicule them?

Why do they show no compassion
for those whom they have made?
Why do they also cause you [your gods]
infirmities, afflictions
many, without number?
Thus you know it well. . . .
And thus, day after day,
they demand blood and hearts.
For this reason they are fearsome to the people,
they provoke a great fear.
Their images, their witchcraft,
are black indeed, filthy,
nauseating.
This is how those you have as gods are,
Those you follow as gods, to whom you make offerings.
They are the ones who greatly afflict the people,
who place their filth in them."[25]

The Indians who had listened to what the friars had to say
through an interpreter responded in turn:

When it was concluded, was terminated,
their speech, that of the twelve fathers,
then some of the lords, the rulers,
stood up, greeted the priests
to a small degree, one lip, two lips,
with that they returned the breath, their word. Saying:

"Our Lords, you have striven greatly,
so you have come to this land
because you have come to rule
in your water, your mountain [chiefdom],
Whence?
What is the land of our Lords like
from which you came?
From among the clouds, from among the mists,

you have emerged. . . .
Yet we,
what is it we can say?
Though we act as lords,
we are the mothers and fathers of the people.
Is it the case that here before you
we should destroy the ancient rule of life?
The one so esteemed
by our grandfathers, by our grandmothers,
what they pondered so,
what they sustained with admiration,
the lord rulers?

"And behold, Our Lords,
here are those who are still our guides,
they bear us on their backs, they rule us,
with regard to the service
to those who are our gods,
of those who are worthy of it,
the tail, the wing [the common people]:
the offering priests, those who offer fire,
also those called *quequetzalcoa*.
Wise in the word,
their office, for which they are zealous,
day and night,
the offering of *copal* incense,
the offering of fire,
thorns, spruce branches,
bleeding themselves,
those who look, who are zealous
for the course and orderly functioning of the heavens,
how the night is parceled out.
Those who are looking [reading],
those who relate [what they have read],
those who unfold

the black ink, the red ink [the books].
Those in charge of paintings,
They carry us,
They guide us,
They show us the way.
Those who order
how the year falls.
How the destinies and days
follow their path,
and each of the twenty-day [months].
They are occupied with this,
this is their charge, their duty,
their responsibility, the divine word.
What is known as divine water and fire [war]
this we also deal with,
we are in charge of tribute
of the tail and the wing [the people].
Allow us to gather the priests,
the *quequetzalcoa*.
That we may give them
the breath, the word,
of Our Lord.
In that way perhaps they will
respond, they will answer."[26]

Even more charged with drama were the words of the surviving native priests and learned men who came to respond to the
friars:

"Our Lords, Lords, esteemed Lords!
You have suffered travails,
thus you have drawn near this land,
we gaze upon you, we *macehuales* [humble people],
because you have been permitted to come by Our Lord,
in truth, you have come to rule
your water, your mountain.

Whence? How
have you come here
from the land of Our Lords,
from the house of the gods?
How in the midst of the clouds, among the mists,
from the depths of the vast waters have you emerged?
You, he has made his eyes,
You, he has made his ears,
You, he has made his lips,
the Lord of the near and close.
And now, what, how shall we speak,
how will we raise [it] to your ears?
Are we perhaps something?
Since we are only *macehualuchos* [pitiful little commoners],
we are dirty, muddy,
tattered, miserable, sickly, afflicted.
Since he only allowed [it to] us on loan, Our Lord,
He who is Our Lord,
the edge of his mat, the edge of his seat [power],
where he has placed us.
With one lip, two lips, we respond,
we return the breath, the word,
of the Owner of the close and the near.
From this we have come, from his head, from his hair, we
    emerged,
for this reason, we plunge into the river, into the ravine.
With that we seek, we obtain,
his anger, his ire.
Perhaps we only go to our perdition,
to our destruction.
Or perhaps we have acted in sloth?
Where in truth are we going?
Where shall we go?
As we are *macehuales,*
we are perishable, we are mortal.

Let us not die,
let us not perish,
though our gods have died.
But becalm your hearts, your flesh,
Our Lords,
we shall break open a little,
we shall uncover,
the chest, the coffer, of Our Lord.

"You have said
that we do not know
the Lord of the near and close,
he who owns the heavens, the earth.
You have said
that ours are not true gods.
This is a new word
which you speak,
and we are perturbed by it,
by it we are frightened.
Since our progenitors,
those who came to be, to live on the earth,
did not speak so.
In truth, they gave us their standards of life,
they held them to be true,
they served,
they revered the gods.
They taught us
all their forms of ritual,
their ways of doing reverence to them [the gods].
In that way, we bring soil to our mouths [we swear oaths],
in this way, we bleed ourselves,
we pay our debts,
we burn incense,
we offer sacrifices.
They used to say [our ancestors]

that they, the gods, are whom we live for,
that they deserved us [gave us life].
How? Where? When it was still night.
And they would say [our ancestors]:
that they [the gods] give us our sustenance, our
    nourishment,
all that is drunk and eaten,
which is our flesh, corn and beans,
wild seeds, *chia*.
They are whom we beg for water, the rain,
which causes things to grow on earth.

"And now, are we
to destroy the ancient rule of life?
The rule of life of the Chichimecas?
The rule of life of the Toltecas?
The rule of life of the Colhuacas?
The rule of life of the Tecpanecas?
For it is thus in our hearts [that we understand]
to whom life is owed,
to whom birth is owed,
to whom growth is owed,
to whom development is owed.
This is why the gods are invoked,
are supplicated.

"Our Lords,
Do not do something
to your tail, your wing [people],
which will bring disgrace down upon them,
which will make them perish.
Thus was the education,
the formation,
of the elder men, of the elder women.
Let the gods not be angry with us,
let their fury not befall us,

let us not incur their anger.

Lest, because of this, the tail, the wing,

rise up against us,

lest we suffer upheaval,

lest we lose our senses

if we were to tell them:

'There is no longer any need to invoke [the gods]

no longer a need to supplicate them.'

Calmly, peaceably,

consider, Our Lords,

what is needed.

We can not be at peace,

and surely we do not follow it,

we do not hold that to be true,

even if we offend you.

Here are those

who have charge of the city,

the lords, those who rule.

What they bear, what they carry on their backs,

the world.

It is enough that we have left,

that we have lost, that it has been taken away from us,

that we are impeded,

the mat, the seat [of power].

If we remain in the same place,

we shall provoke that the lords be imprisoned.

Do with us

what you wish.

This is all we respond,

what we answer

to your revered breath,

to your revered word,

Oh, Our Lords."[27]

The text of the *Coloquios* continues with a presentation mostly of the way in which the first twelve Franciscans began the evangelization of the Indians. It is probable that similar dialogues and indoctrinations took place not only in Mexico-Tenochtitlan but also in several other sites, such as Tetzcoco, Tlaxcala, and Huexotzinco, where the Franciscans had begun their evangelization. This renders comprehensible Sahagún's contribution, which displays this as its complete title: *Coloquios y doctrina christiana con que los doce frailes de San Francisco, enviados por el papa Adriano VI y por el emperador Carlos V, convirtieron a los indios de la Nueva España* (Colloquies and Christian doctrine with which the twelve friars of Saint Francis, sent by Pope Hadrian VI and Emperor Charles V, converted the Indians of New Spain). On reconstructing the prototypes of these dialogues, Bernardino sought to leave a testimony of the first activities of the Franciscans who had preceded him.

A mere three years after the arrival of these friars, one of them, Fray Antonio de Ciudad Rodrigo, returned to Spain in order to bring with him another goodly number of young friars predisposed to taking part in the missionary enterprise in New Spain. As we have already seen, he recruited some twenty Franciscans. Among these were two who, while they were still students at the University of Salamanca, had taken the habit of his order and who freely accepted Fray Antonio's invitation. One, a native of Murcia, was Fray Juan de San Francisco. The other, as Mendieta writes, quite learned in divine things, was Fray Bernardino de Sahagún, at that time a member of the province of Santiago de Compostela. As soon as he departed with Fray Antonio de Ciudad Rodrigo, his life and destiny became one with those of the group of friars who, with Martín de Valencia, had already established in Mexico another custodia, which, like the original one in Extremadura, bore the name of the Holy Gospel.

As Sahagún would reiterate in his writings (especially in his *Coloquios y doctrina christiana,* and as he put into practice Nahuatl versions of the Gospels and Epistles), these friars, who had arrived before the Council of Trent, were concerned above all with spreading the divine word, the contents of the book above all books, the Sacred Scriptures.

An eloquent example of this attitude was offered by Fray Juan de Zumárraga, who as bishop-elect, that is, as yet unconsecrated, had arrived in Mexico in 1528 and had brought with him as a traveling companion Fray Andrés de Olmos, who would later distinguish himself as a precursor of the researchers on native cultures and languages. Zumárraga, in his *Doctrina breve muy provechosa* (Brief and very advantageous doctrine), printed in Mexico in 1543, was inspired by Erasmus of Rotterdam, whose principal works he owned. Zumárraga wrote,

> I do not concur with the opinion that states that the uncultured should not read the divine letters in the language the populace uses because what Jesus Christ desires is that his secrets be widely propagated. And so it would be my wish that any humble woman might read the Gospel and the Epistles of Saint Paul. And I say even more: that it please God that they might be translated into all the languages of the world, so that not only the Indians might read them but other barbarous nations as well.[28]

Fray Bernardino would also strive to propagate the divine word, but he would seek to clear the path with a prolonged and probing investigation of the "natural, human, and divine things" related to the culture of the ancient Mexicans.

As we have seen, the friar who had this as his destiny had set sail with his other companions and with the group of Indian nobles who were returning to Mexico in 1529. There, on board the galleon that was about to weigh anchor, he bid farewell not only to Seville and Sanlúcar de Barrameda but also to Spain, forever. With him he took his education as a humanist, his missionary zeal, and his faith in the Word of the Book of Salvation.

CHAPTER TWO

ENCOUNTER WITH THE
NEW WORLD (1529–1540)

As Bernardino himself would write much later, "On leaving Sanlúcar for the Canaries, from there onward, one continues across an extremely broad gulf of the sea [the Atlantic], which reaches to the islands of Santo Domingo."[1]

In two months, after a stopover in the Canary Islands, Fray Antonio de Ciudad Rodrigo, his Franciscan companions, and the returning group of native nobles landed at the port of Veracruz. It is more than probable that, at some point in the voyage, Bernardino and the other young friars had occasion to speak with personages of such distinction as a son of the great Motecuhzoma and other Nahua nobles who were on board. Their conversations had to have taken place in Spanish because the friars had no knowledge of Nahuatl, but the Indians had by then managed to achieve some mastery of the language of the conquistadors through their contacts with Spaniards in Mexico and after their year on the peninsula.

As regards Sahagún, it is plausible that, in view of his linguistic interests, he would have availed himself of the opportunity to learn a little Nahuatl. We can thus imagine him asking the native speakers all sorts of questions in order to render in written form the manner in which nouns were structured, the verbs with their pronouns, and the various particles of the language that composed the lingua franca of New Spain. This being the case, it would seem to be no exaggeration to claim that Bernardino's linguistic research into the Mexican language actually began before he arrived in the land where his destiny lay.

It is also likely that he was able to add the information provided by Motecuhzoma's son and by the other young Mexicas to the information he already had on the culture of the inhabitants of New Spain, derived from his reading of works such as Cortés's *Cartas de relación* (Letters of relation) and from whatever their leader, Fray Antonio de Ciudad Rodrigo, had been able to tell the friars. The Mexicas were perhaps able to relay to him something about their ancient way of life; their cities, temples, and palaces; the greatness of the land; and the variety of peoples, climates, animals, and plants. Whatever Fray Bernardino was able to become acquainted with beforehand would very soon turn into startling reality for him.

NEW SPAIN IN 1529

After they landed in Veracruz, we only know that from there the twenty friars, led by Antonio de Ciudad Rodrigo, headed into the heart of the country. In his *Historia general*, written years later, Fray Bernardino alludes to places and incidents that he surely observed on his way to Mexico City. Among other things, he remarks on the impressive snow-capped summit of the Pico de Orizaba: "There is a mountain called *Poyauhtecatl* [Lord of the Mist], it is near *Ahuilizapan* [Place of Cheerful Waters, which was corrupted into *Orizaba*] . . . ; its summit was snow covered."[2] It seems plausible that some stops were made along the way, especially in places such as Tlaxcala and Huexotzinco, where there were already Franciscan monasteries. Continuing their trek, after days or weeks they arrived in the region of the lakes.

As had happened with Hernán Cortés and his men a mere ten years before, Bernardino de Sahagún and the other friars must have marveled at the extraordinary beauty of this great basin, fringed by mountains covered with forests, a region of splendid light, water, and verdure. Along the shores of the lake lay numerous population centers. Approaching from the south, the great expanse of water could be traversed along the long and narrow causeway of Iztapalapa. If, however, they had first been in Tetzcoco on the eastern shore of the lake, the crossing to Mexico-Tenochtitlan, which was under construction at that time, would have been accomplished by the friars in canoes.

The ancient metropolis, seat of Motecuhzoma's government, had been destroyed as a result of the eighty-day siege, after which it fell into Cortés's hands. At the arrival of Bernardino and those who came with him, the rebuilding of the city continued apace, in accord with a plan drawn up by the architect Alonso García Bravo. We owe valuable information on the manner of the city's reconstruction to a Franciscan brother, Toribio de Benavente, one of the twelve friars who had arrived in 1524, and who had taken on the Nahuatl name *Motolinía*, "he is poor." Motolinía deals with this precisely as he describes the array of misfortunes that had befallen the natives as a consequence of the Conquest. The title he gave the corresponding chapter was "How This Land Suffered from Ten Plagues That Were Much Crueler than Those of Egypt."

The first of these was the smallpox epidemic that decimated the populace in 1520. Eleven years later there was another, a plague of measles. The Conquest decapitated the native leadership, and the epidemics and famines mortally wounded the masses of commoners, the *macehuales*. The *encomiendas* (grants of Indians, who had to pay tribute) were then established whereby, according to the same Franciscan, the oppressors, "do nothing other than give orders . . . ; they rankle and corrupt, with a stench like that of fly-bitten carrion."[3]

Onto these plagues were heaped those of "the great tributes and servitude that the Indians gave" until "with the great fear that they acquired for the Spaniards from the time of war, they would give whatever they had; but because the levies were so constant, they would sell their children and lands to the merchants in order to satisfy them."[4.] Many of those services and tributes fostered the development of agriculture and the breeding of livestock, though mostly to the benefit of the Spaniards.

Another extremely cruel plague was the work in the mines: "To this day, the Indians who have died in them cannot be counted." On slavery, which was allowed in the first years, Motolinía states that "hordes were brought in from all parts of Mexico and were herded like sheep for the branding iron . . . ; they burned them into their faces, in addition to the King's principal brand, because as each one purchased the slave, he would brand him on the face, so much so that the entire face bore the marks."[5]

He describes other plagues in such dark colors that Bartolomé de las Casas, the great defender of the Indians, would have liked to appropriate them to endow his own denunciations with greater force. Among these was the charge of obliging the Indians to carry such heavy burdens that it caused them to drop dead on the roads. This practice, along with slavery, tributes, work, services, famines, and plagues, was the cause of "many a town being depopulated."[6]

Turning once more to what it meant for the Indians to construct a new city on the ruins of the one that had been razed, Motolinía writes this:

> The seventh plague was the rebuilding of the great city of Mexico, in which more people were employed than were in the time of Solomon on the building of the Temple of Jerusalem; for there were so many people involved in the work, or came bearing materials and bringing tribute and supplies for the Spaniards and for those working at the construction sites, that a person could barely squeeze through some streets and roads, though they are quite broad; at the worksites, some were relieved of the beams while others would fall from some high place; others would have structures collapse on them as they demolished one structure in one spot to build another one elsewhere; and the usual

practice at these sites was that the Indians would build at their own cost, seeking materials and paying the stonecutters and quarry workers as well as the carpenters, and if they brought nothing along to eat, they had to fast.

They carried all the materials on their backs; they hauled the beams and large stones with ropes; and because they lacked the skill and had an abundance of labor, a beam or stone that might have required one hundred men was dragged by four hundred; as is their custom, as they carried the materials, as there are many of them, they go along singing and shouting, and these shouts barely ceased night or day.[7]

It is plausible that already by 1529, after nearly eight years of work, the city was in part rebuilt, though naturally there still remained much to be done. Thanks to evidence preserved by the author of *Monarquía indiana* (Monarchy of the Indies), Fray Juan de Torquemada, who published it for the first time in 1615, we know that Sahagún managed to see much of the ruins of the principal native temple in the former city of Mexico. Before we deal with Torquemada's description, it is worth noting that Bernardino may have been able to contemplate a portion of what had been the *Templo Mayor* (Main Temple) and other structures that made up the great sacred precinct in the heart of the metropolis because even today, many centuries later, the archeological excavations that have been underway there since 1978 have uncovered the impressive remains of these great structures. Juan de Torquemada, writing at the beginning of the seventeenth century, upon pondering the sumptuousness of the Templo Mayor, tells us this:

And so that whoever reads this in the future should not think that I speak idly or unrestrainedly . . . , I wish to set before them here the words of Fray Bernardino de Sahagún, a friar of my Order and one of those who arrived at the very beginning of the discovery of New Spain, which was in the twenty-ninth year; he saw this and other temples, and lived through the conversion of these Indians . . . for more than sixty years, and knew their antiquities in great detail, and wrote of many things in their language.

Who, speaking of the beauty, grandeur, and sumptuousness of this most celebrated temple, though it be evil, being a thing of the Devil, writes these words . . . : "There was much to see in the structures of this temple; its painting held much to behold, and I had it rendered so in this City of Mexico, and it was taken to Spain as a thing very worthy of being seen, and [I] have not had it back since. . . . And though it was so beautiful in the painting, the building itself was more so and more captivating."[8]

The fact that Fray Bernardino, shortly after his arrival in Mexico, would be concerned enough to have a painting made of what could still be seen of the Templo Mayor already reveals a character trait of his. He was a man who from the start was interested in understanding the realities of a culture that was so different. The differences, which he encountered at every step, were great indeed as compared to what he was acquainted with in Spain. A land of acute contrasts, ancient native grandeur, destruction, and reconstruction; the opulence of the new masters and of a few of the native nobility; the misery and profound suffering of the masses of Indians—such was the conquered land that assaulted the eyes of the twenty newly arrived young friars.

His Franciscan brothers, who had arrived a few years before, labored there without rest. After the fall of Mexico, the three Flemings arrived. Shortly thereafter came the twelve friars from the aforementioned province of San Gabriel in Extremadura, with Fray Martín de Valencia at their lead. Others would arrive after that, shortly before the arrival of the twenty friars whom Fray Antonio de Ciudad Rodrigo was bringing. It was thus that, in October 1528, Fray Juan de Zumárraga and Fray Andrés de Olmos had disembarked at Veracruz and immediately gone on to Mexico City.

Upon their arrival, there was much for Bernardino and his companions to hear from the lips of those who were already at work on the evangelization of the Indians. Thus, they learned of the establishment of monasteries in locations outside of the city, such as Tetzcoco, Tlaxcala, Huexotzinco, and Tlalmanalco. Surprisingly enough, Sahagún would later write this:

> As with the Dominican Fathers [who began their labors in Mexico in 1526], we were told that these people [the Indians] had come to the Faith so completely, and were almost all baptized and so wholly in the Catholic Faith of the Roman Church, that there was no need to preach against idolatry because they had truly abandoned it.
>
> We took this information to be quite true and miraculous, for such a multitude of people had been converted with such little mastery of the language and with such little preaching and with no miracles having been performed, such a multitude of the people had been converted.[9]

When Sahagún made this statement many years after his arrival in Mexico, he was, as we shall see, of a very contrary opinion to that which he had heard and recalled in the quotation. For the moment, rather than entering into a disquisition on what had been accomplished in the matter of conversions by the year 1529, we will attend to a number of happenings of great significance, which also formed part of the realities that Bernardino and his companions encountered upon their arrival in Mexican lands. The Franciscans found themselves embroiled in these events with rather grave consequences.

DISSENSION AND FACTIONS AMONG THE SPANIARDS IN MEXICO

With these words, Toribio de Benavente Motolinía described the tenth plague that, in his opinion, afflicted the natives in the years after the Conquest. Commenting on what he had meant by dissension and factions, he wrote this:

> The tenth plague was the dissension and factions among the Spaniards who were in Mexico, and it was not the least

of them but the one that greatly endangered the land, bringing it close to total destruction if God had not kept the Indians as if they were blind; these disagreements and factions were the cause of the trials of many Spaniards, some
condemned to death, others confronted and exiled; others
were wounded in their daring, and there was no one but
the friars to impose peace or get in the middle.[10]

In order to understand what Motolinía meant, it is necessary to
recall what had happened in New Spain once the Conquest had
been consummated, that is, during the eight years prior to 1529,
all of which affected the work of the Franciscans profoundly. The
ultimate consequences of these deeds, as lived by Fray Bernardino, would similarly condition his actions. For this reason, it behooves us to linger over these events.

When the metropolis had been captured on the 13th of August
in 1521, Cortés had to ponder the most advisable course of action
to take. This encompassed several possibilities: to transfer the capital to another site and rebuild it there; to prosecute immediately
the conquest of the whole country; to authorize compensation for
the conquerors; to establish a specific form of government; and to
proceed with the Christianization of the natives.

With regard to the first point, it was decided that the city
should be rebuilt in the same place where it had existed previously. The symbol of the former power would thus survive in
its renewed form. As for the expansion of the conquests, Cortés decided very quickly to send some of his captains to various
regions: Michoacán and Colima toward the west; the hot country (today Morelos and part of Guerrero), Oaxaca, Chiapas, and
Guatemala to the south; and from the Pánuco River to the region
of Tabasco on the Gulf Coast, closing in on the Yucatán Peninsula. The expansion to the north would be undertaken later.

Compensation for the conquerors consisted of a regime of *encomiendas,* which is to say, the Indians were turned over to a specific Spaniard for his use, with the proviso that the conquistador-

encomendero (recipient of an *encomienda*) protect them and foster their conversion to Christianity. With regard to the latter, Cortés furthermore requested of the Crown that friars be sent to labor toward the evangelization of the Indians.

The clearly fundamental issue of organizing a specific form of government was resolved in principle when, in 1522, Hernáno himself was named captain-general and governor of New Spain. Functioning in these two capacities, Cortés would guide the new life of the conquered country. One might say that everything unfolded according to his will. In October 1524, the captain-general and governor decided to absent himself from the city in order to punish Cristóbal de Olid in the faraway country that was Honduras. Cortés delegated the governance of New Spain to three surrogates: the treasurer Alonso de Estrada, the accounts manager Rodrigo de Albornoz, and the municipal functionary or *licenciado* (attorney) Alonso Zuazo. The first two, along with the *factor* (agent) Gonzalo de Salazar and the *veedor* (overseer) Peralmíndez Chirinos, had been named by the Crown to oversee the royal interests in the matter of taxation and to monitor the functioning of Cortés's administration.

Thus Cortés departed, confident in the assumption that Estrada, Albornoz, and Zuazo would govern in harmony. Nevertheless, when he had reached Coatzacoalcos en route to Honduras, he received word of conflicts among those he had left in charge of the government. He decided that Gonzalo de Salazar and Peralmíndez Chirinos should return to Mexico City. The instructions that Cortés issued to them gave rise to a hidden antagonism that provoked the first outbreak of what Motolinía would refer to as dissension and factions. Those returning to Mexico City were to verify whether the treasurer Estrada and the accounts manager Albornoz, along with the attorney Zuazo, were exercising their authority in a harmonious and peaceable manner. If that were the case, Salazar and Chirinos were to associate themselves with them. If there was dissension among these functionaries, however, Salazar and Chirinos were to assume exclusive control of the government.

When they arrived in Mexico City, they determined that the circumstances obliged them to take charge of the government alone. In the opinion of the attorney Zuazo, it would be preferable that they all govern together. At that point, dissension broke out. The treasurer and the accounts manager were both put in prison. Somewhat later, news of Cortés's death while on the expedition was rumored. Many of the old conquistadors who held *encomiendas* granted by Don Hernando began to be persecuted by Salazar and Chirinos. Seeking protection, they requested asylum among the Franciscans.

After the conquistadors were dispossessed of their lands, their *encomienda* Indians passed into other hands, the partisans of Salazar and Chirinos. New forms of exactions were applied to the Indians. Motolinía describes as other plagues the calamities that befell them: slavery, work in the mines, and an increase in tribute and personal services. Under these circumstances, it became very difficult for the Franciscans to impart to the Indians the primitive forms of Christianity, as inspired by their own doctrine in the province of San Gabriel in Extremadura.

The tempest was far from being spent. The treasurer Estrada and the accounts manager Albornoz, who had been deposed from the government, attempted to recuperate it. Further conflicts followed. Having given Cortés up for dead, government officials decided to celebrate a solemn funeral in his honor. His properties were immediately put up for sale at auction. Rodrigo de Paz, who, in addition to being chief constable, was a cousin of Hernando and was the custodian of his properties, was then arrested and submitted to torture so that he might reveal what he knew of the whereabouts of the treasures that, according to rumor, Cortés had hidden. The conquistador's cousin suffered a fate similar to that of Cuauhtemoc, the last ruler of the Mexicas, who was executed by Cortés on the trek to Las Hibueras (Honduras). In addition to having his feet burned in such a way that, according to the chroniclers, the fire charred him up to his ankles, Rodrigo de Paz was hanged in the main square.

The Franciscans became embroiled in the conflict, as much for having pleaded before Salazar and Chirinos in defense of the Indians as for having granted asylum to members of Cortés's party. At some time Salazar and Chirinos extracted by force from the monastery of San Francisco some of those who had sought refuge there. Fray Martín de Valencia placed the city under interdict and decided to leave for Tlaxcala with the rest of the friars. The alarm increased in Mexico City, and Salazar opted to surrender those whom he had imprisoned. All of these events were the beginning of the extremely serious upheavals that Bernardino de Sahagún would witness in 1529.

Well into the year 1526, the dissensions had reached such a point that the attorney Alonso Zuazo sent a letter to Cortés urging his return. Cortés hastened his return and arrived in Mexico City in June 1526. His arrival, far from quieting the situation, only gave rise to new tumults. Nearly at the same time, the attorney Juan Ponce de León arrived from Spain as Cortés's *juez de residencia* (the judge who was to preside over the trial until the end of his term of office). The appointments that Cortés had made as governor and captain-general were put on hold, and in spite of the illness and death of Ponce de León and of the succeeding *juez de residencia*, the suspension of authority remained in force. Treasurer Alonso de Estrada took issue with this situation, confronting Cortés with his objections. The latter, wishing to avoid an open confrontation, withdrew to Tlaxcala. While there, he decided to travel to Spain, where he might personally defend his interests, as much against the *juicio de residencia* (judgment) as against the pillaging of property perpetrated against him and the other conquistadors. It was on this occasion in 1529 that, as we have seen, Motecuhzoma's two sons and several other Indian nobles departed for Spain; on their return to Mexico, they would join Sahagún and the other friars on board the same ship.

When confronted by the conflicts that suddenly had grown worse in New Spain, the immediate decision taken by the Spanish monarch proved the truth of the adage "the cure is worse than the illness." Toward the end of 1528, the Crown created the first *Audiencia* in Mexico, to which the judicial and administrative governance of New Spain would be entrusted.

WITNESSES INCREASING DISSENSION AND VIOLENCE

Though it may seem unbelievable, Nuño Beltrán de Guzmán was named president of the Audiencia. For the previous two years, he had distinguished himself by his sinister actions as governor of the northern province of Panuco. This appointment is difficult to explain. Perhaps he was favored in this way because he counted on the support of many of Cortés's enemies who had fomented reports tending to weaken his prestige and power.

Four additional *oidores* (members of the Audiencia) were also appointed. They arrived at Veracruz on the same ship that brought the first bishop, Fray Juan de Zumárraga, and his colleague, Fray Andrés de Olmos. Having settled in Mexico City, two of the *oidores* died of pneumonia not long afterwards. The other two, attorneys Diego Delgadillo and Martín Ortiz de Matienzo, would come to rival in their misdeeds the president of the Audiencia, Nuño Beltrán de Guzmán. The latter was notorious for his actions as governor of Pánuco. Among other things, he had enslaved thousands of Indians, who were then sent on barges to the island of Santo Domingo, where there was a great demand for cheap labor. It is reported that Nuño had traded twenty Indians for a single horse.

Toward the month of October in 1529, when Fray Antonio de Ciudad Rodrigo entered Mexico City with his young missionaries (among whom was Bernardino de Sahagún), the situation was truly alarming because of the corrupt members of the Audiencia and its president. Different reports of what was happening have been preserved: violence upon violence, which threatened to destroy New Spain. The clashes between Nuño Beltrán de Guzmán and Cortés's supporters were numerous. This was also the case, in a special way, between Nuño and the Franciscans, with Bishop Fray Juan de Zumárraga at their head. There is mention of such conflicts in a lengthy letter, which clandestinely, in an almost picturesque manner, Zumárraga managed to get to the sovereign. Likewise, there are other communiqués, such as the one composed by the royal scribe Jerónimo López, as well as two reports with sworn witnesses on what was happening, one initiated by Nuño Beltrán de Guzmán and the other by Fray Juan de Zumárraga.

The accusations, several of which were terrible, included, on Nuño Beltrán de Guzmán's part, an accusation against the Franciscans of wishing to rise up with the natives of the land in support of an independence movement, and similarly several charges of corruption, such as one claiming that some friars had had sexual intercourse with Indian women.

The first accusation was regarding an action of the Franciscan Juan de Paredes. We do not know of this through the information provided by the chroniclers of the order, Mendieta and Torquemada, who quite plausibly did not wish to speak of it. The report originates with a letter from Paredes addressed to Superior Fray Luis de Fuensalida and is also found in a further denunciation.

Fuensalida, for reasons unknown, had punished Paredes. The latter, being familiar with Nuño Beltrán de Guzmán's accusation about the Franciscans' wishing to rise up with the natives to oust the Spaniards, did not hesitate to throw more fuel on the fire. On the 23rd of August, 1529, he appeared before the scribe of the Audiencia to denounce Fray Luis de Fuensalida, Fray Francisco Ximénez, Fray Toribio de Benavente Motolinía, and Fray Peter of Ghent, accusing them of forging a conspiracy with the principal Indian leaders, just as had been done at Nuño's instigation against Bishop Juan de Zumárraga.[11]

The scandal of the case must have undoubtedly perturbed the many who surely learned of it, as much the friars as the secular priests and society in general. Zumárraga, who was not a man who frightened easily, reacted immediately. Fed up as he was, like so many others, with Nuño's and his cohorts' abuses, he lodged counterdenunciations so serious that they provoked the deposition of Nuño in 1530. This sequence of events constituted one of Fray Bernardino's earliest experiences in New Spain. Despite the repeated decisions of the Council of the Indies to limit Indian slavery to very specific cases, Nuño had continued his old practice and had authorized the trade of a great number of Indians. With regard to the *encomiendas*, Nuño's friendship with the former agent Gonzalo de Salazar had induced him to follow Salazar's example by taking many Indians away from Cortés's followers.

The confrontation between the president of the Audiencia and the Franciscans had been started by the exactions of which the Indians of Huexotzinco were victims. The *encomienda* of that place had been granted to Cortés, a circumstance that helps us to understand why Nuño might take special note of it. Hundreds of Indians were obliged to pass between the two volcanoes Popocatépetl and Iztaccíhuatl to descend into the Valley of Mexico with their tributes. Many of these unfortunates lost their lives because of the heavy loads they carried on their backs. Under such circumstances, Bishop-elect Zumárraga spoke frankly to Nuño. The response of the latter was a refusal, saying that the bishop had no reason to be meddling in issues concerning public administration.

Going further, in order to intimidate Zumárraga, Nuño reminded him of what had befallen the bishop of Zamora, who had been hanged when he had leaned in favor of the *comuneros* (rebels) of Castile. Bernardino de Sahagún, who had doubtless been in Salamanca at the time, recalled how the bishop had died; he must have learned of Nuño's threat, that voracious exploiter of Indians, as soon as he arrived in Mexico.

Zumárraga, far from backing down, instigated a reprimand from the pulpit of the president and other members of the Audiencia who were present at Mass for their abuse of the natives. The most implausible event occurred then. As recounted in a letter to the monarch by the conquistador Jerónimo López, who was an eye-witness,

[The *oidor* Diego Delgadillo] arose and, shouting, demanded that [the preacher] be removed from the pulpit, which was done, casting down the friar from the pulpit; this was accomplished by a constable and a certain Villaroel and others who came on their own, cursing him, which was a great offense before God and the church they were in, and it caused a great commotion among the residents of the City of Mexico and the natives who witnessed it.[12]

The friar vicar-general, on orders from Zumárraga, notified the members of the Audiencia that they had incurred an excommunication. The situation worsened when the vicar-general sought asylum at the monastery of San Francisco. Nuño then prohibited any provisioning of the friars who were there. The peace that had thus been won was fleeting. When the excommunication was lifted, Nuño suspended the siege of the monastery.

The abuses of the president and his followers continued to rise. In addition to opposing any intervention by Zumárraga in support of the Indians, extreme instances arose, such as the pulling of two pretty Indian girls out of a school for young natives in order to turn them into concubines; they also profaned the tombs of Indians and Spaniards to seize whatever offerings or objects of value might be found there. The most serious clash occurred when the president of the Audiencia, with an excessive use of force, decided to free from the Franciscan custody two secular clerics awaiting an ecclesiastical trial for their bad conduct. Zumárraga's reaction was to demand their return to him. In order to accomplish this, he walked in procession with the only other bishop in New Spain, the Dominican Fray Julián Garcés of Tlaxcala, as well as other friars and members of the populace. The *oidor* Delgadillo, after an exchange of harsh words, attacked Zumárraga with the thrust of a lance, which pierced his habit.

On this occasion, the reaction was even more energetic. Zumárraga excommunicated the *oidores*, and with the city under interdiction, he moved with his friars to Tetzcoco. It had become an urgent matter to inform the Crown about what was happening. As Jerónimo López, the king's self-appointed informer, recounts with abundant detail, Nuño had taken measures to impede the delivery of any mail going to Spain. We owe to the same Jerónimo López the description of how the bishop managed to have his denunciations reach the king: "With this, he [Zumárraga] secretly shipped the other dispatches, which he had turned over to a Basque, who carried them in a small barrel of [olive] oil [sealed with] wax and wrapped in a slab of bacon."[13]

In that lengthy letter, written on the 27th of August, 1529, Zumárraga describes with a wealth of detail the numerous outrages already alluded to and many more. It can be affirmed that what Zumárraga informs Charles V about in this letter is of great interest for our knowledge of the situation that prevailed in Mexico in those turbulent years of the first decade after its conquest. This is what he wrote in the last part of his letter, making several recommendations to the emperor. Regarding the *oidores* Matienzo and Delgadillo, he states this:

> That Your Majesty see to it that the attorneys Matienzo and Delgadillo be removed from their charges as *oidores* of your Royal Audiencia because, without a doubt, they have two diabolic extremes [vices], as those who knew them in positions of authority in Spain can testify; one [vice] being that they are very greedy, and this greed is so extreme that there is nothing, however convenient it may be for the service to God or to Your Majesty, that they do not twist or neglect for their own particular interest, which is their primary purpose, all else being secondary to it; they prove what I say with their own deeds, in view of how rich they are and what they have hoarded, and with everyone who is in this land; the other [vice] is that in every case they are friends of partiality and uproarious behavior and indulge themselves [that way], as has been clearly demonstrated; with this can be added that they do not enjoy the reputation they ought

to for the positions they hold and for whom they represent, for they constantly deal and eat with low persons from vile occupations, they are loose and lewd with women and subjugated to them in matters of honor and judgment.[14]

At the same time, with respect to the president of the Audiencia, Nuño Beltrán de Guzmán, Zumárraga recommends this:

> The other and principal thing is that Your Majesty, as soon as possible, should send a wise and most trustworthy person to arrest Nuño de Guzmán and these *oidores* to ascertain and investigate the truth of everything that I have said; for if it were a lie, I desire my punishment to be that Your Majesty not believe me anymore and whatever else Your Majesty might decide, of which, through God's goodness, I am certain; and that You should punish them for the evil they have done, so that those who may preside on the Audiencia might fear Your Majesty's justice and not dare to do anything they ought not, especially as blatantly as these have done and continue to do.[15]

Some paragraphs later, he makes specific mention of one of the crimes perpetrated by Nuño and requests that that kind of behavior, which he characterizes as infernal, be expressly forbidden:

> Item: I have it on good authority that after Nuño de Guzmán became governor of Pánuco, twenty-one ships laden with slaves left the port of that province with his permission and at his behest as trade and that he dispatched nineteen thousand more; for the information I have is from their owners, and for this reason that province is so ravaged and in ruins, for there is nothing left to govern there because, in addition to [Nuño] shipping out the bulk of the populace, those left behind flee to the hills for fear of being spotted by them. Your Majesty, for the reverence [owed to] God, send orders that this extraction, so infernally damaging to the

country, cease, and punish such a great felony and bring a timely remedy there, so that this land not [be ruined; the original manuscript is torn here], as Nuño de Guzmán has begun it [its destruction], I beseech Your Majesty's royal conscience.[16]

The denunciations had their effect. The sovereign and his mother, Queen Juana, saw it as an urgent matter to depose the members of that Audiencia and to name others of tested moral mettle. That is how, toward the end of 1530, the following were designated: as president, the bishop of Santo Domingo Sebastián Ramírez de Fuenleal; and as *oidores*, Vasco de Quiroga, Alonso Maldonado, Juan de Salmerón, and Francisco Ceynos. With their arrival, which nearly coincided with Cortés's own arrival from Spain, things would improve in Mexico. As the Mexican educator and prolific scholar, Justo Sierra (1842–1912) has expressed so concisely, "With Ramírez de Fuenleal, a long period of peace commenced in which the Mexican nation began to take shape."[17]

It is fitting to mention that the other members of the Audiencia were all learned and fair-minded gentlemen. One of them, Vasco de Quiroga, would stand out as the builder of utopias. To him is owed the creation of the famous hospital towns, in which the social and economic aspects of the native communities were an object of particular attention. It has been said about Vasco de Quiroga, who was consecrated bishop of Michoacán a few years later, that through his works he made a reality of the *Utopia* of humanist Thomas More, which he so admired.

Not long before the arrival of the members of the second Audiencia to Mexico, Hernán Cortés had returned with the titles "Marquis of the Valley of Oaxaca" and "Captain-General of New Spain." This took place in July 1530. He would remain until January 1540, when he would return to Spain definitively. The presence of the conquistador in Mexico would be quite significant, not so much in the domain of administration and politics, but in the field of exploration of the South Sea and the "Great Island" to the west, which turned out to be Baja California. Cortés was a perennial supporter of the Franciscans. His nemesis, Nuño Beltrán de Guzmán, in one of the several suits he would make—on this occasion against Zumárraga—sought witnesses to testify that

> Fray Juan de Zumárraga . . . is partial to Hernando Cortés, his things, and his servants, and he favors in all he can, publicly and clandestinely, and has it preached from the pulpits . . . , and this is done [for him] by the Franciscan friars, who take sides with and are partisans of Don Hernando.[18]

Zumárraga, who had confronted Nuño in defense of the Indians, as we have seen, brought out evidence in his own favor. For this purpose, he called together a goodly number of well-known people from the incipient society of New Spain. He placed before them a questionnaire in which he asked them to respond to the best of their knowledge and understanding. This information began to be written down on the 11th of July, 1531, before four of the members of the second Audiencia, including Vasco de Quiroga and the relevant scribe of His Majesty's chamber.[19]

The information focused on the behavior of the Franciscans in their capacity as missionaries: among other matters, their attitude in defense of the Indian peoples, the behavior of the members of the first Audiencia, issues of civil and ecclesiastical jurisdiction, attacks on Zumárraga, the violation of the order of asylum, and the attitude of Zumárraga toward Cortés. A topic of particular interest was one dealing with the acquisition by the Franciscans "of the language of the country and whether they had prepared a grammar in it" and the teaching of reading and writing to the young Indians.[20]

Such well-known people as Gil González de Benavides, mayor of Mexico City; *Comendador* (Commander) Leonel de Cervantes; the Dominican bishop Fray Julián Garcés; Domingo de Betanzos and Vicente de las Casas (also Dominicans); bachelors Alonso Pérez and Juan Ortega; the former conquistador who had arrested Cuauhtemoc, García de Olguín; and the clerics Gaspar López,

Hernán Martín, Rodrigo de Torres, and Pedro Sánchez Farfán were among those responding to these and other questions.

As to the questions about the learning of Nahuatl, the preparation of a grammar, and the teaching of reading and writing to the natives—a matter that must be highlighted here—the answers are of enormous interest. They all converge, with slight deviation, in maintaining something that sounds almost startling. Barely ten years after the Conquest of Mexico City and a mere seven years after the arrival of the twelve Franciscans, according to bachelor Alonso Pérez,

> the friars were working on preparing a grammar to learn the language well . . . , and this witness knows that they preached to the natives in their own language.[21]

And, according to Mayor Gil González de Benavides,

> This witness has observed that among said religious there are great tongues [speakers of the native language], and I have seen many youths learning to read and write in the monastery of My Lord, San Francisco, as well as in other houses and monasteries of the region.[22]

Commander Leonel de Cervantes used very explicit words:

> He has seen in the possession of said religious the grammar that they have prepared to learn the language in order to succeed better in the instruction of these natives in the things of our Holy Catholic Faith, and he has seen in the monastery of this City of Mexico, and this witness counted them one day, approximately five hundred and sixty youths; and in the same way, I have also seen great numbers of them in the houses at Tetzcoco and Cuernavaca . . . , and I have observed that many know how to read and write quite well.[23]

It is also fitting to quote, among others, a final declaration, that of the Dominican friar Vicente de las Casas:

He sees that a grammar has been prepared by the hand of these friars for the learning of the language of this country, which some of the friars speak quite well, with which they gather a great harvest among the natives as they proclaim the Gospel literally in their sermons; and there are many of them [natives] who know how to sing the Mass and to chant vespers [by reading them] and all the hours [of the Divine Office], singing them very well without the friars having to intervene.[24]

Bernardino de Sahagún must have witnessed all of this for himself when he had scarcely spent two years in Mexico. He may well have availed himself of that grammar in learning Nahuatl, in the knowledge of which he would excel as perhaps no other. One can also recall that Fray Peter of Ghent, who had founded a school for young Indians as early as 1524, had progressed rapidly in his knowledge of Nahuatl.

For those who have maintained gratuitously that it was not until the forties and fifties of the sixteenth century that Nahuatl was first transcribed in alphabetic script, it is important to highlight the declarations quoted. Also, as regards Peter of Ghent, he wrote to the friars of the province of Flanders on the 27th of June, 1529. He wrote them about what had been accomplished in evangelization among the natives. He added that he had almost forgotten Flemish but that he spoke Spanish, and to prove that he also knew Nahuatl and could write it, he ended the letter with these words:

> Ca ye ixquich, ma motenehua in toteuh, in totlatocauh Jesu Christo, which can be translated as follows:
> "For the rest, I have nothing more to say; may Our Lord God be praised and His Son Jesus Christ."[25]

Just as he must have heard about all of this, it is probable that Fray Bernardino also learned what the witnesses had declared, those who had been convened by the then bishop-elect Zumárraga.

Sahagún, who dealt with him personally on occasions such as the solemn inauguration of the College of Santa Cruz at Tlatelolco, would come to share with him and with the majority of his Franciscan brothers his admiration, without flattery, of Hernán Cortés. This is what the great majority of witnesses had manifested in their testimony about Zumárraga's behavior with regard to that. Sahagún actually mentioned Cortés in various places in his *Historia general*, especially in the Book of the Conquest and other works, such as the *Coloquios y doctrina christiana*. In referring to Cortés, he does so with a great deal of objectivity. Acknowledging Cortés's courage, he also indicates that because of the Conquest, the Indians were afflicted in the extreme, so much so that "they were a shadow of what they had once been."[26]

Cortés's exploration of the Pacific, though it did involve some of the Franciscans who went along as missionaries, would remain outside Fray Bernardino's scope of interest. Thus the last thing he would write about the conqueror would be related to the Conquest and to the arrival in 1524 of the first twelve Franciscans in Mexico. To this he dedicates the last chapter of the second version of the *Book of the Conquest*, which was composed in 1585 when he was quite elderly.

FIRST ACTIVITIES OF BERNARDINO DE SAHAGÚN

Fray Bernardino must have been shocked and saddened by the experiences he lived through during the first phase of his residence in New Spain. Perhaps recalling the chaos of the first Audiencia, the result of bad government, as compared to the forms of political organization among the ancient Mexicans, as he came to know them, he would later write "in matters of governance, they are a step ahead of many other nations who presume to possess great statecraft."[27]

It is probable that he remained in Mexico City to learn about the realities of New Spain from the older friars, at least for the first few months; nevertheless, it is evident that while still "in his youth, he was the superior of some major monasteries."[24] Some evidence is preserved of his stay in one of these, San Luis Obispo de Tlalmanalco, on the slopes of the two large volcanoes. It was between 1532 and 1533, when the first church was finished in that town. According to Fray Jerónimo de Mendieta and Fray Juan de Torquemada,

> [Fray Bernardino] relates that while he was housed in a monastery in that town of Tlalmanalco, Fray Martín [de Valencia] paid that house a visit; he was custodian for the second time, and it was a widely known and celebrated fact that he became ecstatic while at prayer; one morning, as he completed the canonical hours, noting that the saintly man had moved to a corner next to the choir, he wished to see how he was. Coming to where he could observe him, he saw a light or something of the like (of which he was unable to determine the nature), which dazzled him and impeded his sight so that he was unable to see anything, nor could he see Fray Martín, who was there; he withdrew, confused and frightened by what he had experienced internally and externally.[29]

The proximity to Fray Martín, in whom Sahagún recognized an example of genuine Franciscan virtue, would undoubtedly reinforce in him the ideals that had taken shape since he had become a member of the province of San Gabriel in Extremadura. He had to take advantage of the exceptional opportunity that was offered by the Mexican natives of being guided toward a Christianity in which, instead of greed and envy, purity of life and a profound communal sense would flourish. The recent discord and violent clashes that had erupted among the Spaniards confirmed the idea that, to make the sought-after ideals a reality, one had to separate the Indians from those who had come to subjugate and exploit them. It was an urgent matter to learn about the indigenous soul and its culture. Only in this way could an authentic Christianity be built, as in the earliest times of the church.

As Fray Bernardino labored among the natives of the town of Tlalmanalco, he must have continuously contemplated those ideals, being concerned that he and his brothers transform them, little by little, into a living reality. The idolatry that he encountered at every turn could only be eradicated when the most hidden roots of the thought processes, beliefs and practices of the natives were known. To achieve this would require research, something that was frequently not an easy undertaking. Rumors about the persistence of powerful vestiges of idolatry near the mission of Tlalmanalco (though in a place that was difficult to access) propelled Bernardino to undertake an ascent of nothing less than the two tall volcanoes that set off the eastern fringe of the Valley of Mexico. He himself has left us an account of this climb, if not this impressive feat:

> There is a smoking mountain not too far from the Province of Chalco [in which Tlalmanalco is located], called *Popocatépetl*, which means "Smoking Mountain." It is a monstrous mountain to behold, and I was on top of it.
>
> There is another range next to that, which is the Sierra Nevada, and it is called *Iztactépetl*, which means "White Mountain"; it is monstrous to behold its height, where there used to be much idolatry. I saw it and was on top of it.[30]

Such an ascent of the two elevated volcanoes confirms what has been said about the character of Fray Bernardino, so inclined to investigate the natural and human realities of the land to which he had come. Likewise, his climb of those volcanoes at a height of 5, 500 meters (ca. 16, 500 feet) allows us to see him as a decisive man of good physical constitution. He was emulating the highly vaunted exploit of the conquistador Diego de Ordaz and his two companions, who scaled Popocatépetl in search of sulfur at the time of the Conquest. Regarding various sites where he knew that idolatry was practiced, in an appendix in Book XI of his *Historia general*, Sahagún provides another account of his similarly early stay in Xochimilco, a town situated to the south of Mexico City. There he uncovered evidence of worship offered to the god Tlaloc, Lord of Rain:

> There is another spring that is very clear and beautiful at Xochimilco, which today is called *Santa Cruz*, where there was an idol under the water, where they offered *copal* incense. I entered the water to take it out; I then placed a stone cross there, which is still there in the same spring.[31]

The church that was begun around 1535 next to the Franciscan monastery at Xochimilco was called *San Bernardino*. It is probable that Sahagún sought to honor his patron saint in this manner. We know that he had a great devotion to this saint, as is demonstrated by the fact that some years later he wrote a short work entitled *The Life of Saint Bernard*.[32]

Although Mendieta asserted that in his youth Sahagún had resided in various monasteries, there is evidence that he was at least at those of Tlalmanalco and Xochimilco. At the beginning of 1536, Sahagún's destiny would change. At that time, instead of continuing with his work as a missionary among the natives, he was assigned to be a teacher at the College of Santa Cruz in Tlatelolco, which was formally inaugurated on the 6th of January, 1536.

SAHAGÚN AT THE IMPERIAL COLLEGE OF SANTA CRUZ IN TLATELOLCO

Sahagún's ties would be fertile ones with the College founded to the north of Mexico City at Tlatelolco. The idea of founding an institution of higher learning there for native youths, sons of the nobility or those selected for their talents, was due to Bishop Zumárraga and to Sebastián Ramírez de Fuenleal, president of the second Audiencia. Both were men of the Spanish Renaissance; they perceived the need for a college in which the encounter between the two cultures (the Spanish and the Mexican) would be fostered and in which native youths would be educated at a sophisticated level and would then have a positive influence in their respective communities. The college had been functioning on a probationary basis since 1533, though seemingly not at Tlatelolco but at the monastery of San Francisco in Mexico City. Its solemn inauguration at Tlatelolco, with Zumárraga and Fuenleal in attendance as well as the recently arrived first viceroy Antonio de Mendoza, took place on the Feast of the Epiphany, or the Feast of the Three Kings, in 1536 to symbolize that the college was being opened for the instruction of the gentiles of the New World. Because it was opened under the auspices of Charles V, it was dubbed *imperial*.

In choosing the masters for the college, a special effort was made to seek the most learned who could be found. In addition to having an excellent mastery of the native language, they had to enjoy renown as experts in one or more branches of the humanities, theology, and biblical studies. The masters of rhetoric, logic, and philosophy were Fray Juan de Gaona, who had taught at the Sorbonne, and Fray Juan Focher, who was also a doctor of jurisprudence from the same University of Paris. The master of grammar was Fray Andrés de Olmos, who had immersed himself in the study of native antiquities and would prepare the first broad grammar, or *arte*, of the Mexican language, along with similar studies of Totonac, Tepehuan, and Huaxtec. Fray Arnald de Bassacio and Fray Bernardino de Sahagún were professors of the Latin classics, history, and other humanistic subjects.

Sahagún, who would spend several periods of his life at the College of Santa Cruz at Tlatelolco, where he trained his principal native collaborators, speaks of this research and teaching institution in several places in his works. This is especially the case on several pages of his "Relación del autor digna de ser notada" (Author's account worthy of note), which he intercalated between Chapters 27 and 28 of Book X of his *Historia general*. There, in addition to referring to the abilities and occupations as well as the vices and virtues of the Mexican natives in their pagan past, he discusses what had occurred since the coming of the Spaniards.

In treating this topic several years later, Fray Bernardino did so based on his by then lengthy experience. As a scholar, he knew better than anyone else what the ancient culture had been; as a teacher and missionary, he had plumbed the depths of the soul of the Indians. In treating the abilities of Nahuatl man, he speaks in minute detail of the many ways in which he had distinguished himself in pre-Hispanic times: as an artist working with stone, clay, feathers, and metals; as a wise man and master in the schools, knowledgeable about minerals, plants, and animals; as physician, merchant, astrologer, orator, and poet. As for the period relating to New Spain, Sahagún then notes,

> We hold from experience that they are quick to learn and employ the mechanical arts. . . . Also in trades such as tailor, shoemaker, silkmaker, printer, scribe, reader, accountant, singer of plainsong and with organ accompaniment, flute player, pipe player, sackbut player, trumpeter, organist; he knows grammar, logic, rhetoric, astrology, and theology; all of this we know from experience, that they have talent for it and learn it and know it, and they teach it, and that there is no art for which they do not have the talent to learn and use it.[33]

Moving on to "the ruling of the republic" and to moral and religious topics, he acknowledges that in times past their behavior was even better because they educated their children in close "conformity to natural philosophy and morality." All of that, nevertheless,

> ceased with the arrival of the Spaniards and because they overthrew and cast down to the ground all customs and manner of government that these natives had had and wished to rule them according to the way of life in Spain, as much in divine things as in the human; thinking them to be idolaters and barbarians, the entire regime they had was lost.[34]

It was consequently necessary to impose a remedy, and for that purpose, to implant in the native youth various forms of education. After referring to them, he attends more directly to the College of Santa Cruz:

> When we first arrived in this land to plant the faith, we gathered the youth together in our houses, as has been stated, and we began to teach them to read and write and to sing, and as they did well in this, we managed to set them to learning grammar, for which exercise a College was founded in Mexico [City], in the place called Santiago de Tlatilulco [Tlatelolco], and all the towns and regions selected their most talented youth and those who knew best how to read and write. . . .
>
> [After our] working with them for two or three years, they came to understand all the aspects of the discipline of grammar, to speak Latin and understand it, to write in Latin, and even to compose heroic verse. . . . I was present at the foundation of this College.[35]

In order to assess what began to take shape as the intellectual life of teachers and students, several pieces of evidence can be adduced, some positive and some negative. Among them is one subscribed to by Zumárraga and by Bishop Julián Garcés, who recognized the advances being made in matters intellectual and moral. Others consisted of criticism and alarm, such as the one from the former conquistador Jerónimo López, who in a letter addressed to the sovereign, dated the 25th of February, 1545, describes the dangers he perceives in the acquisition of so much knowledge by the young natives:

> So many gifts and favors have been given to the Indians, which has come to the proverb being hung on them that much conversation brings with it disdain. . . .
>
> In placing the Indians in the culture of the Latin language, having them read science, wherein they have come to know all about the beginnings of our lives through the

books they have read, from whence we come, and how we too were subjugated by the Romans and converted to the Faith from being gentiles, and all the rest that is written about that, which causes them to say that we too arose from gentiles and were subjects and conquered and subjugated and were subject to the Romans, and we rose up and rebelled and were converted to baptism so long ago, and yet we are not good Christians; the Indians thus trained are many. The friars in Mexico City and the hinterlands get it into their heads to preach; they say and preach whatever occurs to them about these and other things.[36]

It is true that under the guidance of masters of such distinction, among them Sahagún, the Nahua youths soon made great progress. There was also something else that was true and remained imperceptible to the self-appointed informant, Jerónimo López. Besides teaching Latin, grammar, history, religion, sacred scripture, and philosophy, subjects relating to the native culture had also been introduced. To accomplish this, native teachers had been located. Joining their efforts to those of the humanist friars, works with truly universal significance were produced at the college.

For Fray Bernardino, the College of Santa Cruz at Tlatelolco would come to be not only a teaching environment, but also an open space for the research to which he would dedicate a good part of his life for the purpose of plumbing the depths of the native culture. Furthermore, there he would be able to count on the presence of wise elders, masters of their antiquities, who became his consultants. Among his students, he would also find effective collaborators in his ultimate enterprise. He would refer to four of them, who, as he stated, were his students: "one is called Antonio Valeriano, resident of Azcapotzalco; another is Alonso Vegerano, resident of Cuauhtitlan; another Martín Jacobita, resident of Tlatelolco; and Andrés Leonardo, also from Tlatelolco."[37]

THE SPIRITUAL CONQUEST AND THE
PERSISTENCE OF ANCIENT BELIEFS

What some have called the "Spiritual Conquest" of Mexico in
the years circa 1536 and following was in the process of expansion, not as deep as some would have it nor as superficial as
others claim. In 1526 the Dominicans had arrived to reinforce
the Franciscans, and by 1533 the Augustinians joined in on the
tasks with the members of the other two orders. Already during
the viceroyalty of Don Antonio de Mendoza, several monasteries were begun in what are today the central states of Mexico
and in more remote regions such as Oaxaca, Chiapas, and Guatemala. Bernardino maintained a profound skepticism before
the optimistic statistics on conversions advertised by friars such
as Toribio de Benavente Motolinía. According to Motolinía, by
the year 1539 it could be said that

> in my judgment and truly, more than nine million Indians
> have been baptized in this period, which must be around
> fifteen years since this time [since 1524].[38]

Bernardino, who many years later in 1585 remained skeptical
regarding these conversions, would come to declare that "this
new Church is founded on falsehood."[39] He, however, had hoped
to develop another form for approaching the native people and
society. In his opinion, the only sure path was through a deep
knowledge of the ancient culture. The missionary must proceed
like the physician who must know the illness of which the patient
complains. When he ascertained that little progress had been
made by the thirties, he denounced the cases in which idolatry
was still alive. Moreover, he participated in trials that Bishop
Zumárraga had opened against Indians who were thought to be
apostates; since having been converted to Christianity (at least by
all appearances), they had returned to the native religion. Famous
among such trials was the one prosecuted in 1539 against Don
Carlos Ometochtzin, lord of Tetzcoco, nothing less than the son

of the celebrated Nezahualpilli and grandson of the most worthy and wise, Lord Nezahualcóyotl.

Zumárraga acted as bishop and apostolic inquisitor then, and three Franciscan friars were the interpreters. One was Antonio de Ciudad Real, with whom Bernardino had traveled to Mexico; another was Alonso de Molina, first lexicographer of the Nahuatl language, who published his *Vocabulario* in 1555; and the other was precisely Sahagún, who by then must have stood out for his knowledge of the indigenous language. He was thus able to see first hand how risky the rapid conversions of the Indians had been. It fell to Sahagún to interpret into Spanish at least a portion of what the accusers and witnesses alleged that Ometochtzin had expressed. Among other things, it was said that Ometochtzin had stated this:

> Look, hear, that my grandfather, Nezahualcóyotl, and my father, Nezahualpilli, never told us anything when they died, nor did they name anyone, nor anyone who was to come; understand, brother, that my grandfather and my father looked in all directions, forward and backward . . . , and they knew what had to be done and what had been done, as the fathers say, and they named the prophets that, in truth, I tell you that my grandfather and my father were prophets who knew what had to be done and what had been done. Therefore, brother, understand me, and let no one put his heart in this law of God and Divinity. . . . What is this Divinity? What is it like? Where did it come from?[40]

If the wisest of the forefathers had said nothing about the new law and the new divinity, however much the friars insisted on them in their schools and their catechisms, there was no reason for the Indians to change their way of thinking.

Another form of criticism consisted of pointing out that, even among the friars, there were distinct forms of religion, from which it followed that the pre-Hispanic beliefs and practices also had their own place:

See that the friars and clerics each have their own form of penance; see that the friars of Saint Francis have one manner of doctrine and sort of life and style of dress and way of praying, and the followers of Saint Augustine have another, and the followers of Saint Dominic have another and the clerics have another, as we all see; and thus it was among those who attended the gods among us: those from Mexico had one manner of dress and one manner of prayer and offering and fasting, and in other nations another; in each town they had their own way of sacrificing, their own way of praying and of offering, and that is the way the friars and clerics do it because no one agrees with the others.[41]

To all of this, Ometochtzin added, according to witnesses, the idea that the new doctrine would interfere in a direct manner with what each person, for his own happiness and solace, might be able to do in his personal life. Among other things he said this:

What do wine and women do to men? By the way, don't the Christians have many women and get drunk without the religious fathers being able to impede them? So, what is this that the fathers do to us? That is not our occupation nor our law to impede anyone from doing what they might wish to. Let us leave them and throw over our backs what they tell us to do.[42]

According to several witnesses, this was the form of argumentation of Don Carlos Ometochtzin, expressions that Sahagún had to translate from Nahuatl into Spanish. It must have been an eye-opening experience for Sahagún to participate in trials such as this one (which ended with Ometochtzin being burned at the stake on the 30th of November, 1539) and others, such as that of Pochtecatl Tlailotlaqui, former leader of the merchants, who was accused of concealing the images of the gods worshipped at the Templo Mayor in Mexico-Tenochtitlan).[43] How could one accomplish the conversion of men whose culture and beliefs were unknown? Could one continue to believe that faith and charity, such as those of the primitive church, could be implanted in that manner? These inquisitorial trials must have been both a revealing and a painful experience for Sahagún, who served as interpreter in the first case and assistant to the defense in the other. He had some consolation years later when natives, as Christians still "tender in the Faith," were excluded from the Inquisition's jurisdiction.

Other approaches to the natives had to be found. Sahagún was able to convince himself even more about this when he interrupted his first stay at the college at Tlatelolco in 1540. He went back to work for nearly five years among the natives of the valley of Puebla. This experience was followed by his return for another stay at Tlatelolco from 1545 until 1558. There, in various ways, he shaped his original plan for evangelization based on the knowledge of the native language and culture.

CHAPTER THREE

ORIGINAL PLAN FOR THE EVANGELIZATION AND RESCUE OF THE INDIGENOUS VOICE (1540–1558)

We know from Fray Bernardino himself that he concluded his first stay at the College of Santa Cruz in Tlatelolco in 1540. On speaking about the college, he writes, "I was the one who worked with them for the first four years [from 1536 to 1540] and set them onto all the subjects relating to the Latin classics."[1] His life as a teacher was interrupted in order to return to that as a missionary. His new destination was the valley of Puebla, to be headquartered at the monastery of Huexotzinco, one of the first Franciscan establishments in New Spain. From Huexotzinco, he visited places of importance, such as Cholula, Tepeaca, Tecamachalco, Tehuacan, Calpan, and others, where in a short time the Franciscans began to build churches and monasteries.

The first work written by Sahagún dates from the same year, 1540, and has remained unpublished to this day, though several copies were made in the sixteenth century. It is a sermonary in Nahuatl for all the Sundays and some saints' days throughout the liturgical year. Sahagún himself, after revising and editing it years later, describes this early work of his as follows:

> The following are some Sunday and Saint's Day sermons in Nahuatl. They were not translated from any sermonary but

rather composed afresh to the measure of the Indians' capacity: brief in subject matter, in congruous language, graceful and straightforward, easy to understand for any who should hear them, high and low, *principales* [lords and leaders] and *macehuales* [commoners], men and women. They were composed in the year of 1540.[2]

The earlier extant copy of this sermonary is preserved in the Ayer Collection of the Newberry Library in Chicago and consists of 202 pages of native paper, that is, made from the bark of an *amate,* a tree of the genus *Ficus* (fig).

Accepting as true this testimony from Fray Bernardino, we must recognize that this sermonary was written when he was already at the monastery in Huexotzinco. It is nevertheless plausible to surmise that he had already begun it while still at Tlatelolco, considering that he had to prepare fifty-two sermons in Nahuatl, one for each Sunday starting with the first Sunday of Advent to the nineteenth Sunday after Pentecost, as well as those in honor of various saints. This sermonary supports the conclusion that, as early as the thirties, lengthy texts were being written in Nahuatl employing the Spanish alphabet. In order to assess the value of this sermonary, it should be looked at, not as an isolated occurrence, but rather in the context of the whole of Sahagún's eventual contributions.

The first thing to be pointed out is that he wrote in Nahuatl. Because it is a certainty that other friars were already preaching in the language, what Bernardino accomplished had a new purpose. He was convinced that it would make no sense to construct mere improvisations or to attempt to translate already existing sermonaries from Latin or Spanish. It is for that reason that he underscores the point that he did not take them from any other sermonary but composed them anew to fit the measure of the Indians' capacity. And he adds that he has made them concise in subject matter, using a *congruous* language, graceful and straightforward, which is to say fitting, opportune (*congrua*), beautiful, graceful (*venusta*), and clear, without complications or subtleties. This sermonary, designed to have all of the above attributes, was the first in a series of works by Sahagún, conceived in harmony with a concept that had probably been germinating in his thoughts since he began teaching at the college in Tlatelolco. It was necessary to accommodate to the cultural realities of those among whom one was to work and whom one wished to evangelize. Only in this way would a presentation of Christianity be possible that would be comprehensible to the native mentality, "for any who should hear them, high and low, *principales* [lords and leaders] and *macehuales* [commoners], men and women."

With time, Sahagún's thinking became more focused until he realized that the above would not be at all sufficient. It would be necessary for the missionaries to have a deep knowledge of the language. It was also indispensable that they truly absorb a knowledge of the ancient culture. This explains why Fray Bernardino would not be satisfied with the sermonary as he had composed it in 1540 and would continue to revise and add to it, in congruity with the native speech patterns and mentality.

HUEXOTZINCO: ITS REGION AND CULTURAL VESTIGES

Sahagún provides several reports of his experiences in the valley of Puebla. He had before his very eyes three distinct forms of reality: there were the numerous native towns virtually untouched by any missionary activity; then there were the head towns such as Huexotzinco, where a center of evangelization had been established; and not too far away there was a purely Spanish settlement, La Puebla de los Angeles, a city founded on the 16th of April, 1531, by members of the second Audiencia. As regards Huexotzinco, situated on the slopes of Iztaccíhuatl, at an altitude of 2,300 meters above sea level (ca. 6,900 feet), it is important to recall that it was a significant head town for an important pre-Hispanic kingdom, at times allied with Tlaxcala and at others leaning toward the sphere of influence of Mexico-Tenochtitlan. Lord Tecayehuatzin had ruled there before the arrival of the Spaniards; according to other evidence, he had also distinguished himself as a composer of songs. Sahagún had heard that art, poetry, and music had flourished there and made reference to compositions designated as *Huexotzincayotl*, that is to say, a work or possession of the people of Huexotzinco.

Once the Conquest was over, Cortés granted the first *encomienda* of Huexotzinco to himself. Around 1532 a *corregidor* (magistrate) was appointed there; somewhat later the town included within its jurisdiction the towns of San Salvador, San Martín Texmelucan to the north, and Calpan, Acapetlahuacan, and Huaquechula to the south. The Franciscans established themselves there around March 1525. Juan Juarez, one of the first twelve friars, was named guardian of a small monastery built there. He was succeeded by Fray Toribio de Benavente Motolinía in 1529, the year Sahagún arrived in Mexico. It was then that Nuño Beltrán de Guzmán raised the taxes on Huexotzinco, calling for Zumárraga's brusque intervention, as we have seen.

Also at that time, the town and monastery changed places. Apparently many thousands of Indians had sought refuge in the ravines nearby, fleeing from the violence that was brought by the Conquest. This relocation involved nearly forty thousand residents according to the chronicler Fray Jerónimo de Mendieta. That task fell to Fray Juan de Alameda, who is also credited with having begun the construction of the magnificent monastery that still stands there to this day.

When Fray Bernardino arrived in Huexotzinco, the monastery and the church were under construction; they would not be completed until 1570. The religious activities described by Sahagún in Huexotzinco bring to mind, once again, the ideals that the Franciscans were seeking to implant. In order to achieve a reflowering of Christianity via the ancient model, in which material things would be nothing more than a means to facilitate a dedication to the life of the spirit, it would be necessary to offer the Indians an environment favorable to that purpose. New forms of communal organization would have to be created, precisely with close ties to the friars, the bearers of the gospel message. Here is what Sahagún noted in that regard:

> An experiment was attempted at the beginning: in some of the towns of this New Spain where the religious resided, as in Cholula and Huexotzinco, they would settle married couples close to the monasteries, and there they dwelt, and there they all attended Mass each day at the monastery, and they would preach to them about Christianity and about the matrimonial state, and this was a good means by which to keep them from the infection of idolatry and other bad habits.[3]

The case of a town called Chocaman deserves mention. The chronicler Mendieta offers specific information about some natives who, on their own, desired to live in the manner they had heard about from the friars, via the ideals of primitive Christianity. He thus recounts this:

> God communicated such a good spirit to an Indian named Balthazar, a native of Cholula, that he was not satisfied with saving his own soul alone but, going around to the surrounding towns, such as Tepeaca, Tecali, Tecamachalco, and Cuauhtinchan, he gathered together all the Indians he could attract to his opinion and devotion, and for what he intended, sought out throughout the mountains that drop behind the Volcano and the Sierra Nevada of Tecamachalco a convenient and appropriate spot; he wished to find quietude to give himself over to God in retirement and in a solitary life without noise. He took those he had persuaded, and they decided to follow him with their wives and children to a setting such as he desired, between two or more rivers that emerge from the same Sierra Nevada. . . .

In this place, he built a settlement with many inhabitants, which he called Chocaman, which means "a place of weeping and penance," and he established good habits, creating by mutual accord certain ordinances and laws by which they would live. . . . I only recall that these Indians had a good reputation, for which reason they were called *beatos* [the devout], and their withdrawal from the world and their mortification was great. . . . Father Juan de Ribas, one of the twelve, was very fond of these Indians and would often go to them and, with his warmth, encouraged and sustained them in the rigor and holy practices they had begun.[4]

In this manner, the experience of the Indians of Chocaman emulated the ideals by which the followers of Fray Martín de Valencia had lived in their monastery at Belvís de Monroy during the time of the *custodia* in Spain. Sahagún, who had known about the people of Chocaman, related how the friars used to preach to them. He himself also had occasion to do so, visiting from Huexotzinco; it is almost certain that he availed himself of his sermonary in Nahuatl. As he had done in Tlatelolco, he especially sought to draw in the young people. In them, Christianity would blossom in a more spontaneous way.

Absorbed in his missionary efforts while visiting nearby locations, he experienced (as he had before the Templo Mayor in Mexico-Tenochtitlan) a very deep admiration for the impressive relics of the ancient spirituality of the natives. In two places in his *Historia general,* he ponders the extraordinary grandeur of Cholula. In the prologue to Book VIII, he states,

> Those who fled this city [referring to Tollan-Teotihuacan] built another very prosperous one, which is called Cholula, which because of its grandeur and edifices, the Spaniards, upon seeing it, called it Rome.[5]

In describing the great pyramid—it bears mentioning that it is the largest known puramid in the world—and in explaining how it could have been built, Sahagún relies on the old and universal persuasion about the existence of giants in a remote past:

> [I]t even seems impossible to say that they were built by hand (the buildings), and indeed they were because those who built them then were giants, and even this is clearly seen in the hill or mountain of Cholula, for it shows evidence of being built by hand because it had adobes [mud bricks] and stucco.[6]

Just as the monuments of the ancient culture provoked great admiration in him, the phenomena of nature were also objects of his attention. For example, he refers to

> A river called *Nexatl*, which means "lye" or "water that has flowed through ashes." There is a river of this kind between Huexotzinco and Acapetlahuacan, which descends from the mountain that smokes, which is the volcano, which springs from its heights; it is water; it melts in the snow and passes through the ashes that spew from the volcano; it sinks [into the earth] very near to it and gushes out again below, between Huexotzinco and Acapetlahuacan. I saw where it sinks [into the earth], which is close to the snow, and the place where it reemerges.[7]

Fray Bernardino's sense of observation is once again revealed. He describes the nature of the water that forms this river. It is melted snow that, upon flowing through ashes spewed out by the volcano (a frequent occurrence), acquires a very special quality, like that of lye in his opinion. And he, whose interest in nature, linguistics, and culture was growing apace, remarks that, for that reason, the river is called *Nexatl*, "water that has flowed through ashes" *a[tl]* 'water' and *nex[tli]* 'ashes').

Likewise, he provides other observations from his treks throughout the region. One of these also refers to streams of water:

I saw two streams, one between Huexotzinco and San Salvador [Texmelucan] and the other between Huexotzinco and Calpan, which spring forth and flow in the rainy season and cease to flow and spring forth in the dry.[8]

This scene, which at first glance might appear to be rather simple, Sahagún describes in a context in which he seeks to collect something of the classification scheme that the Nahua peoples used for different types of streams of water. According to his notes, springs that flow from flat land are called *ameyalli* (from *a[tl]* 'water' and *meya* 'flow'). Streams that are intermittent, with no relation to the season of the year, are designated as *pinahuizatl* (from *a[tl]* 'water' and *pinahuiz[tli]* 'shame'), "for, as they say, shame before the passersby constrains them." Rivers and streams like those he described, whose flow is determined by the rainy season, he notes are occasionally called *teztzauatl* (from *a[tl]* 'water' and *teztzauh[tli]* 'portent') because, since they only flow at certain times, their arrival can alarm the people.

Turning his attention to the mountains, he makes three references to his stay in Huexotzinco. One is the aforementioned *Poyauhtecatl* 'Lord of the Mist,' Orizaba Peak, the tallest in Mexico (5,747 meters; ca. 17, 000 feet):

There is a mountain called *Poyauhtecatl*; it is close to Ahuilizapan [Orizaba, Veracruz]. A few years ago its summit began to burn, and I saw that it had its top covered with snow for many years, and then I saw how it began to burn; the flames were visible night or day from over twenty leagues distance [the approximate distance from Huexotzinco]; and now because the fire has burnt most of the front slope of the mountain, the fire is no longer visible, though it is still burning.[9]

Having made the above observations on the volcanic activity of Orizaba Peak, he alludes briefly to another mountain, not as tall, but which also had several religious connotations for the Nahuas:

There is another mountain near Tlaxcala that is called Matlalcueye, which means 'Woman with Blue Skirts.'[10]

This name, as he well knew, was one of the titles of the Mother
Goddess in her relation to the waters that fertilize the earth. It can
be added in passing that the name of *Matlalcueye* was changed
to another, also a woman's name: *La Malinche,* the famous native
woman who acted as Cortes's interpreter and companion.

Another reference to Popocatépetl brought Fray Bernardino
to denounce what he had uncovered in a town situated on its
slopes. In a note in his *Historia general*, he mentioned this recollection from the period of his stay in Huexotzinco—because the
town fell within its jurisdiction—in which he condemned several religious practices that, in his judgment, were no more than
covert forms of idolatry. The following is his reference to that:

> At the base of the volcano in a town called Tianquizmanal-
> co, San Juan, they celebrated a great feast in honor of whom
> they refer to as *Telpochtli* [The Youth], who is *Tezcatlipoca*
> [Smoking Mirror]; and when the preachers heard tell that
> Saint John the Evangelist was a virgin and that this is called
> *Telpochtli* in their language, they had occasion to hold that
> feast as they had formerly, palliated under the name of San
> Juan Telpochtli, as it sounds on its face, but in honor of the
> ancient Telpochtli, who is Tezcatlipoca, because Saint John
> has performed no miracles there.[11]

Sahagún's comment about the occurrences at Tianquizmanalco
at the foot of the volcano near Huexotzinco, as we shall see, would
come to form part of a much broader denunciation he would lodge
toward the year 1576 of what was occurring in other locations,
where new forms of ritual had been superimposed on practices
formerly in honor of the pre-Hispanic gods. According to Fray
Bernardino, another of these sites was to be found on a small hill,
the Tepeyacac 'On the Nose of the Mountain,' where the cult of the

Virgin of Guadalupe now substituted for or palliated the ancient one in honor of *Tonantzin*, 'Our Mother,' the supreme female deity.

RETURN TO A MUCH CHANGED TLATELOLCO

In 1545, probably obeying an order from his superiors, Sahagún returned to the College of Santa Cruz at Tlatelolco. In five years it had undergone several changes. Sahagún relates the prevailing conditions:

> The friars had taught the students and had been with them for more than ten years (from January 1536 and from even before the official opening), teaching them all the discipline and customs that were to be observed at the College; because there were among them those who read [lectured] and who were seemingly capable of administering the College, they were allowed to lecture and administer by themselves.[12]

Thus the college, when Fray Bernardino returned to it in 1545, had become an institution that could count on a native academic staff, although it continued under the supervision of the friars. Shortly before he departed for Peru, Viceroy Mendoza made a donation to the college. Though there are no data about the identity of the Nahua rector and faculty during 1545, we know from the *Códice de Tlatelolco* (Tlatelolco codex) that five years later the rector was Pablo Nazareo, a native of Xaltocan, who had grown up since childhood with the twelve Franciscans. According to the *oidor* Alonso de Zorita, he was "a good latinist and rhetorician, logician and philosopher, and not a bad poet in all genres of verse."[13] Also at the college as teachers were Martín Espiridión and Antonio Valeriano of Azcapotzalco. The latter was one of Sahagún's best collaborators and came to occupy the position of native governor of Mexico.

What could be seen as the plan's first achievement was to be affected, along with the rest of the city and a good part of the country, by a most serious epidemic of *Matlazahuatl,* an illness related to typhus, which broke out that year. Sahagún speaks of it:

> In the year 1545, there was a most serious and universal pestilence, in which the majority of the people of New Spain died. At the time of the pest, I was in Tlatelolco and buried more than ten thousand corpses; at the end of the pestilence, I caught the disease and was close to my end.[14]

Sahagún's assertion about having buried "more than ten thousand corpses" should obviously be understood as that he participated, by directing or collaborating, in mass burials of the victims of the plague. It is probable that several of his students also took part in this. Perhaps it was this involvement that caused the death of so many through contagion and that caused Sahagún himself to fall so gravely ill that, according to his own description—"I caught the disease and was close to my end"— he came close to death.

In 1576, turning to the same epidemic, Fray Bernardino recalled that "the pestilence that occurred thirty years ago struck a great blow against the College."[15] The disease spread to such an extent that the figures for the dead given by different chroniclers are truly frightening. Thus the Augustinian Fray Juan de Grijalva in his *Crónica* asserts that five-sixths of the population perished, after mentioning that, as a harbinger of the pestilence, flames were seen atop the volcano Popocatépetl and there was a series of evil omens.[16] The aforementioned self-appointed informant of the emperor, Jerónimo López, in a letter dated the 10th of September, 1545, writes to the monarch that, within just a ten-league radius around the capital, nearly four hundred thousand individuals had died.[17] According to the chronicler Torquemada, that number doubled in what was then New Spain.[18]

It was to be expected that, as remarked by Sahagún, this pestilence would strike a great blow against the college. To compensate as much as possible for the loss of students, some of whom were among the most advanced, according to Viceroy Mendoza the doors were opened not only to the former native nobility but also to those from any social rank. The only condition for admission and retention was to demonstrate an adequate intellectual capacity. Thus began anew the original plan for a higher education in which valuable elements of the cultures of both Old and New Spain would converge.

BERNARDINO'S EARLIEST RESEARCH ON THE ANCIENT CULTURE

As we have seen, the idea that Fray Bernardino was developing—that of familiarizing himself deeply with the native culture as a precondition to completing the work of evangelization on a firm foundation—moved him during those years to taking the first anticipatory step toward what would be his research with a global scope. As to what date he undertook the research, he himself provides a note that permits us to fix it with certainty at 1547. This note appears at the end of Book VI of the *Códice florentino* (Florentine codex), which includes the last preparation of what would become his *Historia general* in Nahuatl and Spanish. Book VI contains a collection of texts: examples of the *Ancient Word*, which included orations delivered at important occasions and at highly significant events in the life of native man and society. As we shall see, those texts which are extraordinary examples of the pre-Hispanic literary tradition, are known as *Huehuetlahtolli* 'Ancient Word.' Sahagún places the following note at the end of the book in which they are recorded:

> It was translated into the Spanish language by said Father Fray Bernardino de Sahagún thirty years after it was written in the Mexican language, this year of 1577.[19]

By subtracting thirty years from 1577, we find ourselves with 1547, which is when he collected the forty *Huehuetlahtolli* in the Nahuatl language. The corresponding research he undertook while at Tlatelolco. This provides a basis for the hypothesis that the beginning of Sahagún's research on the ancient culture occurred in 1547 in the context of the College of Santa Cruz at Tlatelolco, where other salvage work on the culture was underway: research on native medicine as well as the elaboration of documents, such as one of a cartographic nature and others related to the *códices*, or books in the ancient style.

It is probable that Fray Bernardino, who was familiar with what another Franciscan, Andrés de Olmos, had collected (he had transcribed other *Huehuetlahtolli*, testimonies of the *Ancient Word*), inquired about them among the native elders who frequented the monastery and college at Tlatelolco. His search was rewarded when he was able to hear from Nahua lips the texts that contained, as he described it, the heart "of the rhetoric, moral philosophy, and theology of the Mexican people, in which there are many curious things exhibiting the beauties of the language and very delicate things relating to the moral virtues."[20]

Overflowing with admiration for the spiritual significance and literary worth of the *Huehuetlahtolli*, Sahagún did not hesitate to compare these to testimonies he considered akin to them from other nations of classical antiquity as well as from modern times. All peoples, he tells us, "have set their eyes on the wise and powerful to persuade them and also on men who are exemplars of moral virtue." He then compares them: "There are so many examples of this among the Greeks, Romans, French, Spanish, and Italians that the books are full of them." Such an appreciation for rhetoric, moral philosophy, and theology flourished in those cultures; "it was also the custom in this Indian nation and most especially among the Mexicans, among whom the wise, eloquent, virtuous, and courageous are held in high esteem."[21]

These testimonies of the *Ancient Word* are indeed an example of the most elevated level of wisdom from pre-Hispanic Mexico. There are among them several examples of prayers to the supreme god *Tloque Nahuaque*, 'Lord of the Near and Close'; appeals to Tezcatlipoca during tribulations, such as times of pestilence, famine, or war, and to Tlaloc in times of drought; orations on the death of one ruler and the election or enthroning of another; advice from parents to their sons and daughters, revealing to them what is good and what is bad on earth; and another body of exhortations and reflections that were uttered at the principal moments in the life cycle, from birth, entry into school, graduation, matrimony, and news of the pregnancy of a young wife to sickness and death.

In collecting these texts, Fray Bernardino experienced a growing admiration for what presented itself as an unsuspected spirituality in the conquered people. As these *Huehuetlahtolli* became better known among the Spaniards, especially the friars, there were some who doubted their authenticity and suspected that they were the creation of Bernardino, a truly learned man; he, however, became angry and wrote what has been quoted here:

> In this book it shall be seen very clearly that what has been affirmed by some skeptics, that all of what is written down in these books, before the present one and after it, are fictions and lies: they speak driven by passion and mendacity because what is written in this book, no one is capable of inventing, nor could any living man fabricate the language it contains. And all the knowledgeable Indians, if asked, would affirm that the language is their ancestors' own and works that they composed.[22]

Another critical argument must be adduced in favor of the authenticity of the *Huehuetlahtolli*. As we have seen, Fray Andrés de Olmos several years prior had had other *Huehuetlahtolli* transcribed alphabetically. These texts, with Christianizing interpolations, are preserved in a manuscript that is housed at the Library of Congress in Washington, D.C.; they were also published in 1600 by Fray Juan Bautista de Viseo. That book, which became extremely rare, was reproduced in 1988 by the Comisión Conmemorativa del Encuentro de Dos Mundos (Commemorative Committee for the Encounter of Two Worlds) and again in 1991 with a release of 615,000 copies by the Mexican Ministry of Public

Education and the Fondo de Cultura Económica (Fund for Economic Culture).[23] The *Huehuetlahtolli* can now be enjoyed by many. A comparison between several *Hueheutlahtolli* included in these texts and those that Sahagún collected and transcribed independently demonstrates that there are notable similarities between many of them. This fact corroborates the authenticity of these texts.

The harvest of testimonies in the very language of the ancient wise men came to be a valuable contribution to, and also a powerful incentive for, the continuation of research. One had to deepen the familiarity with the thought of the ancient indigenous people, as an indispensable precondition for guiding the development of a pure and true Christianity like that of the church in the times of the apostles, an ideal pursued by the first Franciscans who arrived in Mexico.

Sahagún came to appreciate these testimonies so much (as the revelation of an unsuspected humanism) that he did not hesitate to ponder their style and content. As he affixed a title or heading to each of them, in several instances he added expressions such as these:

> The language and affection as they prayed to their principal god, called *Tezcatlipoca* . . . , when there was a plague . . . [i]s the prayer of the priests in which they confess him to be all-powerful, invisible, and intangible. They employ beautiful metaphors and figures of speech.[24]

Time and time again, he praised the language employed in these prayers and orations, he also did not hold back from vaunting their content, in particular, that of the *Huehuetlahtolli* in which the father and mother exhort their daughter:

> Due to their language and style (*mutatis mutandis*), were these speeches to be delivered from the pulpit to the boys and girls, they might be more efficacious than many another sermon.[25]

It is certainly the case that what was affirmed by Sahagún might have struck some as not only hyperbolic but even rash. He was, after all, praising pagan prayers and native wisdom.

The following words come from a talk delivered by a Nahua father to a daughter who has reached the age of reason. I have striven to render them faithfully from the Nahuatl as an example of the wisdom that so impressed Sahagún:

> Here you are, my little daughter, my necklace of precious stones, my quetzal plume, my human creation, born of me. You are my blood, my color; my image resides in you.
>
> Now accept this; listen to it: you live, have been born; Our Lord has sent you to this earth, he who is the Lord of the Near and Close, the creator of humanity, inventor of humankind.
>
> Now that you can see for yourself, take account of things as they are. Here it is thus: there is no happiness, there is no joy. There is anguish, worry. Here suffering springs forth, as does worry.
>
> Here on earth, it is a place of much weeping, a place where the breath gives out, where bitterness and exhaustion are too familiar. A wind like obsidian blows and slashes us.
>
> They say that the burning of the sun and wind truly torments us. It is a place in which one nearly perishes of thirst and hunger. So it is here on earth.
>
> Hear me well, my darling daughter, my little girl: this world is not a place of ease; there is no joy, there is no happiness. It is said that the earth is a place of painful joy, of a happiness that pierces us.
>
> It is thus that the elders speak: so that we not go about groaning, so that we not be filled with sadness, Our Lord gave us laughter, slumber, food, our strength, our power, and finally sexual intercourse, by which we sow the seeds of humanity.
>
> All of this softens life on earth so that we not go about groaning. Yet, though it were so, if it were true that we only suffer, if things on earth were truly so, should we live in fear? Must we remain in dread? Must we live a life of tears?
>
> For as we live on earth, there are rulers, there is authority, there are nobility, eagles, and tigers. And who goes about

saying that life on earth is so? Who goes about attempting to seek death? There is striving, there is life, there is struggle. A wife is sought; a husband.[26]

With this approximation to the Nahuatl version of this discourse, it would not be superfluous to ascertain how Bernardino transposed the content of the same expressions in his paraphrastic translation with addenda of his own. Comparing one version with others casts a light with which one can appreciate the procedures he adopted in his preparation of the Spanish text in his *Historia general*. What follows is his version:

> You, my little daughter, like a precious bead of gold and like a rich plume, issued forth from my bowels, whom I engendered and who are my blood and my image, who are here present, hear well what I wish to tell you, for you are now at the age of reason: the creator has given you the use of reason and the ability to understand, he who is everywhere and is the creator of everyone; and because it is so that you now understand, and have the use of reason to know and understand how things of this world are and that in this world there is no true pleasure nor real rest, much rather there are labor and afflictions and fatigue in the extreme, and an abundance of misery and poverty.
>
> Oh, daughter of mine! This world is for weeping and suffering and for the woeful, where there are cold and harsh winds and the great heat of the sun, which punishes us, and it is a place of hunger and thirst! This is a great truth, and we know it from experience.
>
> Note well what I tell you, my daughter, that this world is evil and painful, where there are no pleasures, but only woes. There is a proverb that says that there is no joy that is not mixed with sadness, that there is no rest that does not come with travail here in this world; this was said by the ancients, who left it for us so that no one should be burdened with too much weeping and with too much sadness.

Our Lord gave us laughter, slumber, food, and drink with which we grow and live; he gave us also the work of generation, through which we multiply in this world; all of these things provide our lives with some brief solace in this world so that we not be afflicted with constant weeping and grief; and even though it is so, and this is the way of the world, where pleasures are mixed with woes, we take no note of it; nor is it feared, nor is there even weeping, for we live in this world, and there are kingdoms and realms, dignities and honors, some are close to rule and kingdoms, others are close to war.

What is said is a great truth that happens here on earth, yet no one considers it, no one thinks of death, only the present, in which they seek food and drink and life, build houses and work to live, seek wives to marry; and women are married, passing from girlhood to the married state; this, my daughter, is as I have said.[27]

These two versions of this brief text reflect in two different ways the beauty and profundity of native expression. Beyond the differences, they are two approaches to a text that is an authentic example of Nahuatl literature in the pre-Hispanic tradition.

TEACHING, FURTHER RESEARCH, AND OTHER UNDERTAKINGS IN TLATELOLCO

Fray Bernardino continued his stay at the College of Santa Cruz, which this time would last until 1558. Aside from working alongside the new native teachers as a master of grammar and the Latin classics, he was able to draw much closer to some of his former students, the *trilinguals* (speaking Nahuatl, Latin, and Spanish), who years later would collaborate with him in his most ambitious research.

Viceroy Antonio de Mendoza, who had promoted and achieved so many initiatives—founding new towns and cities; organizing expeditions to the northern regions of the land; suppressing rebel

groups, such as the famous one involved with the so-called Mix-
ton War of 1541 in Jalisco and Zacatecas, to which Sahagún alludes in Chapter 2 of Book VIII in his *Historia general*,—had lent
his support to projects promoting intellectual culture.[28] Among
these, the establishment of a printing press in 1539 stands out, as
well as the creation of new schools, such as the Colegio de San
Juan de Letrán (College of Saint John Lateran) for young *mestizos*
(persons of mixed ethnicity), and the procurement of the *cédula*
(order of approval) from Charles V on the 21st of September,
1551, for the creation of the University of Mexico, with the same
statutes and privileges as those of Salamanca.

It should be recalled that it was Mendoza who decided on
the preparation of the codex that still bears his name in order to
inform the emperor about the native culture. In the three component parts of the manuscript, the stages of the expansion of
the ancient Mexicans are laid out in the native style, during the
period of each of the supreme rulers. Also described, according
to quality and quantity, are the tributes that were received from
the diverse provinces; and finally, a picture of what today might
be called a pre-Hispanic ethnography is offered, including forms
of government, education, foods, wardrobe, etc.[29]

Around 1548 or 1549, it fell to the viceroy (who had demonstrated considerable interest in everything related to the higher
expressions of culture, as much indigenous as Hispanic) to request
of the College of Santa Cruz the preparation of a map of Mexico
City and its environs. It is relevant to recall what gave rise to
the preparation of this map, given that it is likely that Sahagún
and his closest collaborators took part in it. In April 1546, Prince
Philip, who was regent in the absence of Charles, had asked Don
Antonio de Mendoza to have cartographic work done in order to
structure better the administration of the viceroyalty. Furthermore,
he and his father had expressed a desire to become acquainted with
the celebrated City of Mexico. Upon hearing of this interest, the
viceroy realized that the preparation of the desired map could
be carried out at Tlatelolco because he was aware that important

work was being done at the college he inaugurated, including the copying of ancient codices. In due course, circa 1550, the viceroy would forward the result of his order to the royal cartographer Alonso de Santa Cruz, with whom he maintained frequent correspondence, in order for him to review and submit it to Charles V if he thought it worthy.

The map, conceived in the Renaissance style with the idea of recreating the landscape in which the city found itself in New Spain, was effectively painted onto two pieces of skin joined together, with an area consisting of 1.74 meters in length and 78 centimeters in width. In this very colorful map, two cartographic traditions converged, that of ancient Mexico and that of Renaissance Spain. In it are represented the island upon which Mexico- Tenochtitlan was located, and to the north, Tlatelolco, with its monastery and college, in a disproportionately large scale, as if to underscore the fact that the map had been drawn there. The lakes surround the island, and beyond these can be seen the shoreline regions of the great Basin of Mexico. The map, which can be referred to as that of Mexico-Tenochtitlan and its environs circa 1550, also includes two hundred toponymic glyphs after the native fashion, as well as many scenes depicting life and daily activities on the island and in the region of the lakes. As a product executed by natives under the probable guidance of a friar, a master at the College of Santa Cruz, the map highlights the talents of those engaged in works of higher culture there.[30]

The *Libellus de Medicinalibus Indorum Herbis* (Booklet on medicinal herbs of the Indians), also known as the *Códice badiano* (Badianus codex), was completed at about the same time. Two former masters at the college, Martín de la Cruz and Juan Badiano, participated in the elaboration of this work. The first was a *tepahtiani*, a physician of recognized prestige. The second was an outstanding Latinist. The herbarium consists of 140 pages, 89 of these showing miniature pictures illustrating the many different plants whose names and medicinal properties are described there. It is relevant to note that, in many of these miniatures, the types of soil in which the respective plants are rooted are indicated in the native manner: stony, moist, boggy, or abounding in insects.

Sahagún must have known the physician Martín de la Cruz because the preparation of the codex coincided with his own stay at the College of Santa Cruz. In fact, years later, when Bernardino had acquired an interest in native pharmacology, he obtained from other Tlatelolco physicians copious information, which he later included among the fruits of his own research. One of these physicians, Francisco de la Cruz, may well have been a relative of Martín.

When Martín de la Cruz had concluded his work in Nahuatl, it is very likely that *tlahcuilos* (native painters) at the college proceeded to illustrate the manuscript with the miniatures, which then became an integral part of the codex. It then fell to Juan Badiano to translate the Nahuatl text into a correct and even elegant Latin. Badiano entitled the codex *Libellus de Medicinalibus Indorum Herbis*.

When the work was finished, it was dedicated and submitted to Don Francisco de Mendoza, son of the viceroy, in 1552. This date coincided with the death of the viceroy, who had departed New Spain in 1550 and had proceeded to Lima to assume the viceroyalty of Peru.

The submittal of the herbarium to Don Francisco, who had remained behind in Mexico to attend to various affairs of his father, may have been due as much to the grateful acknowledgment of the viceroy, who had supported the existence of the college, as to the interest that Don Francisco had evinced for native pharmacology. Upon his departure, he took the herbarium to Spain.

Martín de la Cruz himself, upon dedicating the herbarium to Don Francisco, who was still in Mexico, explained to him his motives for writing it. To begin with, he declares, "The benefits your father has provided me with cannot be exaggerated." These included the entire college that he had sponsored and endowed with financial support. Furthermore, he adds that if Don Francisco had insistently requested the booklet of him, he sees no other motive for it but "to commend the Indians to His Sacred Catholic and Royal Majesty, though they are undeserving of it." He submits the herbarium to Don Francisco, therefore, to express his gratitude and to seek new favors from the emperor, to whom, Martín de la Cruz assumes, he will show it and perhaps use it to regale him.

There is no indication that Charles V or his son Philip ever saw the codex. It is known, however, that a well-known and well-connected pharmacologist at the court, Diego de Cortavila y Sanabria, owned it. Proof of this is offered by his inscription on the first page, which reads, "ex libris Didaci Cortavila." The herbarium had other owners, one of whom, in fact, permitted a copy to be made of it. Today we know that the copy is housed at the Windsor Castle Library in England.

It was Cardinal Francesco Barberini, a devout bibliophile and former apostolic nuncio in Spain, who later came to possess this codex. Because he was the Vatican librarian, at his death the precious manuscript remained in that library. It was preserved there and rediscovered, almost simultaneously in 1929, by the Englishman Charles Upson Clark, the Italian Giuseppe Gabrieli, and the North American Lynd Thorndike. They communicated to other scholars the interest that the codex aroused in them; among these were the collector and historian William Gates, the specialist in medical history William Welch, and Dr. Emily Walcott Emmart. In this way, the manuscript that had originated at the College of Santa Cruz at Tlatelolco came to attract the interest, not only of bibliophiles such as Francesco Barberini, but also of specialists in various fields from a variety of nations.

This entire account, which may seem to be a digression, seeks to highlight the universal significance that the college, in which Sahagún had labored as a teacher and researcher of Nahuatl culture, had come to garner through several of its contributions. The codex was published in 1940 with a study by Dr. Emmart.[31] Years later, in 1964, it reappeared along with numerous works by distinguished specialists.[32] Finally in 1990, the *Libellus de Medicinalibus Indorum Herbis* was returned to Mexico by Pope John Paul II, thus being the only native codex that has fortunately found its way back to its country of origin.

The various interactions that Don Antonio de Mendoza, the viceroy, had with the college and the various forms of economic support that he provided would be recalled by Fray Bernardino many years later when speaking about the financial state of the institution:

> If Don Antonio de Mendoza, may he rest in Glory, Viceroy of this New Spain, had not provided for it from his own estate, and a small income it receives, with which a few are poorly supported, there would not even be a memory of the College and its students.[33]

Bernardino held Viceroy Mendoza in high esteem; he had met him on the 6th of January, 1536, when the College of Santa Cruz was solemnly inaugurated. For diverse reasons, throughout his life Bernardino would have dealings with several viceroys. After the departure of Mendoza for Peru, with Luis de Velasco I already at the helm of government, we find that Sahagún and other Franciscans—among whom were Provincial Fray Juan de San Francisco, Commissioner General Francisco de Bustamante, Guardian of Mexico Diego de Olarte, Antonio de Ciudad Rodrigo, and Toribio de Benavente Motolinía—having gathered together, as they say, "in our capitular congregation," addressed a letter to Emperor Charles V, dated the 20th of October, 1552.

In that letter, they beseech the sovereign to demarcate the authority of the viceroy from that which the Audiencia enjoyed so that the former, "who has a great desire and will to defend these poor natives," might rule more freely.[34] The fact that Fray Bernardino appears as a signatory to this letter further confirms what the chronicler Jerónimo de Mendieta had expressed about him: "at times he was *definidor* [president or chair of the order chapter] of this Province of the Holy Gospel."[35] The exercise of this charge implicated participation in the *definitorio*, the consultative and governing body of the Franciscans, along with the superior, or provincial, and others, such as the commissioner and some of the principal guardians and monastery superiors. This position, though it did require time, did not distract Sahagún from his projects at Tlatelolco.

THE *BOOK OF THE CONQUEST*: THE "VISION OF THE VANQUISHED"

Just about that time, Fray Bernardino, in his efforts to understand the emotions and thoughts of the native people, attacked another project: that of gathering together testimonies from the lips of those who had witnessed or participated in the events of the Conquest. We know from the researcher himself that this took place at Tlatelolco sometime between 1553 and 1555. Much later, in 1585, reviewing what remained of his papers, Sahagún attempted to edit and enrich his ancient Nahua testimonies dealing with the Conquest. At the beginning of what would be his new version, he noted the following:

> When this writing [about the Conquest] was done, now more than thirty years ago, it was all in the Mexican language. Those who assisted me with this writing were all leading elders and very knowledgeable men . . . who had found themselves in the midst of the war when this city was conquered.
> In the book wherein the Conquest is treated, there were several errors: some things were included there about this Conquest that should not have been; others were left out. For this reason, this year of fifteen hundred and eighty five, I have emended this book.[36]

If we subtract a bit more than thirty years from 1585, we arrive at a date between 1553 and 1555, which is when the scholarly friar collected the evidence he gathered from the elders who had been present in the war when Tenochtitlan was conquered. These testimonies, in which it is clear that it is *Tlatelolcas* (the people of Tlatelolco) who are speaking, he would incorporate later as Book XII in the *Historia general* in Nahuatl and Spanish. In a brief prologue titled "To the Reader," Bernardino indicates, with a certain amount of reticence and obvious hesitancy, what his actual purpose had been:

> Though many have written in Romance about the Conquest of this New Spain according to the account of those who conquered it, I wished to write it in the Mexican language, not so much to extract certain truths from the accounts of the Indians themselves who found themselves in the Conquest, but rather to secure samples of the language relating to warfare and weaponry that the natives use, in order that from this, I could obtain appropriate words and expressions in the Mexican language about this subject matter.[37]

Bernardino's declared intention was basically linguistic because he states that, in that manner, words and expressions related to war could be extracted. From this it might seem that war was a particularly appealing topic for him, which is something he contradicts at various points throughout his works because he holds it to be tyrannical and destructive.[38] Further on in the same prologue, however, he cannot conceal what was, in reality, his guiding idea: to learn what the drama of the Conquest signified in the native mind:

> Those who were conquered and knew about and provided information about many things that happened among them during the war, which are unknown to the conquerors, for which reason it seems to me the writing of this history is not superfluous, which was written when those who were alive at the time of the Conquest provided this narrative, leaders and persons of good judgment and who can be certain to have told the whole truth.[39]

The Nahuatl narrative of the conquered begins with an evocation of the "signs and omens" that were said to have appeared prior to the coming of the men of Castile, and it concludes with the surrender of the Mexicans after eighty days of siege of their city; the imprisonment of Cuauhtemoc; and the admonition of the lords of Mexico, Tetzcoco, and Tlacopan (The Triple Alliance) by Cortés, who demanded the surrender of gold that he insisted they had concealed. This is certainly not the oldest native testimony from Tlatelolco; there exits another in what are called the *Anales de la nación mexicana* (Annals of the Mexican nation). It is, however, the most complete text and the one with the greatest impact, in which the conquered people speaks for itself and expresses what the clash with and defeat at the hands of the men from Castile signified for it.

This account, dramatic testimony derived from Sahagún's research, has aroused considerable interest since the sixteenth century. Fray Juan de Torquemada edited it in his *Monarquía indiana* and proclaimed that no one could understand what the Conquest had been like if he did not take into account the opinion of the natives. The royal chronicler Antonio de Herrera also availed himself of it, though without crediting Sahagún. For my part I can say that, under the title of *Vision of the Vanquished*, I have broadcast this testimony, which continues to captivate the attention to such a degree that it has been reprinted many times, as well as being translated into fifteen languages.

To place in doubt, or even more, to deny the veracity of these testimonies would be a gratuitous rejection of what Sahagún has stated about those who provided "this narrative, leaders . . . of good judgment . . . who can be certain to have told the whole truth." Furthermore, it would amount to ignoring the internal evidence in the account, in which the astonishment that the Spanish invasion provoked and the trauma of the Nahuas' defeat are patently obvious. Similarly, such a doubt or denial would imply setting aside the concurrence among the testimonies that exists between this text and that of the *Anales de Tlatelolco* (Annals of

Tlatelolco), works that did not originate with the Mexica-Teno-
chcas but with the people of Tlatelolco, who, as can be perceived
there, exhibited a great deal of animus against the Aztec neigh-
bors who dominated them. It would indicate that everyone who
was acquainted with this account, who held it to be true, and
who had quoted from it had acted precipitously and naively;
among these would be Juan de Torquemada, the chronicler Antonio de Herrera, the court physician Francisco Hernández, and
the grammarian Horacio Carochi.

It is important to recall three of Bernardino's projects undertaken before 1558, when, broadening his goals, he initiated his
global research on the ancient culture. One of these was his approach to Nahuatl, which had become increasingly penetrating.
An indication of how well known and admired this interest of
his was is evidenced by the fact that, when Fray Alonso de Molina published his *Vocabulario en la lengua castellana y mexicana*
(Dictionary in the Spanish and Mexican languages) in 1555, he
wrote the following inscription in the book:

> This work was seen and examined by the Reverend Father
> Francisco de Litorne, guardian of the Monastery of San
> Francisco in Mexico, and by Father Friar Bernardino de Sa-
> hagún of said Order, to whom its review was commended.[40]

The second type of activity consisted in continuing with the
task of translating the biblical texts into Nahuatl, as part of the
plan he had undertaken of drawing close to indigenous man. As
is expressed in the prologue to his book *Coloquios y doctrina christiana*, he thought that the word of the Sacred Scriptures should
be made accessible to the native people. In fact, as we shall see,
in 1561 he completed his translation into Nahuatl of all of the
Epistles and Gospels that are to be read on all the Sundays and
principal feasts of the liturgical year.

His last act prior to beginning his broader research seems to
have taken place in 1558. This was when he moved to Michoacán
as a father visitor of the friars who labored there and who formed

part of a *custodia*, a Franciscan administrative entity that is of lesser rank than that of a province. He would inquire further about the indigenous inhabitants of Michoacán; later, when gathering together the texts for his *Historia general*, he transcribed his notes on the principal native groups of New Spain. He would then bring together all the testimonies of the Nahua elders on the realms and kingdoms that had flourished in antiquity, such as Teotihuacan, Cholula, Tula, and others, as well as what they thought of peoples with different languages and cultures. Such testimonies were, as we shall see, only one small part of what would come to make up the *Historia general*.

CHAPTER FOUR

BEGINNING OF SYSTEMATIC AND GLOBAL RESEARCH IN TEPEPULCO (1558–1561)

The beginning of the long phase of global research undertaken by Sahagún consisted of the convergence of two efforts. One was his long-standing interest in deepening his knowledge of the indigenous culture so as to build a new Christianity on this foundation. The other determining factor (as he stated in his prologues to Books I and II of his *Historia general*) was the order he had received from Fray Francisco de Toral, the newly appointed tenth provincial of the Holy Gospel Province:

> I was compelled in holy obedience [writes Fray Bernardino] by my Major Prelate to write in the Mexican language whatever it seemed to me to be of use for the doctrine, culture, and preservation of Christianity among these natives of New Spain and for the aid of the ministers who catechize them.[1]

Elsewhere, as he specifies more clearly the meaning of the mandate, he states,

> By the order of the Most Reverend Father, Fray Francisco de Toral, Provincial of this Province of the Holy Gospel and later Bishop of Campeche and Yucatán, I wrote twelve

books on the divine or, better said, idolatrous, human, and natural things of this New Spain.[2]

The chronicler Mendieta provides data on the life and work of Fray Francisco de Toral. We know that he was born in Ubeda, Andalusia. Years after entering the Franciscan Order, he arrived in Mexico. There he was the first to learn the Popoloca and Nahuatl languages as they were spoken in the region of Tecamachalco in the modern state of Puebla. It is quite reasonable to imagine that, between 1540 and 1545, he had close dealings with Fray Bernardino during the phase of his life when he was working as a missionary in Huexotzinco, at not too great a distance from Tecamachalco. Being familiar with and sharing his interest in the Nahuatl language and in his project for deepening his knowledge of the native culture, upon being appointed provincial for the three-year period from 1558 to 1561, and of common accord with Sahagún, Toral gave him the formal charge to undertake "in holy obedience" the research that so interested Bernardino.

SAHAGÚN'S MOTIVATIONS

Before we look at how Sahagún initiated his work, it is necessary to inquire further about the motivations that induced him to address himself to it. It would be wrong to postulate that he was moved primarily by what today we would qualify as scientific interest, as some would have it. Nevertheless, it would be equally far from the truth to affirm that in his work he was driven exclusively by his missionary zeal. It is certain that his initial motivation was religious. He declares as much unambiguously in his prologue to Book I of his *Historia general*. There, comparing the evangelizer to a physician, as we have seen, he writes this:

> Preachers and confessors are physicians for the soul; in curing spiritual illnesses, it is essential that they have expertise in spiritual medicines and illnesses. The preacher treating the vices of the republic in order to enlist his doctrine

against them; the confessor, in order to know to ask what is needed and to understand what is said with regard to his duty; it is indeed necessary that they know what is needed for the exercise of their occupations.[3]

Bernardino then insists on what he has been able to ascertain regarding the persistence of idolatry, asserting the following:

It is inappropriate for the ministers of this conversion to state that, among this people, there are no other sins but drunkenness, theft, and carnality. For there are many other much graver sins in need of remedy. The sins of idolatry and idolatrous rites, superstitions and omens, and superstitions and idolatrous ceremonies have not disappeared altogether.

In order to preach against these things or even to be aware of their existence, we must be familiar with how they were practiced in pagan times, [because] through our ignorance, they do many idolatrous things without our understanding it.[4]

According to what he says, it is clear that Bernardino was especially motivated by his role as a missionary, who must know the ancient culture and all its rites and idolatries in order to banish them and be better able to implant Christianity. Further on in the same prologue, he himself manifests other reasons that motivated him. One of these is his linguistic interest, closely tied to the previously mentioned motive (of fostering evangelization), yet clearly becoming a predominant point of attraction for him:

This work is like a great dragnet bringing to light all the words of this language with their literal and metaphoric meanings and all their manners of speech and the greater part of their antiquities, good and evil; in order to save a great deal of effort in the future for, with a great deal less strain than I have had, those who may wish to will be able in a short time to learn about their antiquities and the entire language of this Mexican people.[5]

Knowing the words with their metaphorical meanings, all their manners of speaking, and their language and antiquities is an objective that would seem to be appealing in its own right, though, naturally, achieving this would be a great boon to any missionary. Abounding in this knowledge, Sahagún adds the following near the end of a "Note to the Sincere Reader":

> When this work was initiated, it began to be said by those who knew of it that a *Calepino* was being prepared; and to this day, there are many who will still ask me, "How is the Calepino coming along?" Of course, it would be a very useful thing to do, preparing so practical a work for those who might wish to learn the Mexican language, as Ambrosio Calepino did for those wishing to learn Latin and the meaning of its words. However, there has certainly been no time for that, for Calepino was able to abstract the vocabulary and its meanings, its nuances and metaphors, from the reading of the poets and orators and other authors in the Latin language, basing what he says about them on the authority of these authors; which basis has been lacking for me because there is no alphabet nor writing among these people, thus it was impossible for me to construct a Calepino.[6]

Though Sahagún asserts here that the natives had "no alphabet nor writing," elsewhere he acknowledges that they possessed paintings or symbols and characters "by which they understood." In fact, he reproduced some of these pictures and signs alongside the Nahuatl texts. When he was writing the prologue to a work consisting of twelve volumes, he insisted that then, using what he had gathered, something like a Calepino might be feasible:

> Yet I laid the foundation so that whoever might wish to do so can make one with ease. Through my industry, twelve books have been written in a proper and natural form of this Mexican language, where, beyond being very tasteful

and beneficial writing, will also be found in it all the manners of speaking, all the vocabulary that the language uses: as well founded and true as what Virgil and Cicero wrote, along with the other authors of the Latin language.[7]

As much as the linguistic interest meant to Sahagún, as he penetrated more deeply into his research, the appeal of learning about the ancient culture in and of itself also grew stronger. He speaks a great deal about this throughout his *Historia general* and in the prologue to Book I, from which I have been quoting. In it, he also states this:

> I shall avail myself of all this work to assay the carat [worth] of this Mexican people, which has remained unknown up to now. . . . They thus are held to be barbarians and of very little worth; in truth, however, in matters of culture and refinement, they are a step ahead of other nations that presume to be quite politic.[8]

In the context in which he wrote this, he offers a brief synthesis of pre-Hispanic history, which must be seen as startlingly close to what has been revealed by modern archaeology. In speaking about the antiquity of various peoples, he adduces the testimony of the native paintings and codices. He ponders the monuments left behind by the different inhabitants, founders of kingdoms and realms that succeeded one another, from Tula-Teotihuacan (*Tula* in the sense of 'city'), Cholula, Xochicalco, and Tula-Xicocotitlan, up to Mexico-Tenochtitlan. Deep into the matter of history and culture, he does not conceal his admiration in his writing:

> There are great signs of the antiquities of this people, as [can be seen] today at Tula, Tulantzinco, and a structure known as Xochicalco in the vicinity of Cuauhnahuac [Cuernavaca]. And almost in the entire land, there are signs and traces of extremely ancient buildings and treasures [jewels]. . . . The learning and wisdom of these peoples are manifest for

being great, as it appears in the Tenth Book, where in Chapter 29 the first inhabitants of this land are discussed; it is asserted that they were accomplished philosophers and astrologers and very adroit in all the mechanical arts. . . . In religion and the adoration of their gods, I do not believe that there have ever been idolaters more devoted to their gods, nor at such great cost to themselves as these [people] of New Spain.[9]

From the prologue to Book I of the *Historia general*, the three primary motivations for Fray Bernardino de Sahagún's research efforts are revealed in religious, linguistic, and, as we would say today, historical-anthropological veins. Now it is time to turn to how he got the project underway.

Sahagún's assertion that he "wrote twelve books" and that he had been ordered to "write in the Mexican language whatever it seemed to me to be of use" deserves some scrutiny here, although it anticipates what will be discussed more fully further on. What does he mean by this? Does he really consider himself to be the author of the texts that he has identified elsewhere (such as in the prologue to Book VI of his *Historia general*) as the testimonies contributed by the Indians: "all of what is written in these books, before and after this one, . . . is in a language that is their ancestors' own"?[10] In fact, he even gives the names of some of the elderly men who had provided him with these and other texts, such as Diego Mendoza de Tepepulco, also known as Tlaltentzin, "an elderly man of great dignity and ability," and the healers who provided ample information about their field of competence.[11]

Dealing with the beginnings of Sahagún's research presupposes becoming aware, from the start, of the critical problem his work presents. One must discern between what can be considered purely indigenous and what is due to the friar, or more broadly, to his Hispanic, humanistic, and evangelizing Christian cultural baggage. With this critical focus, at the same time that one must describe the results obtained by Bernardino in the various phases of his research, one must also inquire about what the different testimonies gathered by him are and actually convey. With respect to the methodology he adopted or to the way he proceeded to carry out his research, Sahagún himself declared,

> Having received this order [from Provincial Francisco de Toral], I wrote up an agenda or memorandum of all the subjects that I would treat, that is what is written down in the twelve books, the *Postilla* [commentary], and the *Cánticos* [canticles].[12]

These words certainly deserve some comment. It is desirable to reconstruct, as far as possible, the agenda or memorandum, which is to say, the schema and structure of what he proposed to gather into his work. Sahagún adds that what was included is, in fact, the content of the twelve books into which, in the end, the *Historia general* was divided, in addition to the *Postilla* and the *Cánticos*. One must not forget that Bernardino, on writing this in the decade of the seventies, alludes to the major portion of what he had achieved since 1558. Over the years, it had all been the object of revisions and elaborations: what he had been gathering as indigenous texts, the ordering he imposed on them, and what he would write in Nahuatl and Spanish on his own account. All of the richness and complexity that specialists in the ancient history of Mexico acknowledge in his work are a product of his perfectionist striving to improve the whole of his work with each restructuring.

THE AGENDA OR SCHEMA OF TOPICS TO BE STUDIED

The examination of the oldest documentation that has been preserved as part of the Nahuatl texts collected by Sahagún on the indigenous culture is a good route to learning about how he structured the agenda or memorandum. The folios that belong to that oldest documentation obtained in Tepepulco have the characteristic of including numerous paintings in the native style and texts that are the elucidation or reading of the same. Sahagún himself distributed those *Primeros memoriales* (First memoranda, as Francisco del Paso y Troncoso designated them on reproducing them in facsimile form in 1906) in five lengthy chapters. Though only four of them are preserved, their examination reveals what he originally sought to encompass in pursuit of information about the native culture.

The first two chapters in Nahuatl address "divine things," one on the gods and the other on what lies in heaven and in the netherworld. The next two chapters encompass "human things": the third concerns itself with "Rulership," and the fourth is about other realities related to human beings. There was also a fifth chapter, which included texts on the things of nature and of the earth, as we shall see.

If one compares the arrangement of subject matter that constitutes the oldest texts collected and organized by Fray Bernardino with what he himself, in his prologue to Book I, described as an objective of his research, we shall see that there is complete agreement between them. There he declared that his intention was to inquire about the "divine or, better said, idolatrous, human, and natural things of this New Spain."

Some Sahagún scholars have asked themselves where our friar could have derived the conceptualization and organization of his work. Given its nature as an approach to a culture, some think that he might have taken his model from Pliny's *Natural History*. According to others, the work of Saint Isidore of Seville in his encyclopedic *Etymologies*, and *De Propietatibus Rerum* (On the properties of things), written in the thirteenth century by Bartholomeus Anglicus, contain many of the themes that Sahagún found appealing.[13] It is not possible to provide a conclusive response to the question of what possible works read by Fray Bernardino were for him a wellspring of inspiration; it will suffice to recall that in the Renaissance context in which he had been educated at the University of Salamanca, the interest was palpable in a universal approach to the knowledge of the cultural and natural realities of the peoples of classical antiquity and those of modern times.

SAHAGÚN IN TEPEPULCO

Toward the end of 1558 or at the start of the following year, Bernardino, along with his agenda or memorandum, moved to the town of Tepepulco (today called *Tepeapulco*, located toward the southwest in the state of Hidalgo), which then belonged to the province of Aculhuacan or Tetzcoco. Fray Toribio de Benavente Motolinía recalled that the town was one of the first visited by the Franciscans:

> Among these, Tepepulco did it quite well, and it grew constantly in profiting from and deepening its knowledge of the Faith. . . . This town is set in a small highland valley, where there had been one of the largest and most attractive of the temples of the Demon; it was then cast down [by the friars]; because it is a large town it had many *teocallis*, or temples of the Devil, and this is in general the rule by which a town could be said to be large or small, whether it had many temples.[14]

From a very early date, the Franciscans began the construction of a church and monastery in Tepepulco. The date of 1530 carved into the south wall of the church's bell tower testifies to this. Fray Andrés de Olmos was working there as a missionary about that time. It was probably he and the Franciscans who followed who saw the already initiated construction through to completion during the decade of the fifties in the sixteenth century. The new religious structures were raised on top of a high platform that had formed the principal part of the main *teocalli*, or native temple. Today the remains of other pyramids may be seen nearby, along with numerous archaeological relics, which are gathered together in a small museum on the ground floor of the monastery.

Hernán Cortés had set his eyes on Tepepulco before the construction of the church and monastery. Attracted by the abundance of broad, open fields surrounding the town, which he thought would make good pasture land for the breeding of live-stock, he began construction of a country house, a sort of large castle. The members of the first Audiencia, enemies of Cortés, impeded the consummation of his plans. Although Cortés's plans did not prosper, the Franciscans managed to build a hospital for natives and Spaniards. It should be recalled that one of the roads that joined Mexico City with the port of Veracruz passed through Tepepulco, so a hospital could also offer solace to travelers in need of rest.

Besides the hospital, a water supply system to bring water from springs about twenty-two kilometers away was built not too long afterward with the participation of the Franciscans. The work was an aqueduct emptying into a "water box," which is still visible near the monastery. This box, which still serves as a water storage tank, was completed in 1545, according to a legend that can be seen on the inside of the cornice of the box, which reads, "When D. Antonio de Mendoza was viceroy, and Charles V *tlatoani* [king], and D. Diego Belázquez governor, the true Faith and the Immaculate God arrived by water."

With regard to the church and monastery, where Fray Bernardino stayed when he initiated his research at Tepepulco in 1558 or the beginning of 1559, it can be stated that they are very well built. Today's visitors can assess this for themselves. As many scholars of Mexican colonial art have noted, the hand of the native artist is visible in various aspects of the church and monastery. For example, the ornamentation carved into the stone of the church façade, despite its plateresque character, includes elements of the local flora, and the church's archivolt displays little angels mounted atop jaguars, whose fur resembles the plumage of a bird.

The monastery and church of San Francisco Tepepulco, without ostentation, constitute a good example of the early architectural style introduced by the Franciscans in central Mexico.[15] The ample halls that house the refectory and kitchen, as well as the De Profundis Hall, can be viewed today as part of a tour through the monastery cloister, with its two floors and its *mediopunto*

arcades of columns reminiscent of the Doric style. Climbing to
the upper level, one can access the cells in which the religious
lived and can also admire the frescoes along the corridor that
depict scenes from the life of Christ. To approach all of this at
Tepepulco is, at the same time, to draw close to Bernardino, who
spent some two years there, to see what he saw and to feel what
his life was like in these peaceful surroundings, so propitious for
prayer and study.

RESEARCH METHODOLOGY

Although his interest in evangelization might well explain Sahagún's move to Tepepulco, it must not be forgotten that his intention at that moment was not so much to act as a missionary but
rather to obey the order of his superior, to inquire about "the divine
or, better said, idolatrous, human, and natural things of this New
Spain." In light of such a purpose, it is appropriate to ask oneself
precisely why he selected the town of Tepepulco. The most distinguished biographer and editor of chronicles, Don Joaquín García
Icazbalceta (1825–1899), in his valuable article about Sahagún, alludes to the circumstance that the native lord of Tepepulco was at
that time married to the daughter of the former ruler of Tetzcoco,
Ixtlilxochitl the Second.[16] This princess had taken with her several
important Tetzcocans, some of them men well-versed in their history and traditions. The lord of the town himself, also mentioned
in some Tetzcocan chronicles, was the person who congratulated
Bernardino at the beginning of his research:

> In said town, I had all the principal men gathered togeth-
> er with the ruler of the town, Don Diego de Mendoza (al-
> ready known by his Spanish name but previously called
> Tlaltentzin), an elderly man of great dignity and ability,
> very experienced in matters religious, politic, and even idol-
> atrous. Having gathered them together, I proposed to them
> what I intended to do and asked them to refer me to ca-
> pable and experienced persons with whom I might speak

and who could provide me with information about which I might ask. They answered that they would discuss what I had proposed and that on the next day they would give me their answer. Thus they bid me farewell.[17]

Don Diego de Mendoza Tlaltentzin is described by the Tetzcocan chronicler Fernando de Alva Ixtlilxochitl, who was to meet him later, as being "from Tepepulco, about ninety years of age [in Ixtlilxochitl's time, circa 1590], a very well-read man ... who is also familiar with histories and accounts, who saw the city of Tetzcoco, and the children of Nezahualpilli, they declared to him."[18]

Another reference of considerable interest can be adduced about this Don Diego de Mendoza Tlaltentzin. It originates in the parish archive in the town of Tepepulco. The only book in Nahuatl preserved there is one containing registry entries of weddings from 1590. The first of these entries lists the marriage of Pedro Hernandez, a single young man who contracted matrimony with María Jacome, an unmarried girl also of the same town, "daughter of Don Jacobo de Metoza," that is, Diego or Jacobo (two forms of the same name) de Mendoza.[19]

It would be fitting to ask oneself whether this Mendoza was the same person to whom Sahagún spoke in 1559 and Alva Ixtlilxochitl spoke between 1585 and 1590, or a son of his. According to the Tetzcocan chronicler, he was "about ninety years of age" around 1590, which means that he had been born around 1500. At the time when Sahagún met him, he must have been around fifty-nine years old, an age that in those days could have seemed to Sahagún to be that of an "elderly man." Furthermore, the fact that his name is preceded by the title "Don," which does not occur with the names of others, appears to corroborate the identity of this long-lived and prolific personage, who in 1590 had a daughter of marriageable age.

This Don Diego de Mendoza agreed to collaborate with Sahagún:

> They came on the next day, this elderly man with the principals, and pronounced a solemn speech, as they were wont

to do in those days, and they pointed out for me some ten or twelve leading elders and told me that I could communicate with them and that they would be able to respond to whatever I asked about. There were also as many as four Latin students, to whom a few years prior I had taught grammar at the College of Santa Cruz at Tlatelolco. With these elders and the Latin grammarians, I spoke for many days over the course of more than two years, following the order of the questionnaire that I had prepared.

Everything we conferred about, they gave me in pictures, which was the form of writing that they used in ancient times. The grammarians would relate them in their language, writing the declaration under the paintings. I still have these originals.[20]

These succinct words are a description of the method that Sahagún had conceived and implemented. Following the schema or questionnaire (the agenda), Bernardino sought out his sources of information. These consisted of the oral testimony of those who were knowledgeable about the native culture and its history, as well as some codices or books of paintings, which, after gaining the trust of the elders, he managed to have revealed to him; of this there is no doubt because he copied several images and glyphs. As we might say today, after the manner of modern cultural anthropologists, he sought out his "consultants." Because of this, he showed no disdain for the written sources: the native pictures with characters. In order to carry out his task, he worked assisted by his *trilinguals*, his former students at the College of Santa Cruz at Tlatelolco. The names of these men are well known to us. He reiterates them in various parts of his works : Antonio Valeriano, "the principal one and most knowledgeable," a resident of Cuauhtitlan; Alonso Vegerano, "a bit less than the latter," from Cuauhtitlan; Martín Jacobita, who became the rector of the college at Tlatelolco; and Pedro de San Buenaventura, also from Cuauhtitlan.

Working with these collaborators and inquiring in Nahuatl via those long-winded *parlamentos* (parleys, speechifying) of which the Nahuas were so fond, Sahagún began penetrating a world of culture that was unknown to him. The harvest seemed to him to be extremely interesting, as can be seen from his descriptions of it. Yet, as Bernardino was gathering these testimonies on the native beliefs and traditions, he was also planting the seeds of Christianity, which, we must not forget, was his main concern. He refers to this when, after mentioning the texts and paintings he had copied at Tepepulco, he adds, "at that time, I dictated the *Commentary* [*Postilla*] and the hymns, which my former students wrote down in Nahuatl in the same town of Tepepulco."[21]

The *Commentary* to which he alludes so often throughout his writings is nothing other than a collection of commentaries on the Gospels and Epistles in the form of homilies. It is in this sense that the word *postilla* was used, as is revealed in a citation from the *Diccionario de autoridades* (Dictionary of authorities) of the Spanish Royal Academy, which references the work of Fray Damián Cornejo: "He wrote *postillas* on the Sacred Scriptures . . . ; he commented on the four Gospels and the Epistles of Paul."[22] As we have seen, toward the year 1540 Bernardino had completed a first version of his sermons for the Sundays and feast days of the year. Now, finding himself in Tepepulco, he revised and expanded, in his perfectionist way, the older work. There are references that allow us to confirm that the sermons were accompanied by the biblical fragments from the New Testament that corresponded to the Sunday readings during the celebration of the Mass.

With regard to what are referred to as *hymns* and *psalms*, based on their form of expression, including turns of phrase and metaphors from the ancient songs of the natives, Sahagún composed these during his stay in Tepepulco so that the Indians might intone them instead of others from their pagan past. Their dictation, which was his own, was transcribed for him by his native students. The compositions from Tepepulco were soon broadcast throughout many communities with the authorization of Viceroy Luis de Velasco. Sahagún remarks on this in his "Prologue to the Reader," which introduces these hymns in the *Psalmodia christiana*, the only book of his that Sahagún saw in print. (It was published in 1583.)

Bernardino worked in Tepepulco until the completion of what he referred to as his *hebdomada*, his "week" or period of three years as superior, as ordered by his provincial, Fray Francisco de Toral, who had mandated his research. Sahagún relates what occurred in 1561: "They transferred me from Tepepulco; taking along all my writings, I went to live at Santiago de Tlatelolco [that is, at the monastery next to the College of Santa Cruz]."[23] There he would set to work on the testimonies he had collected. At this point, it is important for us to acquaint ourselves with the content of what he refers to as "my writings."

THE TESTIMONIES COLLECTED IN TEPEPULCO

Though none of the oldest papers with the paintings and Sahagún's declarations that were written underneath in Nahuatl have been preserved—that is, the originals that Sahagún mentions as the fruit of his research at Tepepulco—there does exist a transcription of them executed under his supervision. This was probably done at Tlatelolco. Bernardino has left us the names of those who accomplished this for him; they were also former students from the College of Santa Cruz:

> The scribes who made the clean copy of all these works were Diego de Grado, resident of Tlatelolco, *barrio* [city ward] of La Concepción; Bonifacio Maximiliano of Tlatelolco, barrio of San Martín; Matheo Severino from Xochimilco, from the Ullac district.[24]

That old copy made of the texts collected at Tepepulco (in which are contained the seeds of the work that would continue to grow) is preserved today, bound in two volumes but not in its original order; each volume is at a different library in Madrid. Those two volumes, which also include texts collected later, are known among specialists as the *Códices matritenses* (*Historia general de las cosas de la Nueva España*, by Fray Bernardino de Sahagún). They encompass a good portion of the Nahuatl documentation collected by Sahagún and only a small part of the Spanish version. Further on, we shall see under what circumstances these manuscripts were taken to Spain. For the moment, it is enough to recall that one part of these Sahagún documents is at the *Biblioteca del Real Palacio* (Library of the Royal Palace); the other is at the library of the *Real Academia de la Historia* (Royal Academy of History).

Toward the end of the nineteenth century, the indefatigable tracker of documents, Francisco del Paso y Troncoso (1846–1916), devoted a good deal of time to Sahagún's *Códices matritenses*. His intention was to publish them with the text translated from the Nahuatl. He died, however, before being able to undertake this project. Upon studying them, he was able to uncover the disarray in which they had been bound because the documents corresponded to different phases of Bernardino's research. He decided on a facsimile reproduction and, with sound instinct and a critical common sense, he reordered the texts according to what appeared to reflect the various phases of their preparation. He published these in a facsimile edition of four large volumes in Madrid (1905–1908), adjudging to each group of documents the designation that seemed most suitable to him.

The oldest manuscripts, that is, those from Tepepulco, received the title *Primeros memoriales* (First memoranda). We shall deal with the remaining texts in due course. These *Primeros memoriales*, together with the already described *Huehuetlahtolli*, expressions of the *Ancient Word*, are thus the oldest testimonies collected by the friar at Tepepulco between 1558 and 1561. Their thematic domains correspond to those of the agenda or questionnaire that Sahagún had proposed to investigate: divine, human, and natural things. The texts and paintings that have been preserved are included in only the first two of these. With respect to the third domain, the one dealing with natural things, there are indications that toward the eighteenth century the respective chapter was in the possession of a Madrid printer, Antonio Sanz, who attempted to sell it to the Real Academia de la Historia. Since this date, the trail indicating its ultimate location has grown cold. In subsequent periods of his research, the topic of "natural things" would attract Sahagún's attention, thus there is ample evidence of them in the native language.

The whole of the texts in the *Primeros memoriales* comprises 88 folios written on both sides (numbered by Del Paso y Troncoso as pages 1–176). All the texts included are in Nahuatl. Similarly, there are numerous paintings, the style of which suggests a pre-Hispanic influence. In Spanish there are only a few glosses and annotations by Sahagún himself organizing his materials into "chapters and paragraphs."

The testimonies that deal with "divine things" encompass 112 pages (that is, 56 folios on both sides). They begin with an account of the feasts throughout the eighteen twenty-day ritual "months" ($18 \times 20 = 360$, plus 5 days held to be unlucky or evil at the end). Each feast is accompanied by a painting in color. Though Sahagún subsequently enriched his data on these celebrations, the texts already contain considerable information. The religious life of the natives vividly emerges in these testimonies, with their sacrifices, songs, dances, and other ceremonies.

As a liturgical manual, this is followed by a collection of texts on the forms of the services and ceremonies for the gods, such as offerings, the lighting of the sacred fire, the act of ritual sweeping, the ceremonial eating of earth (that is, touching it to the mouth in swearing an oath), and the sacrifice of birds and, of course, human beings. The great majority of the texts are accompanied by paintings in color. Another two sections likewise deal with "the liturgy," including the list of the diverse types or classes of priests and the description of the regalia of the principal gods. A schematic painting of the Templo Mayor in Mexico-Tenochtitlan is included in this section.

In what follows, there are some minor texts, a residue of the oldest documentation transcribed in the same Tepepulco. They deal with offenses to the gods, the gods' attributes, the hourly rites for each day, temple rituals, vows, and oaths.

Sections that are very different from the above and yet are bound up with indigenous thought and the universe of the gods are those relating to "what is above us," the celestial realities, and that which is beneath the earth, the netherworld. Thus we encounter first a segment on the sun, the moon, the great star (Quetzalcoatl, that is, Venus), other stars, comets, and eclipses.

The counts of periods of time, that is, calendrical computations, occupy considerable space because they relate to the cycles of feasts, sacrifices, and other rituals as well as to the fates of people, which are always tied to the gods. On the one hand, Sahagún had the *xiuhmolpilli* transcribed; this is the "bundle of years," the cycle of fifty-two solar years that appear with their ancient hieroglyphic signs and alphabetic transcriptions. On the other hand, several folios are dedicated to the presentation of the *tonalpohualli* 'the count of days and destinies.' This system, based on twenty signs and thirteen numerals, had a fundamental importance. Based on the *tonalpohualli,* each day of the year and the years themselves were given a name. By consulting this count, the good and bad omens for whatever mattered in human life could be predicted. In a conclusion to his rather lengthy first chapter, Sahagún transcribed some texts dealing with auguries and the interpretation of dreams.

In the same section on "divine things," he included another chapter, which, in contrast to the first, ended up being rather brief. In this he deals with the netherworld, the region of the dead and others in the hereafter, "destinies and dwellings of the dead." The first part of what Francisco del Paso y Troncoso called the *Primeros memoriales* concludes with this second chapter.

Frontispiece of the *Vocabulario en la lengua castellana y mexicana,* published by Fray Alonso de Molina in 1555. The colophon states that Fray Bernardino reviewed and approved the manuscript.

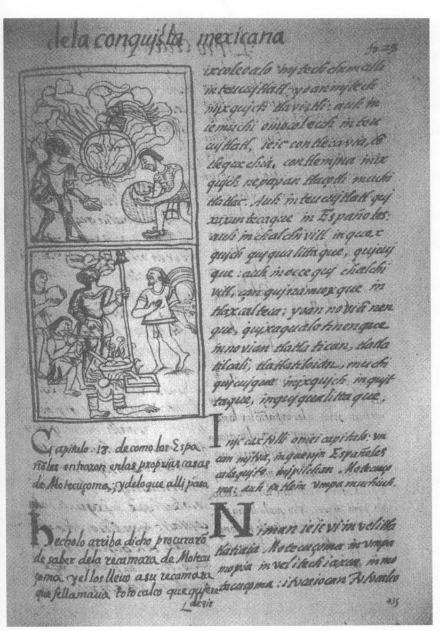

Nahuatl text collected by Sahagún from Tlatelolcan elders ca. 1555. It was later transcribed in the *Florentine Codex*, of which folio 28r is reproduced here.

Remains of a pre-Hispanic temple in Tepepulco, state of Hidalgo.

Stairway to the convent and church in Tepepulco.

Entrance to the church of San Francisco in Tepepulco.

Water box in Tepepulco, from 1545.

Inscription along the interior cornice of the water box, which reads, "When D. Antonio de Mendoza was viceroy, and Charles V *tlatoani* [king], and D. Diego Belázquez governor, the true Faith and the Immaculate God arrived by water."

Folio 2r of the *Primeros memoriales* collected by Sahagún in Tepepulco. The paintings depict the feasts from the pre-Hispanic calendar described in the Nahuatl text on the left (From Bernardino de Sahagún, *Primeros memoriales*, University of Oklahoma Press, 1993).

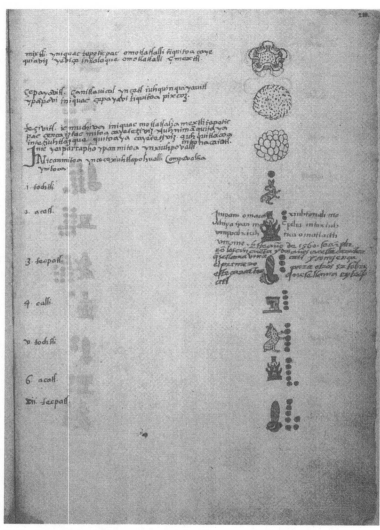

Folio 288r of the *Primeros memoriales*. The upper part represents clouds, snow, and hail. Below these texts and drawings begins the count of the solar year. One reads, in Sahagún's hand, on the sign for the year 3-Flint, "This year of 1560 concluded the fifty-two years with this sign called *ume acatl* and begins with the sign called *ey tecpatl*, first of the fifty-two" (From Bernardino de Sahagún, *Primeros memoriales,* University of Oklahoma Press, 1993).

This approach to the spiritual world of the ancient Mexicans reveals a paradoxical people who practiced what were held to be repulsive sacrifices of human beings but at the same time showed them to be possessed of a deep and elevated spirituality. It would be necessary to penetrate deeply into the indigenous soul to set it free of the devil until the true religion, a Christianity such as that of the apostles, could be implanted.

The second part, on "human things," was also divided into two chapters. The first begins with three lists of rulers, accompanied by brief commentaries in Nahuatl, such as the one about the effigies of the sovereigns: those of Mexico-Tenochtitlan, Tetzcoco, and Huexotla. In speaking about those of the metropolis, the text includes an annotation in Nahuatl about the native ruler, who was maintained by the Spaniards to rule over the Nahuas of Huexotla: *In ipan xihuitl ticate, in motenehuaya ome acatl,* 'in the year that is called 2-Reed,' that is, this lord ruled at the time in which these texts were being transcribed, corresponding to 1559. As we have seen, this was when Sahagún was collecting his texts in Tepepulco.

The lifestyle of the rulers is also taken up in the sections dealing with the principal occupations, cuisine, and beverages. Included there are several color paintings of the clothing and adornments appropriate for noble men and women. There follow several lists summarizing the utensils, furnishings, household items, and architectural structures. Del Paso y Troncoso, who had reordered the *Primeros memoriales* (because, as noted above, they are in an arbitrary sequence in the *Códices matritenses*), included other materials at that point, likewise a by-product of the zeal for learning that Bernardino had exhibited at Tepepulco These materials, which are also in Nahuatl, are two listings of men and women, good and evil. Though indubitably these texts and others that appeared later all originated in Tepepulco, their ordering must have been quite difficult. Fray Bernardino was himself unsure of their place in regard to the whole of the work, which he was to reorganize and expand several times.

These texts focus on education: the origin of the Chichimecs, seminomadic peoples from the north who, mixed with the Toltecs, the creators of a high culture, were held to be the ancestors of the Nahuas. The power of the rulers was also an object of attention. The chapter approaches its conclusion with further examples of the *Huehuetlahtolli*, testimonies of the *Ancient Word*, as warnings to the people, and with the enunciation of the principal causes of the anger and sadness that may afflict those who rule.

The second chapter of this part on "human things" surpasses the confines of the topic concerning those who rule and allows entry to a number of, albeit brief, data on kinship terminology, parts of the body, illnesses, and cures. Two sections are included that again deal with the rulers and the nobility. One, accompanied by numerous paintings in color, provides the designations for weapons and insignias such as headdresses, feather crests, and shields; another, at the end of what has been preserved of the *Primeros memoriales*, presents some of the "modes of courtesy and vituperation," as much for the nobles as for the populace at large.

We can say little more about the third part on "natural things" aside from the aforementioned vague reference to the fact that it included paintings of plants and animals. Any scholar, historian, anthropologist, or insightful person who has read the *Historia general de la cosas de la Nueva España* by Fray Bernardino, as it has been published several times in Spanish, will recognize in what has been described up to now that the texts in Nahuatl from the *Primeros memoriales* are like a seed or nucleus of the restructured and vastly expanded work.

CATEGORIES TO WHICH THESE TESTIMONIES CAN BE ASSIGNED CRITICALLY

The testimonies originating in Tepepulco are of great interest within the whole of Sahagún's contribution, in and of themselves and as indicators of the themes that were researched and would be researched by him. These materials can be assessed more correctly from the perspectives that were of interest to Bernardino while he pursued his investigations: that is, from an emphasis that was at one and the same time ethnological, historical, philological, and linguistic. They can also be divided critically into several categories.

Many of these texts, most of which are accompanied by paintings, have a fundamentally ethnographic interest inasmuch as they reveal several aspects of the ancient culture. Such is the case with the account of the feasts, as well as those that speak of the priesthood and the diverse rituals, the omens and dreams, the heavenly bodies, death, education, the origin of the Chichimecs, weapons and insignia of the nobility, and what relates to illnesses and remedies.

There are other testimonies in which a historical interest predominates. These are the annotated lists of the supreme rulers of Mexico-Tenochtitlan, Tetzcoco, and Huexotla. It is also worth noting that the linguistic preoccupation surfaces here as part of an effort to enrich lexical knowledge: the garments of each lord in the paintings are accompanied by glosses providing their corresponding names.

Of cultural as well as textual interest, that is to say philological interest, are the twenty sacred hymns with their linguistic annotation. Also in this category are the exhortations of the elders, that is, the examples of the *Huehuetlahtolli*, testimonies of the *Ancient Word*, which Bernardino collected at Tepepulco.

Finally, though they always had a cultural importance for Sahagún, the linguistic interest is blatant in the registers of names accompanied by their morphemic variants or in the verbs with which phrases and sentences were constructed. An example of this can be seen in the lists of foods and beverages, clothing and ornaments, ladies' pastimes, women's utensils, buildings, furniture, the external and internal organs of the human body, and styles of courtesy and vituperation among the nobility and the masses.

CRITICAL ASSESSMENT OF THE
TEXTS ORIGINATING IN TEPEPULCO

Another point of view, one concerned with the ultimate source of the texts, weighed critically, states that some are responses to the questionnaires employed by Sahagún. One example is the text about the feasts. Next to the paintings are indicated the name of each feast, rituals related to it, how it was celebrated, and on what date of the Christian calendar it was celebrated. Another group of responses includes those that accompany the paintings of the regalia of the gods. They are described succinctly, from headdress to sandals. This is also the case with the text about the lords of Mexico-Tenochtitlan, Tetzcoco, and Huexotla. The questions whose responses are provided are as follows: What is his name? How many years did he rule? What did he do?

Other texts, however, provide what was said by consultants in a quite spontaneous manner, without following a questionnaire. There are numerous examples of this in the *Primeros memoriales* concerning the tolling of the different hours at the temples and the temple rituals; vows and oaths; heavenly bodies; *Mictlan*, or 'the Land of the Dead'; the woman who came back to life; the origin of the Chichimecs; and other accounts. The spontaneous responses are likewise the ones that provide linguistic information.

Finally one can discuss from a critical perspective a third group of testimonies. These are the ones that bear, with greater or lesser fidelity, textual expressions from the pre-Hispanic tradition. There are two examples of this in the *Primeros memoriales*. One consists of the twenty hymns to the gods, and the other includes the speeches of *Huehuetlahtolli*. In both cases, though there may have been fortuitous alterations to the original versions, it is possible to assert that we stand before "canonical" testimonies of the ancient culture. They constitute genuine examples of pre-Hispanic literature in Nahuatl.

It would be grotesque to claim that Sahagún composed or induced the composition of the twenty hymns, which are so difficult to understand that he did not even attempt to translate them into Spanish, and the content of which pertains to pre-Hispanic religious thought. As concerns the *Huehuetlahtolli*, also transcribed in Tepepulco, it is fitting to repeat what Sahagún said years later about those collected in Tlatelolco: "[I]t does not befit human understanding to fabricate them" because they are "their own language and the work of Nahua learned men and priests."

One can already appreciate the method adopted by Sahagún through the material collected at Tepepulco. Adapting himself to the pre-Hispanic cultural tradition, he reproduced the paintings from the codices and transcribed the corresponding "readings" of these with their glyphs, as the elders had provided them. Likewise, he obtained specific responses to his questionnaires and listened to other accounts freely communicated by his consultants. He inquired about a great many words, as much from a lexico-morphological motivation as from a cultural one. Finally, he transcribed texts, which also related to paintings and glyphs, that constituted "canonical " expressions, that is, imprecatory formulas or those of praise as in the sacred hymns and in some oratory, in the manner of *Huehuetlahtolli*. It should be emphasized that what he accomplished at Tepepulco, set the framework for his ultimate research. The ethnological-historical-philological-linguistic method would yield even more abundant fruit in the years to come.

Two editions of these testimonies exist. The first, a facsimile, is owed to the aforementioned Francisco del Paso y Troncoso, who wished to bring order to the disheveled state in which these testimonies had been bound in the two volumes of the *Códices matritenses*.[25] When he reorganized the different folios in his reproduction of texts and paintings, Don Francisco kept in mind the sequence indicated by Sahagún: "divine and human things," because the section on "natural things," which almost certainly did exist, has gone missing.

In this reordering, the testimonies of Tepepulco, because they were the oldest, receive the name *Primeros memoriales* and comprise

pages 1 to 176 of volume VI in the facsimile edition achieved by
Del Paso y Troncoso. In order to identify the materials from Tepepulco in the two volumes of the Madrid codices and to reorder
them in his edition, he also took into account the annotations, several of them in Sahagún's own hand, that precede its different sections, parts, chapters, and paragraphs.

The other edition, which is much more recent, comprises a
reproduction, likewise in facsimile, and a paleographic version
with an English translation. Ferdinand Anders prepared the reproduction in color.[26] Thelma D. Sullivan did the paleography
and English translation. Upon her death, her work was revised
and completed by other scholars.[27] It can be added that years
before, scholars such as Eduard Seler, Angel María Garibay K.,
Wigberto Jiménez Moreno, Alfredo López Austin, and Miguel
León-Portilla had translated and published (the first in German,
the rest in Spanish) several of these texts collected by Sahagún
at Tepepulco.[28]

CHAPTER FIVE

EDITING AND EXPANSION OF THE TEPEPULCO MATERIAL AND RETURN TO TLATELOLCO (1561–1575)

Installed in the monastery at Santiago Tlatelolco, very close to the College of Santa Cruz, Bernardino continued writing his works on what one might call his "three fronts": doctrinal, linguistic, and historical-cultural. Recently returned from Tepepulco, he comments on his approach:

> I went to live at Santiago of Tlatelolco where, gathering the native principals together, I proposed the matter of my writings to them, and I asked them to indicate to me some capable persons with whom I might examine and converse about the writings, which I had brought from Tepepulco. The governor, along with the mayors, indicated up to eight or ten elders chosen from among them who were very fluent in the language and familiar with the matter of antiquities; with them and some four or five students, all trilinguals, for a year or somewhat longer, shut up in the College, everything I brought in writing from Tepepulco was edited, declared, and added to. And everything was rewritten anew in a bad hand, as it was done in great haste. In this perusal or examination, the student who worked most of all was Martín Jacobita, who was then the Rector of the College, a resident of Tlatelolco from the *barrio* of Santa Ana.[1]

Sahagún applied the same method he had employed at Tepepulco. As he had done there, he sought out persons with whom to confer, in this case those who were also "very fluent in the language and familiar with . . . antiquities." He again relied on the assistance of his trilingual students and, in a special way, on Martín Jacobita, then rector of the College of Santa Cruz. He dedicated much time to his research. He describes the result in the following way: "[E]verything I brought in writing from Tepepulco was edited, declared, and added to." The elders of Tlatelolco made it possible for Sahagún to emend or correct several points with their testimonies. With his students he made a declaration of the new contributions, that is to say, he commented on them until he understood them adequately because at that time he had not yet proceeded to a Spanish translation. The friar- researcher informs us that it was "added to," that is, there was a considerable enrichment of the materials. And yet, "as it was done in great haste," the manuscript is "in a bad hand."

Searching through the *Códices matritenses*, modern scholars have sought to identify whether it is there that the texts are included, written in a "bad hand." It seems probable that some folios that correspond to this phase of the first revision and other addenda might be preserved there, also bound out of order. Indeed, in the collection of texts already treated here that make up the *Primeros memoriales*, a discrimination can be made. Most of them are composed in very neat handwriting along with the colorful paintings. Perhaps they came that way from Tepepulco, where, quite plausibly, a copy based on the first notes and drafts was made. Nevertheless, there are some pages in a "bad hand" that might coincide with those to which Bernardino refers. Other folios in bad handwriting are included in the *Códices matritenses*; these differ in their manner of presentation from all the others. As we shall see, all of the other folios are arranged in columns. The sloppily written folios, however, which are in Nahuatl, take up the entire width of the page. They deal especially with the goddess, Tlazolteotl, fomenter of lust, and are related to the rite of confession that was addressed to her. There are also adages to the sun and the moon, traditions about their restoration in the Fifth Cosmic Age, and stories about Mexican rulers up to Don Diego Huitznahuatlailotlac, who ruled in Tetzcoco at the time Sahagún was working there. Don Francisco del Paso y Troncoso, editor of the facsimile of the *Códices matritenses* and organizer of their contents, designated these texts as the *Segundos memoriales* (Second memoranda).

As can be seen, Sahagún scholars have on occasion almost been obliged to take on the role of detectives in approaching Bernardino's greatest contribution. The associated problems are far from few in number, and they arise constantly in the volumes that constitute the *Códices matritenses*.

Many other texts are included in these *códices*; they are the fruit of the revision and reelaboration that Bernardino continued at the College of Santa Cruz. One group of folios in Nahuatl stands out; Sahagún had annotated them heavily in order to sequence them in various ways. In each of these folios there are three columns, though only the middle one is in the Indian language. Sahagún reserved the other two: the one on the left for the Spanish version, and the one on the right for linguistic annotations. In the same *Códices matritenses,* there are a few other folios in which the three columns managed to be completed.

Francisco del Paso y Troncoso, that perspicacious scrutinizer of documents, dubbed the group of texts in three columns, with only the middle one filled in, *Memoriales en tres columnas* (Memoranda in three columns). This body of documents (fruit of Sahagún's new stay in Tlatelolco until 1565) was targeted by him for further work. The trove of data was growing apace; indeed, it entirely surpassed what had previously been collected at Tepepulco. It was in reality the fruit of a parallel but distinct investigation. The world of the ancient gods seemed a little less dark to Sahagún. The subtleties of the calendar, the astrology, the feasts, and the omens were becoming a bit less mysterious.

The matters related to the phenomena of nature were also beginning to be perceived in all their complexity and richness.

Illnesses and cures had been a matter of protracted research at Tlatelolco. Fray Bernardino, conscious of the significance of his compilation of *materia medica*, preserved the names of the *titicih*, the native physicians who regaled him with their ancient lore; he wrote:

> The aforementioned was examined by the Mexican physicians whose names follow: Juan Pérez de Sanct Pablo, Pedro Pérez de Sanct Juan, Pedro Hernández de San Joan, Joséph Hernández de San Joan, Miguel García de San Sebastián, Francisco de la Cruz de Xihuitenco, Balthasar Juárez de San Sebastián, Antonio Martínez de San Joan.[2]

In another place, on concluding his transcription of the texts on the remedies for the illnesses, he adds to the list of physicians the following:

> The account above, on the medicinal herbs . . . was provided by the physicians of Santiago Tlatelolco, elders and very experienced in everything concerning medicine for they all heal publicly . . . : Gaspar García, resident of La Concepción; Pedro de Santiago, resident of Santa Inés; Francisco Simón and Miguel Damián, residents of Santo Toribio; Felipe Hernández, resident of Santa Ana; Pedro de Requena, resident of La Concepción; Miguel García, resident of Santo Toribio; and Miguel García, resident of Santa Inés.[3]

Bernardino's attitude before these native physicians was that of one wishing to learn. Years before, when another great pestilence had assailed New Spain, he would lament that there were no longer any native physicians at the college, indicating that he valued their remedies and procedures.

FIRST DIVISION OF THE TLATELOLCO TESTIMONIES

It is important to keep in mind the division imposed on the content of the texts that were contained in the manuscripts prepared at Tlatelolco: at first, they were also divided into five lengthy chapters. Contrary to what might be expected, though they maintained a relationship with the five chapters into which the Tepepulco texts had been divided, they were not incorporated with them. As has been stated, they constituted a different compilation. Consequently, the result would be two parallel but distinct collections of testimonies. Sahagún would only add some of the Tepepulco texts to the Tlatelolco manuscripts in the several reorganizations of his materials that he carried out. Examples of this are the text containing the description of the feast of *Atamalcualiztli*, when "water tamales" were eaten, and the twenty hymns to the gods. Let us attend to the contents of each of the five chapters into which Bernardino initially divided those new texts collected at Tlatelolco.

The first chapter is composed of folios from 33r to 159v of the codex preserved at the Royal Palace in Madrid. These include the description of the gods, accounts of the feasts throughout the year, the aforementioned twenty sacred hymns, the birth of Huitzilopochtli, the attributes of Tezcatlipoca, the legend of Quetzalcoatl and Tula, the different fates in the afterlife, and education in the schools.

The second chapter consists of folios 160r to 249v in the same *Códice del Real Palacio* (Royal Palace codex). The texts on "natural history" are to be found there, that is, the celestial bodies and the origin of the fifth sun at Teotihuacan; "astrology," or the count of two hundred days of the *tonalpohualli*; and the auguries and superstitions. As can be seen, the organization of the Tlatelolco manuscripts coincides with that of those brought from Tepepulco.

The third chapter encompasses folios 2r to 50r in the codex housed at the Royal Academy of History in Madrid. These folios depict the nobility, its attributes, and its pastimes, as well as the merchants.

The fourth chapter contains folios 88r to 197v of the same Royal Academy codex. It covers the broad field of *Tlacáyotl* 'human things,' that is, people's virtues and vices, parts of the body, and illnesses and remedies as well as a section on "the nations that have come to people this land."

The fifth and last chapter, from folio 200r to 342v, is also included in the codex at the Royal Academy of History. It seems to bear a similarity to the lost fifth chapter of the *Primeros memoriales* from Tepepulco; that is, it deals with *Tlalticpacáyotl* 'natural things,' such as animals, trees, plants, and different kinds of rocks and minerals.

COMPOSITION OF THE *SEGUNDOS MEMORIALES* AND THE *MEMORIALES CON ESCOLIOS*

In addition to this great collection of folios in the *códices* of the Royal Palace and the Royal Academy of History, bearers of what Del Paso y Troncoso referred to as *Memoriales en tres columnas*, the fruit of research at Tlatelolco, there are other materials in the same codices. They are the ones named *Segundos memoriales* (or *Complementarios*) by the same scholar, along with *Memoriales con escolios*. It has not been an easy task to fix precisely the dates of the respective elaborations; there are differences of opinion among those who have undertaken it.

The so-called *Segundos memoriales*, written in Nahuatl but encompassing the entire breadth of the folio (as has already been mentioned), are an indication of a first form of presentation written about 1562 consequently, prior to the one in three columns. It is possible that such vestiges are only a part of more extensive manuscripts that have disappeared today.

The *Memoriales con escolios* occupy folios 160r to 178v of the *Royal Palace Codex*, as well as folios 88r to 96v of the one housed at the Royal Academy of History. Such folios are an example of the manner in which Sahagún intended to present his manuscripts in a definitive fashion. He stated this himself in the already cited note at the top of folio 160r of the *Royal Palace Codex*: "The entire work should go the way this notebook is arranged."[4] As has been described above, it should show the Nahuatl text in the middle, the nonliteral, Spanish paraphrased version on the left, and linguistic annotations on the right. This is confirmed by another of his annotations in folio 178r where the same texts appear, but in a "bad hand." The note reads, "This is the draft of the first notebook." This notebook, now written in a good hand, was the only attempt to copy "in a good hand" the three columns with testimonies that refer to "celestial bodies" and "fathers, mothers, children, grandparents," etc., as much the "good" as the "bad" and "vice-ridden."

Put another way, these testimonies deal with part of what constituted the second and fourth chapters in the original division of the "five lengthy chapters." Thus, there are references, though struck through, to that first ordering. In folio 160r of the manuscript from the Royal Palace, one reads *Inic ome cap* (second chapter); placed before the *ome* there is a *chic*, so that *inic chicome* (seventh) results and joins the word *amuxtli* over the *cap*, now struck through, to indicate that the text belongs to Book VII in the new ordering. Something similar appears in folio 88v of the Royal Academy manuscript. There the words *nahui cap* (chapter four) are obliterated and, in Sahagún's handwriting, it is indicated above that this text belongs to the "tenth book." In these notes the reorganization of the manuscripts completed after Sahagún's stay at the monastery of San Francisco in Mexico is manifest.

If we accept what Sahagún states in his second prologue to the *Códice florentino*, one might think that the copy "in a good hand" was an attempt at transcription carried out toward the end of his stay at Tlatelolco toward 1564 or 1565. Another hypothesis would be to suppose that it belongs to the manuscript, though it is lost today, known as "from 1569," without implying that in this transcription the three columns had been completed according to the original intention. In such a case, it would still need to be explained why the native assistants, on copying the manuscript in a "bad hand," did not suppress the original note that referred to the original ordering in five lengthy chapters. At least it is clear that Sahagún corrected this, indicating in which book each of these texts belonged in the definitive reorganization of his manuscripts.

This is what Bernardino accomplished during his stay in Tlatelolco from 1561 to 1565. The five chapters into which he had divided the texts transcribed in Tepepulco were not just an object for revision. Indeed, they served as a kind of model for a new, broader, and in reality, different compilation from the one carried out in Tepepulco. It may consequently be asserted that the major portion of what came to constitute the work in Nahuatl, according to how Sahagún divided his texts, arises from what was compiled in those years. He had completed very little paraphrased translation into Spanish. Whichever way one looks at this, the stay at Tlatelolco was decisive in the totality of his research. I will take up next the critical assessment of the texts collected at Tlatelolco.

THE *COLOQUIOS Y DOCTRINA CHRISTIANA*

We return here to the *Coloquios y doctrina christiana* from which several paragraphs have been adduced to illustrate the first confrontations between friars and native priests and to exemplify an early form of indoctrination by the friars. Bernardino comments on this:

> It will be done for the purpose . . . of knowing that this doctrine of those twelve apostolic preachers [the friars who arrived in 1524] began to convert this people of New Spain; it has been in papers and memoranda until this year of fifteen hundred and sixty-four; because previously there had been no opportunity to set in order nor to convert it into the Mexican language in a polished and reasoned manner, which was brought back and polished at this College of Santa Cruz in Tlatelolco in the aforementioned year with the students who were the most capable and knowledgeable in the Mexican language and in the Latin language, who up to

now have been raised in this College; whose names are Antonio Valeriano, resident of Azcapotzalco; another Alonso Vegerano, resident of Cuauhtitlan; another Martín Jacobita, resident of Tlatelolco; and Andrés Leonardo, also of Tlatelolco. It was likewise polished with four very fluent elders, as knowledgeable about language as about antiquities.[5]

The work to which Sahagún alludes encompassed several parts. The first included "the conversations and confabulations (speechifying, parleys) that took place between the twelve religious and the leaders, lords, and satraps of the idols," that is, the native priests. This first part, in Nahuatl with a Spanish version, is of enormous interest. In it the colloquies and dialogues are recreated archetypically, which implied a clash of beliefs. As we have already seen, there is a deep drama in the responses of the priests. With great accuracy, Sahagún managed to reconstruct there, as best he could, the defense that the Nahua wise men credibly presented of their own beliefs and conceptualization of the world.

The text of these dialogues or "confabulations" is accompanied by another two parts: one, a Christian doctrine, and the other a "*Postilla* [commentary] of all the Epistles and Gospels for the Sundays of the entire year (which is the sermonizing used up to now), very appropriate in language and subject matter for the capacity of the Indians, which is being polished and shall form another volume in its own right, so that this one not be too long."[6]

Although portions of the *Coloquios* and the *Postilla*, that is, the Sunday sermonary and commentaries on the versions of the Epistles and Gospels, have been preserved, the *Doctrina christiana* has not come down to us. Sahagún managed to secure permission to publish his transcription of the dialogues, or *Coloquios*, although he was never able to see that work in print. I must say that I have had the privilege of bringing to light a facsimile of the manuscript with a Spanish version of the Nahuatl text of these same dialogues. This work appeared in 1986, 422 years after Bernardino had prepared it.

A PAUSE AT THE MONASTERY OF
SAN FRANCISCO IN MEXICO CITY

As usual, it is Sahagún who furnishes us with information about his latest move:

> Having done what I have mentioned in Tlatelolco, I came to live at San Francisco in Mexico [City] with all my writings; where, for a space of three years, on my own, I repeatedly went over all my writings, and I emended them once more, and divided them into books, into twelve books, and each book into chapters, and some books into chapters and paragraphs.[7]

Thus, in a few words we have what was Bernardino's principal occupation from 1565 to 1568. His "writings" in Nahuatl now included an impressive array of indigenous testimonies. At least by their appearance, they could be seen as basic knowledge about the pre-Hispanic culture of Mexico. The good friar must have felt impressed with such a mountain of texts. He had not neglected to attend to his commentary (*postilla*), the versions of the Epistles and Gospels, or the Christian doctrine; neither had he slackened off in his research on "the divine, human, and natural things" of the ancient peoples of "this New Spain." It would be natural to imagine that Bernardino might have asked himself at some time whether it was excessive of him to continue transcribing in Nahuatl, thus preserving texts with dire idolatrous consequences. Though Sahagún may not have credited this thought, there would soon be others, including some friars, who did hold his great life's work to be an extreme danger.

In the monastery of San Francisco, on his own, always the perfectionist, Sahagún "repeatedly went over all [his] writings." The best evidence for this three-year process lies in the hundreds of annotations he included, most of all on the texts in three columns, which made up the major portion of the *Códices matritenses*. These annotations are at times difficult to read precisely because from that time, Bernardino began to suffer from a trembling in his hands, a condition that was to recur a few years later; in referring to the year 1570, he would declare that "I can write nothing due to the shaking in my hands."

A perusal of the annotations and reordering done by Sahagún on his writings makes clear that he conceived of at least five different forms of organization, though always guided by the idea of encompassing themes of a religious, human, and natural character. Thus, for example, in one phase of work he introduced annotations in his texts to divide them into nine books. In the end, he decided to incorporate with his writings the oldest materials compiled since 1547, that is, the *Huehuetlahtolli*, or testimonies of the *Ancient Word*, and the book dealing with the Conquest. Furthermore, he divided in two the book dealing with "Rulership." Thus, his *magnum opus* would consist of twelve books. It should be noted that he signed his name at the end of each book, with an obvious indication of a hand tremor, as if to leave clear evidence of his wish that this be the arrangement.

After a series of changes (evident in his annotations, allowing a reconstruction of the complex process of reorganization of the texts), the thematic content of each book was as follows: I. The gods worshipped by the Mexicans; II. The feasts and sacrifices to the gods every twenty days, with the transcription of twenty sacred hymns; III. The origin of the gods, in particular Tezcatlipoca and Quetzalcoatl, with appendices on the different fates after death and on education; IV. The book of the *tonalpohualli*, or count of 260 days; V. Auguries and superstitions; VI. The book of the *Huehuetlahtolli*, testimonies of the Ancient Word; VII. The sun, the moon, the stars, and the "binding of the years"; VIII. Kings and nobles, the forms of government, elections of the rulers, and their manner of life; IX. The merchants, officials for gold and precious stones, and featherworking; X. The virtues and vices of the people, parts of the human body, disease, and medicine, with a

final chapter on "the nations who have come to inhabit this land";
XI. Nature, animals, trees, plants, metals, and diverse stones; and
XII. The Conquest of Mexico.

CRITICAL ASSESSMENT OF THE NATIVE TESTIMONIES

To evaluate critically the materials included in the *Primeros memoriales*, that is, the texts from Tepepulco, we formulated a three-
way distinction. In the first instance, we identified texts that per-
tain to the ancient forms of expression, can be conceived of as
"canonical," and were systematically assigned to genres such as
oratory, prayers, songs, and historical and legendary accounts.
Other texts we saw were responses on the part of the Indians to
the Franciscan's questionnaires. Finally, we placed in a third category the testimonies that were a spontaneous expression of what
the native consultants thought about a particular issue. This cat-
egorization can also be applied to the manuscript from Tlatelolco
reexamined at the monastery of San Francisco in Mexico City.

Let us examine the first category, the one consisting of those
texts that constitute a recollection of "canonical" manifestations
of the ancient indigenous tradition. It can be asserted that, with
the exception of the contents of Book XII (which is a recollection
of what the witnesses of the Conquest saw), in the rest of the
books, there are examples of these "canonical" manifestations of
the ancient indigenous tradition.

In Book I, dealing with the gods, we find an enormously interesting account of how sexual transgressions were confessed to
Tlazolteotl. In that account are transcribed what we might call the
"sacramental" words of the *tonalpouhqui,* or astrologer, addressed
to the person wishing to make his declaration of sinfulness and
thereby purify his own being. Book II includes the twenty sacred
canticles to the gods transcribed in Tepepulco, which were so eso-
teric that Sahagún abstained from attempting to translate them.
In Book III are several texts that, because of their rhythm and
expressive force, seem to be ancient poems, which might today

qualify as epics. One of these deals with the portentous birth of Huitzilopochtli. Another more extensive one was designated by Angel María Garibay Kintana as one of the original versions of the "Cycle of Quetzalcoatl." In the same book in the form of appendices are other texts dealing with the hereafter and with education. Here and there are also included several speeches in the manner of the *Huehuetlahtolli*, testimonies of the *Ancient Word*.

In Book IV, on the art of divination, two canonical *Huehuetlahtolli*, or examples of the *Ancient Word*, enunciated by merchants are cited. In the following Book V, canonical expressions of the ancient native traditions are uttered by those pronouncing specific omens. Their words are cited there, in several cases literally.

It is almost idle to state that Book VI is a preeminent example of the native pre-Hispanic literary tradition, dealing as it does with "Rhetoric and Moral Philosophy," that is the *Huehuetlahtolli*. The same can be said of the adages, riddles, and metaphors that are included as appendices in this book. Consideration must be given, however, to the manner in which some of the *Huehuetlahtolli* were modified or adapted to differing contexts and interlocutors. In this sense, it must be asserted that several of these examples of the *Ancient Word*, as they were traditionally composed, were a type of "living literature." This can be proved by comparing those Sahagún had transcribed to those collected previously by Fray Andrés de Olmos.[8] Furthermore, Hernando Alvarado Tezozomoc and Fray Diego Durán, in their respective works,[9] include Spanish versions of *Huehuetlahtolli* in the form of speeches addressed to several *Huey tlahtoque*, or supreme rulers of the Mexicas, at the time of their enthronement. The adaptations and modifications to an original text can be identified in these speeches that are addressed to specific persons.

Examples of the ancient tradition are less abundant in Books VII and VIII, the former on the phenomena of nature, the latter on the kings and rulers of the earth. Included in Book VII is the account of the creation of the sun and moon in the Fifth Age of the world. This account, like the one in Book III dealing with Quetzalcoatl—by virtue of its expressiveness, richness in parallel phrasing, and other stylistic devices—can also be seen, at least in part, as an ancient poem. Book VIII reveals but a few short texts that seem to emanate from the ancient tradition, chiefly in Chapter 20, where the procedure for selecting a ruler is discussed. In Book IX, there are once again several speeches, after the fashion of the *Huehuetlahtolli,* uttered by merchants. It is of considerable interest to compare its content with what is represented graphically in the pre-Hispanic *Fejérváry-Meyer Codex* . Though it seems likely that the codex was painted in the Mixteca, it is a book in which the deities and context correspond to the culture of the Nahua peoples. In an edition by the same name, which I prepared, I designated it as a *tonalámatl* of the Pochteca, the Book of Days and Destinies frequently consulted, though not exclusively, by the merchants.[10]

In the copious and varied data furnished in Book X, three types of texts from the ancient native tradition can be discerned. The first of these appears in the context of descriptions of the qualities and manners of being of different people, due as much to their kinship as to their occupations. In the majority of these texts, the natives' responses were guided by the general outline of the questionnaires that Sahagún presented to his consultants. Nevertheless, in some of the testimonies they gave, they intercalated expressions of the *Ancient Word.* These same expressions are to be found elsewhere in other Nahuatl sources. As examples of these, we can cite the constellations of metaphors and conceptualizations referring to the *tlamatini* 'the wise man,' to the *tlahcuilo* 'the painter-scribe,' and various other artists. This also occurs in some texts with a moral dimension, as is the case with those dealing with vice-ridden people, strong and noble men, and women of ill repute.

The second group of testimonies, in which traces of the ancient tradition can be perceived, is the one referring to the maladies of the human body and the medicines to cure them. These were furnished to Sahagún by native physicians specializing in the healing of diverse ailments, the names of which he recorded, as we have seen.

Finally, in the last chapter of Book X, which speaks about the nations inhabiting the earth, undoubtedly stimulated by Sahagún's questionnaires, there are two rather lengthy texts that provide evidence of the historical accounts transmitted in the ancient native schools. One tells of Quetzalcoatl and the Toltecs; the other is a panoramic overview of the cultural evolution of the Nahua peoples and even, to a certain extent, of all of Mesoamerica. Sahagún had asked his consultants about who they, the Mexicas, were. These testimonies, after offering a dubious etymology for the word *Mexicatl*, evoke an ancient account. This tale begins with the appearance of wise men on the coasts of the Gulf of Mexico who were already in possession of a writing system and calendar. It continues with the rise of Teotihuacan and later of Tula and concludes with the arrival of the Nahua groups in central Mexico. Based on the content of the codices, this account seems to be an example of the testimonies transmitted in the pre-Hispanic schools.

The most extensive of the books is XI, dealing as it does with "natural things"; in the *Florentine Codex*, Book XI occupies 253 folios, both front (recto) and back (verso) pages. It is a description of animals, plants, and all types of minerals. In the greater portion of the text, it is evident that the responses aligned themselves according to Sahagún's schemata. Nevertheless, there are two types of texts that are tied to the ancient tradition. One treats medicinal herbs and minerals. The evidence included in it was provided by the physicians who were still active in their profession and whose names are recorded by Sahagún. It can be said that the data provided there are an example of pre-Hispanic pharmacology. The other genre that relates to the *Ancient Word* consists of legends interspersed throughout the description of the animals. Some of these texts can be considered the seed of what would be a bestiary of ancient Mexico. Among them are narratives about various types of strange serpents, as well as those dealing with the *ahuítzotl* (a mythical creature), the *tlacuatzin* (opossum), and the coyote.

Bernardino incorporated the account about the Conquest as Book XII of his *Historia general*; he had obtained it around the year 1555 while he resided in Tlatelolco. As Sahagún indicates, this account was provided by men who were present during the Conquest. We have seen the reasons that can be adduced about its veracity. The words of these witnesses about the events they describe, often in intensely dramatic terms, offer what today is often considered the point of view of "the Other." They allow us a perspective on what the Mexica-Tlatelolcas experienced as they observed those alien and never-before-imagined men, who, after their sudden appearance, showed that they were determined to impose themselves on those who had ruled in Mexico for so long.

The account that describes the end of Tenochtitlan and antici-pates the coming to an end of the autonomous existence of the indigenous universe must have seemed to Sahagún a worthy conclusion to his *Historia general*. Thus, after some hesitation, it was to become Book XII. Bernardino placed such significance on this book that, as we shall see, it was the only one that, years later in 1585, would be the object of important revisions and changes.

It should also be kept in mind that another considerable por-tion of the materials included in the *Historia general* contains the responses, more or less spontaneous, that his consultants pro-vided, also in Nahuatl. These texts, though not an example of pre-Hispanic literature, can be considered to be a reflection of the traditions and thought patterns that prevailed in the cultural mi-lieu of the Nahua peoples. To this category belong the following accounts in the books into which Sahagún divided his texts: the descriptions of certain feasts; recollections of omens delivered in set circumstances; reports on some of the rulers; popular anec-dotes and folk beliefs; treatises on some of the animals, plants, and minerals; diverse narratives; and obviously everything re-counted in Book XII about the Conquest.

Many other texts, however, can be identified as responses to Sahagún's questionnaires.[11] Among these are the testimonies dealing with the gods in Book I. In those accounts, the following questions are answered: What were the names and attributes of the god? How did he behave? How was he venerated? What were his apparel and adornments? Of course, exceptions were made, as in the case of the goddess Tlazolteotl, as has already been mentioned. Though they may seem to introduce considerations extraneous to the questionnaires, the descriptions of the feasts throughout the solar year in Book II also follow a schema. By contrast, the contents of Book III, rather than appearing to be responses to questionnaires, evoke the accounts and commentaries of the ancient tradition. Although in Book IV, with its "diagnoses" of the signs or days of the *tonalpohualli*, the astrological count, the texts do accommodate Sahagún's questioning, some offer a canonical flavor, such as the *Huehuetlahtolli* of the merchants prior to undertaking a trading expedition. There is greater latitude in Book V on the omens.

According to Sahagún, the descriptions of the heavenly bodies in Book VII are in a "low form of speech"; this description, however, cannot be applied to the narrative of the Fifth Sun, which has the tone of a text from the ancient canonical tradition. Book VIII was also written as a response to questioning about the apparel of the rulers and other issues relating to them.

In Book IX, there are narratives about the merchants reminiscent of ancient testimonies and also responses to questions in the form of queries concerning the different artisans. The theme treated in Book X on the different social rankings and occupations, including that of the hawkers, follow a questionnaire format. The opposite is true of the responses about maladies and their cures provided by the native physicians, whose names are recorded. Questionnaire responses reemerge in the discussion of the diverse nations with which the Nahuas were acquainted. This is evident in the reconstruction of the questionnaires related to the Huaxtecs.[12] Finally, the issues investigated by Sahagún in

Book XI, which deal with animals, trees, herbs, metals, stones, and colors, are presented in accord with the heuristic schema he adopted.

As can be seen, contained in Sahagún's magnum opus is an entire gamut of data, the comprehension of which demands several forms of analysis based on the sources. In gathering his evidence, Sahagún had to admit expressions with differing origins as communicated by diverse people in varying circumstances.

When he had concluded the revision and reorganization of his "writings," all of which were in Nahuatl, he would make new strides in relation to his *Historia general* and to other works he had in hand, which he was also submitting to revision and enrichment. In order to accomplish this, he left the monastery of San Francisco and returned to the College of Santa Cruz.

It is probable that during his stay at San Francisco, Bernardino undertook other works of a religious nature. An indication of this is furnished by the fact that his name appears in print, along with Fray Alonso de Molina, at the end of the prologue of the booklet entitled *Sumario de las indulgencias concedidas a los cofrades del Sanctíssimo Sacramento* (Summary of the indulgences granted to the members of the Confraternity of the Most Holy Sacrament), which was published in Mexico City on an unknown date but approximately in 1570. This booklet in Nahuatl confirms that Molina and Sahagún were in the habit of collaborating on various works, as they had on past occasions.

CONSULTATION ON THE CALENDAR

Before returning to Tlatelolco, Bernardino consulted his former student, Pedro de San Buenaventura of Cuauhtitlan, on the date (in the Christian calendar) on which the Nahua new year began. The answer is preserved in a letter from his student, which is clearly addressed to the monastery of San Francisco in Mexico City, where Sahagún was to be found at that time, that is, probably between 1566 and 1570. The letter shows the signatures of both Pedro de San Buenaventura and Pedro González, who plausibly served as scribe because the letter is not in the handwriting of the former.

Study of this letter reveals two things. The first is the continued confidence that Bernardino exhibits in the learning of his Nahua collaborators. The other is the content of the letter itself. It confirms the wide divergence of opinions on the issue, seemingly originating in the differences that existed among the various Nahua regions and realms, as exists today between the Roman (Western) calendar and that of the Greek Orthodox.

Aside from this, Pedro de San Buenaventura's letter offers estimable data on various aspects of the Nahua calendar. What it reveals about the twenty-day time periods is quite interesting. Sahagún's correspondent notes that the first of these was called *Cuahuitl ehua*, as he "had read in the books." He deals with several days within this first period. It can be added that this letter provides a good description of the *Xihuitl*, that is, the Nahuatl solar year. Sahagún held on to this letter without comments of his own. Today it is preserved in folio 53 of the *Códice matritense* of the Royal Palace in Madrid.

Aside from this letter, Sahagún himself tells us what he took with him to the College of Santa Cruz around 1570 as well as what was an object of interest for him there, recalling what he had been able to accomplish up to then:

> After this, with Fray Miguel Navarro being the Provincial and Father Diego de Mendoza Guardian of the Monastery in Mexico, with their favor, a clean copy of all the twelve books was made in a good hand. And the Commentary and Hymns were emended and copied afresh, and a grammar of the Mexican language was done with a vocabulary appendix, and the Mexicans emended it and added many things to the twelve books as a clean copy was being made of them.

Memoriales en tres columnas, written in Tlatelolco. This page deals with "the seventeenth sign called *ce acatl*" and was included in Book IV of the *Historia general* (*Códice matritense del Real Palacio*, fol. 230r).

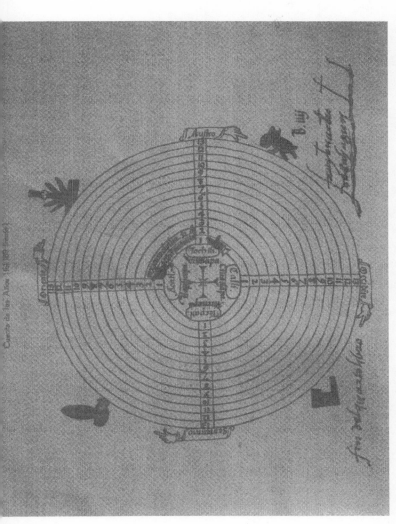

Wheel of Years, with the glyphs Reed, Flint, House, and Rabbit. Fray Bernardino's signature is accompanied by a note he wrote, indicating that this wheel would be included at the end of Book IV of the *Historia general* (*Códice matritense del Real Palacio*, fol. 242v).

COLLOQVIOS Y DOCTRI-

na christian conque los do
ze frayles de san francis
co enbiados por el papa
Adriano sesto y por el Em
perador Carlo quinto:
cô vertierô alos indi-
os de la Nueua Espa-
na. êlêgua Mexica-
na y Española.

Frontispiece of the *Coloquios y doctrina christiana*.

¶ A qui empieça[n] la doctrina christiana, conque fueron conuerti dos los indios
desta nueua españa, por los doze frayles de san fran[cis]co, que primeram[en]te los predicaron.

¶ El primer Cap[itul]o, halla, dela Relacion, que dierõ los doze frayles de S. fran[cis]co
alos principales de mexico, declarandoles la razon de su benjda.

Señores y principales de mexico (que aqui estais juntos) oyd con atencion, y
nota lo que os queremos dizir: que os dar os a entender la causa de n[uest]ra benjda,
A. Ante todas cosas os rogamos, que no os turbeis, nj espanteis de nosotros,
nj penseis que somos mas que hombres mortales y passibles como vosotros:
no somos dioses, nj emos descendido del cielo: enla tierra somos nacidos y cria-
dos. comemos y bebemos y somos passibles y mortales, como vosotros no somos mas que nescieuos. embiados a esta tierra: tenemos ar vna grã Baxi-
da, de aquel gran señor. que tiene iurisdicion. espual sobre todos qua les
biben enel mundo: el qual sellama Santo padre, el qual esta acongoxado y
cuidadoso por la salud de v[uest]ras almas, veis aqui loque dize. B. Sepa yeh
en dã mjs hijos, todos los que habitã en aquellas tierras region descubier tas
(que sellama la nueua españa) ansi los mexicanos, como los tlaxcalte-
cas y todos los demas que viue en las yndias occidentales: que los dias pa-
sados (muy poco a) que aviendo mj noticia su fama, a res dado noticia
dellas, n[uest]ro muy amado hijo el emperador don Carlos Rey delas españas
(quinto deste nombre) escriuio me, esto en sentencia. C. sepa V[uest]ra santidad
padre n[uest]ro muy amado, que mjs españoles, andescubierto vna tierra muy
grande (muy lexos de nosotros, hazia el occidente,) llena de muchas gen
tus pueblos y reynos: los quales son yndios: y los conquistarõ a su volun.
tud, ya son mjs basallos: suplico a v[uest]ra santidad que mandais embiar pre
dicadores, queles prediquen lapalabra de dios: y los ynstruyã enla religion
xpiana (porque todos son ydolatras gentiles) esto es loque avia sentido
suplica. D. Como vue visto esta peticion, luego junte a todos mjs hijos los
cardenales: y los di noticia deste negocio que n[uest]ro amado hijo el emperador
pedia: y luego entramos en cõ sejo: y determjnamos de embiar nños de
confiança para que prediassen la fe de n[uest]ro señor Jesu xp[ist]o alos dichos yn
dios infieles, para que mediante ella se saluassen: y los demos toda la
n[uest]ra authoridad que para la prosecucion de la dha conuersiõ les fuesse
necessaria. E. Pues agora amjgos nños, aqui estamos en v[uest]ra presencia
los que emos sido elegidos y embiados, a nosotros nos a embiado el
gran señor que tiene authoridad espual sobre todo el mundo: el qual habi
ta en la gran ciudad de Roma: dio nos su poder y authoridad: y tambien
traemos la sacrada escriptura donde esta escriptas las palabras del solo
verdadero dios señor del cielo y de la tierra, que es vida a todas las cosas:
al qual nun abeis conocido. F. Esta, y njnguna otra es la cusa d[e] n[uest]ra
benjda: y para esto somos embiados, para que os ayudemos a saluar, y para que
teabais la mjsericordia que dios os haze: el gran señor que nos embio, no q[uie]
en oro nj plata nj piedras preciosas: solamente quiere y desea v[uest]ra saluacio

Attempt at a Spanish translation of part of the *Historia general*. Chapter 16 of this text became Book I (*Códice matritense del Real Palacio*, fol. 11v).

HISTORIA DE LAS COSAS DE NUEVA ESPAÑA

(Códice matritense del Real Palacio, fol. 160 No.)

Folio from the *Memoriales con escolios,* with three complete columns
(*Códice matritense del Real Palacio,* fol. 160r).

Page from the *Breve compendio de los ritos idolátricos que los indios de esta Nueva España usaban en tiempos de su infidelidad,* sent by Sahagún to Pope Pius V and signed on 20 May 1570.

Auh yntla camo nican tlalticpac titlamaceuaznequi
titlaibiyouiznequi, ca monequi ompa Purgatorio titla
maceuazuiritlaibiyouitiuh: auh yn ompa tlaibiyouiliz
tli ca occeca tlapanauia ynicvei, ynictemamauhti, ynic
tetlaibiyouilti. Auh ynic titomaquixtizque ynitechca
yn nican tlalticpac tlaybiyouiliztli, yuan ynitechca
yn Purgatorio tonebuiztli chichinaquiliztli, quimc pie
lia yn tonantzinfancta Y glefia cenca yey necuiltonoliz
tli: (auh ynoccenca tlapanauia) yebuatl ynitlaybiyeui
liztin yni Pafsiontotemaquixticatzin Jefu chrifto moye
buatl ynin tlaybiyouiliz yn Sanctome. Auh yni necuil
tonoliztli, quimopielia yn fancto Padre, çanvel yneix
cauil ynic quimotemaquilliz: yn aço quezquixiuitl ynano
ço quezquilbuitl, ynitechpouitetlapopolbuiliz:auh, (yn
tla quichiuazque yn tlein yemotlanauatili), yniubca
ytetlaocoliliz,) quitozneouica zinuezqui iuitl nican
tlalticpac, yn añoce ompa Purgatorio, intlama renau
quia; çannoi zquixiuitl ye mixiptlayotia yn tlamaceua
liztli, yniubca ytetlaocolilitzin fancto Padre. Auh yn
tla yebuatl quimotemaquilliz yn Indulgencia plenaria
(quitoznequi, tecentlapopolbuiliztli,) ca muchipoliui
yn tlaybiyouiliztli, yn tiqbiyouizqnia ipampa totlatla
col. Yuan monequi ticmatizque, ca ynic veltictemacuaz
que tiquicnopilbuizque ynin necuiltonoliztli, initechpo
ui tetlaocoliliztli tetlapopolbuiliztli, yuan ynic titono
ma palebuizque, monequitotecbyez yn gracia, quitoz
nequi. Yntla ipan otuezque yntla oticchiubque temic
tiani tlatlacolli, cenca totechmoneq ynicipampa titote
quipacbozque titoyolcocozque, yuan ticcemitozque yn
yctitoyolmelauazque yniquacmotlananatilia yn tona
tzin fancta Y glefia, yuan ynic aocmo ceppa tictoyoli
tlacalbuizque yn toteculyo Dios.

Fray Bernardino   Fray Alonso
De Sahagun   De Molina.

Page concluding the prologue, signed by Fray Alonso de Molina and
Fray Bernardino de Sahagún, from the book *Summario de las indulgencias concedidas a los confrades del Santísimo Sacramento*, which was translated into the Mexican language by Fray Alonso de Molina. Printed in
Mexico between 1568 and 1572.

Prologo.

El aver añadido estas veynte y vna addiciones a esta postilla, parece que
sirviran de muchas cosas. Lo primero es, tener en summa y bien declarado todo
aquello a que es obligado qualquier christiano. Lo segundo, aprouecharan de tener muy a la mano, la declaracion delas tres virtudes theologales; las quales so-
las bastan para hazer a vno perfecto christiano; juntamente con esto se contiene la declaracion o doctrina delas penas del infierno, y dela gloria del Para-
yso: la qual doctrina predicada conel spiritu que ella demanda. Es sufficiente
informacion de vno christianismo. Lo tercero, aprouechara para que el predicador, tenga mucha oportunidad demeter estas addiciones, o alguna dellas,
en qualquier sermon que predicare: porque no ay epistola, ni euangelio en
la postilla, cuya letra no demande alguna dellas: y donde el predicador, pueda
muy a proposito dela letra aprouecharse de alguna o algunas dellas. Las quales
aprouechara de dar motiuo y ocasion al predicador, para que en todos sus
sermones pueda tocar materia muy prouechosa, y muy compendiosa, sin tener
tornar muchos libros. Lo quinto, aprouechara deque los oyentes doctrinados
y apacentados con esta doctrina, tendran intelligencia delo que son obligados
a saber, y apetito deponer lo por obra, pues veran quanto les va en hazerlo,
o dexar lo de hazer, segun parece por las dos vltimas addiciones: que son del
infierno, y dela gloria. Las quales en todos los sermones se deuen tocar en parte
o enel todo.

¶ Este mismo año de 1579. se puso por apendiz a esta postilla, enlo vltimo
vn tratado que contiene siete Collationes en lengua mexicana: enlas quales
se contienen muchos secretos, delas costumbres destos naturales: y tambien
muchos secretos y primores desta lengua mexicana: y pues que este volumen
no aprovechar, sino entodos Sacerdotes, y predicadores, no ay porque tener miedo
delas antiguallas, que enel se contienen, antes daran mucha lumbre, y con-
tento alos predicadores del santo Euangelio.

Vigesima septima addicion de la muerte, y del juyzio.

Folio 93 of the *Adiciones a la postilla*. Fray Bernardino's signature appears at the bottom in a very tremulous hand.

mjra que no todos aquien noco[n]oces, que es como viandante, que anda vellaqueando, y es vellaco: mjra hija, que no te iu[n]tes con otro, sino co[n] solo aquel que te mando, persevera conel, hasta que muera, no lo dexes, aunque el te quiera dexar, aunque sea pobrecito labrador, o oficial, o algun hombre comun, debaxo linaje, au[n]q[ue] no tenga que comer, no le menos pre cies, no le dexes, porque poderoso es nuestro señor, de proveeros, y hon rraros, porque es sabidor de todas las cosas, y haze mercedes aquien quiere. Esto que edicho hija mja, te doy para tu doctrina, paraque te sepas valer: y con esto hago conf[i] eo, lo que deuo delante dios: y si lo perdieres, y lo oluidares, sea a tu cargo, que yo ia hize mjdeuer. O hija mja, muy amada, primogenjta, palo mjta: seas bienauenturada, y nro señor te tenga en su paz, y reposo.

¶ Capitulo dezinueue, que en acabando el padre, de exortar ala hija, luego

---

mocpac maitz: jnotlequjtzi y naquja amjoan, amontean anmopopoliwtiz que: matlacauh xicticitzquj, itech ximopilo, ma nel icnotlacatl, manel icnoquja uhtli, icno ocelutl, manel ic notlacauh, inanozo renonpil tzin, inaço ietlaciauj, maic tiqujhix: ca amech mjmachti liz, amechmochichiujlis into tecujo, in tehtmatinj, in teio coianj, amechichioanj. O ya qujchiu, in njmjtzonmaca, in noten, in tlotlatole intje juic tzinco, ixpantzinco njnoqujx tia intotecujo: aço cana to con tlatlaçatz, caietehdarton matl: iece canoneqjxtil njc chioa. O nochpuchtle, nopil tze, cocitze, topitze: tlacamatl catzintli, majnja mahdacazi eutlatic in totecujo ...

¶ Ic caxtolli onnaui capitulo, vncan mjtua injquenjn iquac oontlato tetn: njman nehoatl

Libro duodecimo

Otro dia los españoles, hirieron lo mjs
mo, vinjeron enlos vergantines, có
muchos amjgos indios, al mjsmo ba
rrio de nonoalco: començaron apele
ar con los del tlatilulco, y trauose
reciamente labatalla, y pelearon to
do eldia, hasta lanoche: y murierõ
muchos indios, de ambas partes, y
retiraronse alli, entonce tres indios
del tlatilulco muy valientes: el vno
llamauan Tzoyectzin, y el otro llamauã

manjan inic mjxpaloc, cẽ
gujaia ihujtzoncalli, quetzal
quauhtlalpiloni iceuex coch,
tlampa tentiuh, ic tlalpitiuh
ieoatl injc tetlepan tlaxoia,
iuh quin tetlepan tlazquj ipã
qujztiuh, quintla ieie caltzaj
tiuh in tlatlapan tlazq̃ in
teucujtla ma temecauh ne
cocampa in ieitiuh y iõ ca
ti ietiuh injmac, cauh in teo
cujtla ma temecatl cuccuentic
auh noie injc xic ieie tiuh, co
tzcoatl, teucujtla cotzcoatl
gan petlanquj, auh njmã
imuz tlaioc in ieiacatl cõpa
quiçaco, injmaial cauauacõ
co nonoalca, aiauh caltitla
auh njman noqujçaco in
tlacxipan via yoan in ieie
qujch tlaxcaltecatl yoã ẽ
tomjtl, val tonac in qujqñ
po vietivitze, in Españoles

Thus the first sieve through which my works were sifted was the people of Tepepulco; the second, the people of Tlatelolco; and the third, the people of Mexico [City]. And in all these scrutinies, the Nahua students were present.[13]

ANOTHER STAY IN TLATELOLCO

The fruits of the first years of this most recent stay at Tlatelolco were the revised copies of the *Postilla* and the *Cantares* (with the text that Sahagún would publish as *Psalmodia christiana* in 1583), along with an *Arte y vocabulario* of the Mexican language. Of this latter work, mentioned several times by Sahagún, only a kind of sketch is preserved. In contrast, he was able to have a clean copy made of his Nahuatl texts, which was apparently completed in 1569; lost today, it probably served as an original, years later, in the transcription of the texts into Spanish based on the Nahuatl version. Sahagún comments, with a certain facetiousness, that in elaborating the clean copy of the manuscript, "many *tomines* were spent," which were coins current in Mexico at that time.

This was a propitious time for him, when he could count on the favor of Provincial Fray Miguel Navarro and of Father Diego de Mendoza, guardian of the monastery in Mexico City. This is confirmed by the *Relación y descripción de la provincia del Santo Evangelio de México* (Relation and description of the province of the Holy Gospel of Mexico), addressed in 1569 by the visitors of the province to *Licenciado* Juan de Ovando, president of the Council of the Indies. In this document, among other things, they declare the following:

> Said religious, Fray Alonso de Molina [the lexicographer], and another, whose name is Fray Bernardino de Sahagún, are the ones who can turn anything into the Mexican language and write in it, as they have been doing for many years hence and continue to do today without tiring. It would be a great service to God and to Your Majesty and for the good of the natives to order the Viceroy and the prelates of the Or-

der, while these two religious are still alive because they are now rather aged, that they should furnish them with all possible favor and warmth so that they can occupy themselves in writing in the Mexican language, for it will leave much light for those who later might come to take up preaching and administering the sacraments to the natives of New Spain, because, as I understand it, no one understands better than do these two, the secrets and propriety of this language, who received it from the speech of the elders.[14]

There are occasions, however, when favorable times and circumstances are followed by adversities. Thus, despite such as positive recommendation as this one addressed to Juan de Ovando, a series of obstacles would soon emerge to afflict Bernardino. This also seems to have begun with a change in provincial, a position for which Alonso de Escalona was selected. He was far from wishing to support and assist Sahagún. Envy, which often corrodes the spirit of the mediocre, had arisen against the friar- scholar. Aware of this, Sahagún makes frequent reference to some "opponents and envious persons" who were among his very own Franciscan brothers.

Having made fresh copies of his "writings," Sahagún himself attempted a preventative defense: "The author of these demanded of the Father Commissioner . . . that three or four religious be assigned to determine what to say about them in the next Provincial Chapter [meeting]."[15] The response and judgment were favorable: "[T]hey reported on them to the *definitorio* [the Board of Franciscan Superiors], telling it that it seemed to them that these writings were to be highly esteemed and should be favored so that they might be completed."[16] In spite of this, it was in this same *definitorio* that the storm that would arise against Bernardino began to brew:

> It seemed to some of the members [*definidores*] that it was an act against [the vow of] poverty that money should be spent on those writings, and so they ordered the author to dismiss

the scribes and to, by himself, take up the task of writing, in his own hand, whatever he wished in them.[17]

This cessation of support, so contrary to the recommendation made to Don Juan de Ovando, would prove to be fatal for Sahagún. He mentions this himself: "Nothing more was done with these writings for more than five years because I am past seventy, and due to the shaking in my hands, I cannot write, nor could a dispensation from this order be secured."[18]

At this juncture, it is of interest to quote from a document originating with Fray Jerónimo de Mendieta, entitled "The Names of the Friars of Saint Francis Remaining at the Beginning of This Year of 1570 in the Province of Mexico, Known as [the Province of] the Holy Gospel, Their Qualities Are the Following."[19] Written in Spain, where Mendieta was at that time, this document was composed for Ovando's information.

The document furnishes succinct information about 150 Franciscan priests, lay brothers, choir members, and religious students not yet ordained as priests. Among the first mentioned is Fray Bernardino. He is said to be

> Seventy or more years of age, a confessor and preacher for Spaniards and Indians, and second only to Fray Alonso de Molina in the Mexican language and in the secrets and antiquities of the language; he has even achieved more than he and any other because he has much given himself over to it. He has written and is writing in the language some works on which I have reported to Your Majesty. He has been Guardian in the principal houses.[20]

There is another anonymous document preserved along with the above, which provides complementary data, though very sketchy, about the same friar priests. Apropos Sahagún, it makes the following rather harsh comment: "He is old and toothless and good for very little."[21] This was the judgment about someone who, in the twenty years of life remaining to him, would accomplish works of the highest significance.

APPEALS TO THE COUNCIL OF THE INDIES
AND TO THE POPE AMIDST ADVERSITIES

Provincial Superior Alonso de Escalona, incited perhaps by other friars, ordered Sahagún to turn in all his books, and these "were dispersed over the whole province."[22] There was perhaps a dual purpose in this. Firstly, new judgments were sought that might prove adverse to those books in which so many idolatrous things were preserved. Secondly, Escalona may have thought that dispersing the books would make it difficult for Sahagún to recover all of them, and consequently he might desist from translating them into Spanish.

In obedience, Sahagún turned over his Nahuatl writings, yet he also attempted to forward information to the Council of the Indies and to the pope about that which he was researching:

> At this time [circa 1570], the author made a summary of all his books, and of all the chapters of each book, and of the prologues, in which everything contained in the books was listed briefly. Father Miguel Navarro [a former provincial favorable to Sahagún] took this inventory to Spain with his companion, Father Jerónimo de Mendieta, and thus, it was learned in Spain what had been written about the things of this land.[23]

Perhaps Fray Bernardino was familiar with the recommendation made on his behalf by his superiors in the report of 1569, cited above; this was addressed to the same Ovando in his capacity as president of the Council of the Indies. Bernardino at least knew that Ovando was pleased with the "Summary" turned over to him by Fathers Navarro and Mendieta. He also attempted to have his own voice reach Rome in order to inform the pontiff. Aware that a forthcoming chapter or general meeting of the Franciscan Order was about to take place in Italy, he also gave Fathers Navarro and Mendieta a booklet, with the petition that it be submitted to the pope. The title of this document was *For Our Most Holy Father Pius V, Pope; A Brief Compendium of the Idolatrous Rites*

That the Indians of This New Spain Practiced in the Times of Their Infidelity.[24]

Although the "Summary" addressed to Juan de Ovando has disappeared, the *Compendium* destined for Pius V has been preserved up to the present in the secret archive of the Vatican. We are thus able to ascertain that in the *Compendium* Sahagún included, in addition to a preface addressed to the pope, a portion of the first book of his *Historia general*, which he had already translated into Spanish—that is, the one dealing with the gods of the Nahua peoples—as well as several sections or chapters of the second book about the "Calendar of the Feasts of These Natives." The booklet was dated the 25th of December, 1570, by Bernardino. Although we know that his "Summary" brought him the favorable attention of Juan de Ovando, it was never known how Pius V expressed himself about the *Compendium*, if he ever did say anything about it.

Many years passed and, according to the indefatigable researcher, "at that time (from 1571 to 1575) nothing was done with them," that is, with his writings. These remained dispersed, running the serious risk of being lost forever. It was then that Philip II's celebrated court physician, Dr. Francisco Hernández, finding himself in New Spain, became aware of some of those manuscripts and took advantage of them. He had arrived in Mexico in 1571 and stayed until 1577, with the mission of studying the natural history of the country and, in particular, its pharmacology. On his return to Spain, based on his research, he wrote his great *Historia natural de la Nueva España* (Natural history of New Spain). In this document, and especially in other works such as his *Antigüedades de la Nueva España* (Antiquities of New Spain), he appropriated several of Sahagún's reports. Because Hernandez knew only a little Nahuatl, he relied on interpreters for his works and for all of his research.[25]

A probable indication of the bitterness that afflicted Sahagún was an action he took in 1572 that seems a bit strange. The celebrated Fray Toribio de Benavente Motolinía had died in Mexico three years before. Sahagún had sung his praises in the prologue to his work entitled *Coloquios y doctrina christiana*. As if there had been a change in his appreciation for the friar, one of the twelve who had arrived in 1524, Sahagún appeared before the Holy Office of the Inquisition, which had recently been established in Mexico City. His purpose was to denounce as contrary to the faith a work by Motolinía. This was his declaration:

> In Mexico, fourteen days of the month of August of fifteen hundred seventy-two, before the Lord Inquisitor, Doctor Moya de Contreras [the archbishop], during his morning audience, Fray Bernardino de Sahagún of the Order of Saint Francis, resident of the Monastery at Tlatelolco, at seventy-three years of age, appeared without a summons and swore under the law to tell the truth; he stated that he had come to denounce and make manifest, as an unburdening of his conscience, that there is a work circulating in New Spain, well known to be by Fray Toribio de Benavente Motolinía, a friar of his Order, in which he justifies the divinatory art the natives of this New Spain had, which is declared as a warning and for it to be remedied, if it be convenient. This passed before me, Pedro de los Ríos.[26]

Such a denunciation must have been known to many, including the Franciscans living in Mexico City and especially Provincial Superior Alonso de Escalona. It was he who had ordered Sahagún a short time before (around 1570) to turn all his documents in to him, as Sahagún described it, deciding to have them "dispersed over the whole province" so that the friars could pass judgment on their content.

The provincial acted in this way after having given ear to the complaints and accusations of the "rival" friars acting against Sahagún; they saw in his work a waste of resources and a risk of reviving idolatrous beliefs and practices. It is also probable that Escalona was moved by the hostility that Sahagún had begun to display against Fray Toribio, who was the last to die of the twelve and was widely respected in the province of the Holy Gospel.

As Bernardino found himself afflicted and perhaps depressed, unable to foresee the fate of his work of so many years, he felt moved as "an unburdening of his conscience," as he had declared before the Holy office of the Inquisition, to denounce this work of Motolinía. Not only on this occasion but also later, he would turn to harsh criticism of Fray Toribio, though without mentioning him by name; this he would do when he had recovered his own manuscripts and was working on the Spanish version of the Nahuatl texts in an appendix to Book IV of his *Historia general* ("On Judiciary Astrology"). At first, he remarked that

> The zeal for the truth and for the Catholic Faith compel me to set down here the same words of a Treatise that a certain religious wrote in praise of this Art of Divination, saying that it was a calendar, so that wherever it may be sighted, it be known that it is prejudicial to our Catholic Faith and it be destroyed and burned.[27]

After such harsh recrimination, Bernardino transcribes a portion of the introduction to this treatise as if to facilitate its identification. Having done this, he adds a paragraph entitled "Refutation of What Is Said Above." In it, he uses expressions such as "in the first thing that he says that, by this count, the Indians counted their weeks, months, and years, this is most false. . . . What he says about Olympiads and five-year periods and convening synods, for the same reason, is false and mere fiction."[28] The words "false" and "most false" appear several times with respect to the assertions of the "religious" whose name he does not give; yet by his denunciation before the Inquisition, we know this to be Motolinía and his treatise, from which he then copies another paragraph. This new condemnation of what Motolinía had written dates from 1576.

However, before Sahagún could write this and return to his texts, being still deprived of them because they were dispersed throughout the Franciscan province and being without assistance, he managed to accomplish something in the period between 1570 and 1575. This is evidenced by certain dates that appear in the *Historia general*, which allow us to see that he had held on to some of his papers. While still assigned to the College of Santa Cruz at Tlatelolco, he made some forays to towns that were know to him. There is evidence, for example, that around February 1573 he spent some time at his former mission of Tlalmanalco near the volcanoes. Fray Cristóbal de Briviesca mentions this stay in a letter, made known by Alfonso Toro, another scholar who devoted attention to the life and work of Bernardino.[29]

ARRIVAL OF RODRIGO DE SEQUERA AND COMPOSITION OF THE *HISTORIA GENERAL*, OR THE *FLORENTINE CODEX* (1575–1580)

The arrival in Mexico of Fray Rodrigo de Sequera, commissioner general of the Franciscans, was a fortunate event for Sahagún in 1575. Another two events occurred at about the same time. One was adverse, namely the death of Juan de Ovando, president of the Council of the Indies, who had taken such an interest in Sahagún's works. The other occurred a short time before the arrival of Fray Sequera. This was the arrival of Fray Miguel Navarro, longtime protector of Bernardino. Thanks to him, the documents that had been scattered throughout the Franciscan province were returned to Sahagún.

> After some years, on returning from the general chapter [convened in Rome, as we have seen, where he submitted the *Compendium* to Pope Pius V], Father Miguel Navarro . . . , in censures [imposing penalties in case of lack of obedience], once again gathered together those books as requested by the author and, once gathered, in a year, more or less, these returned to the possession of the author.[1]

In the span of perhaps a year, from the recovery of his papers to the arrival of Rodrigo de Sequera in 1575, Sahagún was able to achieve something with his writings. It was probably at about this time that he began the Spanish translation of his texts and also started to arrange them into three columns according to the format he had developed, at least for a portion of his work. The Nahuatl would be in the middle, the Spanish version to the left, and the linguistic glosses on the right.

We have already seen that two sections are preserved that give evidence of this in the documentary corpus of the *Códices matritenses*. One includes a Spanish version of what were to become Books I and V, the former on the gods, and the latter on omens and superstitions from the *Historia general*. In his facsimile of these codices, Francisco del Paso y Troncoso designated these texts with the title *Memoriales en español* (Memoranda in Spanish). The other section (with the text in three columns) he named *Memoriales con escolios* (Memoranda with commentaries), that is, with a linguistic commentary. As has been stated, these *Memoriales* comprise just a few chapters from Book VII (on the sun, the moon, their restoration at Teotihuacan, eclipses, and other celestial phenomena) and from Book X (on kinship and persons of different ages and conditions).

In September 1575, the commissioner general of the order, Rodrigo de Sequera, arrived just as Bernardino found himself in possession of his recuperated writings and was attempting to apply the format that he had conceived. He might very well have viewed Sequera's arrival as providential. This is how Sahagún expresses himself about this:

> The Father Commissioner General, Fray Rodrigo de Sequera, came to these parts and saw it [the books of the *Historia general*]; he was very pleased by them and ordered this author to translate them into Spanish.[2]

With respect to the translation, Bernardino himself had written not too long before that there was no one who supported him in finishing the translation into Spanish, which implies, as we have seen, that he had already initiated the translation, of which the *Memoriales en español* and the *Memoriales con escolios* are examples. Here is Father Sequera:

He provided all that was needed to have them rewritten again, with the Mexican language in one column and the Romance [Spanish] in another, in order to send them on to Spain because Don Juan de Ovando, President of the Council of the Indies, had requested them as a result of the Summary that Father Miguel Navarro had taken to Spain.[3]

What Sahagún did not know was that, despite such good fortune, Ovando's death and the complaints that other friars had sent to Spain (denouncing his work as a carrier of idolatrous beliefs) would bring more adversity. Another factor in all of this would be the dispositions of the Council of Trent, for which the Holy Office of the Inquisition was demanding strict enforcement.

A NEW MANUSCRIPT IS PREPARED
AMIDST GREAT CALAMITIES

It was in the month of August in 1576 when a terrible plague known as *huey cocoliztli* 'great sickness' would begin to afflict especially the indigenous population of New Spain. Dr. Francisco Hernández, the previously mentioned court physician, describes, as an eyewitness, the symptoms that the affected suffered:

The fevers were contagious, fiery, and continuous; all were pestilential and, in large measure, lethal. The tongue, black and dry. Intense thirst; the urine, sea-green, but now and again turning a paler color. Rapid and frequent pulse, but faint and weak, sometimes even null. The eyes and entire body, yellow. And then delirium and convulsions; boils behind one or both ears; a hard and painful tumor; pains in the heart, chest, and abdomen; shaking and great anguish and dysentery. The blood flowing from a cut vein was green and very pale, dry and without any serosity. The lips gangrenous; the pudenda and other regions of the body, with putrefying members and hemorrhaging ears; many with hemorrhaging noses; those who fell ill hardly ever recovered. Many were saved by a bleeding from the nose; the rest perished. . . . It especially attacked the young, rarely the old, who even when infected, more often than not, managed to beat it and were saved. . . . Though this was apparently the beginning because, a little at a time, it affected all groups in the population, regardless of age or sex.[4]

Fray Bernardino, who found himself at the College of Santa Cruz and was already working on the preparation of his new manuscript of the *Historia general,* thanks to the support he had received from Fray Rodrigo de Sequera, also wrote about the *huey cocoliztli* of 1576 in passing, alluding to the other plague of 1545, in which he had fallen ill:

> The pestilence that struck some thirty years ago now was a great blow to the College, and it has been no less with this plague of 1576, so that there is hardly anyone left at the College; dead and sick, almost all have gone. . . .
>
> I have seen it with my own eyes . . . , the plague of thirty years ago; most died because there was no one who understood how to bleed or to administer medicines properly and from hunger; the same is happening in this pest, and in all others that may occur it will be the same until all the [Indians] are gone.[5]

The lash of the plague continued to assail the population until nearly the end of 1577. Sahagún, who was immersed in the work of transcribing and translating the *Historia general,* felt himself to be quite affected by it; for, in addition to witnessing the death of thousands, he also watched close at hand how many of the students perished at the college, which was also in a state of crisis financially, academically, and demographically.

According to Bernardino, it had declined financially because of the poor administration "of the Majordomo, a Spaniard, who was in charge of the College."[6] As far as the academics were concerned, there had been "negligence and inattention on the part of the Rector and Counselors [who were now natives] and also from the neglect of the friars, who failed to monitor how things were developing until everything had been run into the ground."[7] Demographically, the plague had run rampant through the student body that remained. This was all very painful for Bernardino and others who had dedicated so many years to the college. They viewed it as a seedbed from which would sprout many among the natives as genuine Christians, humanists, and guides for their people. Only men with that formation would make it possible to implant a true Christianity. Now reality seemed to cause such goals to vanish. Sahagún's pessimism grew. Nevertheless, he did not resign himself to abandoning the college. According to Fray Juan de Torquemada, "the walls of the College are good and sound, and there are many good classrooms and other useful spaces; these were expanded by Fray Bernardino de Sahagún, who, until his death, continued to support and augment what he was able."[8]

OTHER WORKS

In the midst of these tasks and woes, Sahagún stole some time to perfect another group of writings in Nahuatl with a religious theme. These were the ones he referred to as *Adiciones y apéndice a la postilla* (Additions and appendix to the commentary). Among others things, these included some *Ejercicios cotidianos en lengua mexicana* (Daily exercises in the Mexican language), a *Declaración breve de las virtudes teologales* (Brief declaration of the theological virtues), and other texts that were conceived as separate booklets, among which was a *Manual del cristiano* (Manual for the Christian).[9]

Preoccupied as he was with revising and enriching these manuscripts and, above all, with his main project of making a clean copy of the *Historia general*, all the while caring for the victims of the plague, in that same year of 1577, Sahagún received some news that would inevitably shake him. The first was the publication of an edict in which the Holy Office of the Inquisition prohibited the printing, copying, and dissemination of any part of the Sacred Scriptures in the native languages or any other vernacular. The consequence of this would be the requisitioning of any text of the Epistles and Gospels and even of a book of Ecclesiastes in Nahuatl or any other native language. In this regard, Fray Bernardino would recall that five years prior, in 1572, the same Holy Office of the Inquisition had requested that he, as well as Fray Alonso de Molina, Fray Juan de la Cruz, and the Dominican Fray Domingo de la Anunciación, indicate which books from the Scriptures they knew were in a native language. They were also asked whether the prohibition should impede the teaching of doctrine to the Indians, and whether it would be appropriate for at least the ministers of the gospel to have access to them or whether it would be necessary to totally forbid such translations.

Fray Bernardino had responded that he knew of some chapters of Proverbs that had been translated into Nahuatl, and that he had also heard that Ecclesiastes had been translated in a paraphrased version into that language. Concerning the need for priests to have access to texts of the Epistles and Gospels for the Sundays of the year as well as to commentaries on these, his opinion was that both seemed necessary. His comments follow:

> It seems to me that the preachers are in need of a great deal of help; consequently, it appears that a Commentary with the sermons, as has been prepared in recent years, should be in the hands of the preachers, for it will be of great assistance to them, especially as pertains to the Gospels and Epistles for the Sundays and principal feasts of the year.[10]

He was obviously referring to his own works here, that is, his celebrated *Postilla* as well as his Nahuatl versions of the Gospels and Epistles for the Sundays of the year. Now, in 1577, the edict issued by the Holy Office demonstrated that his opinion was not being taken into account and that the translations that he himself had done had become dangerous materials. They thus would have to be turned over to the ministers of the Inquisition, who would certainly confiscate and eventually destroy them. It is not known whether this occurred with any of Sahagún's copies of portions of the Bible in Nahuatl. What is known is that if he did have to turn over some of his works to the Holy Office of the Inquisition, other copies of those works have survived. These are preserved in many libraries, including the National Library of Mexico and the Newberry Library of Chicago.[11]

Another report, which Sahagún did not manage to interpret correctly, was that Viceroy Don Martín Enríquez had received a royal order, dated the 22nd of April, 1577, in which Philip II commanded Sahagún to forward all texts in Nahuatl and Spanish that he had prepared. When Sahagún learned of the royal request, he misinterpreted it, naively imagining that the monarch and his officers on the Council of the Indies were very interested in learning more about the antiquities of the peoples of New Spain. Ignorant of the actual content of the order, he quickly placed in the viceroy's hands everything that seemed appropriate to him. Unfortunately, the true meaning of the royal order was quite different. In it could be glimpsed the old envies of those other friars, who had accused him of fostering the preservation of idolatry and that who had been persecuting him for some time—of this Bernardino was certainly aware. The text of the royal order, of which Sahagún would never know, was as follows:

> [From] The King. [To] Don Martín Enríquez, our Viceroy, Governor and Captain General of New Spain, and President of our Royal Audience there. By means of some letters written to us from those provinces, we have learned that Fray Bernardino de Sahagún of the Order of Saint Francis has composed a Universal History of the most significant things of that New Spain, which is a very copious computation of all the rites, ceremonies, and idolatries that the Indians practiced during their infidelity, divided into twelve books and in the Mexican language; and although it is un-

derstood that Fray Bernardino de Sahagún's zeal may have been good, and although wishing his work to be useful, it seems that it is inappropriate that this book be printed or that it be in any way disseminated in those parts, due to some causes for concern; and thus we order you that as soon as you receive this our order, you very carefully and diligently seek to take possession of these books, without allowing any original or transcript of them at all, and to send them by safe conduct at the earliest opportunity to our Council of the Indies to be examined by it; and be advised that you must not consent to absolutely any person writing about things that deal with superstitions and the ways of life that the Indians had in any language, for that is the appropriate thing in the service of Our Lord God and of ourselves. Dated in Madrid, the twenty-second of April of fifteen hundred seventy seven. I the King. By order of H. M., Antonio de Eraso.[12]

The immediate consequence of this order was that the indefatigable Franciscan researcher handed over a manuscript that was then forwarded to Spain. Modern Sahagún scholars have racked their brains, asking themselves precisely which manuscript was the one turned in by Sahagún. It is true that, with Fray Sequera's support, he was in the process of having a clean copy made of the twelve books of his *Historia general*, with the Nahuatl text in one column and the Spanish version in another, along with handsome illustrations. However, that was not the manuscript that was turned over to Viceroy Enríquez. The reason for this is obvious. Its preparation was not completed until the end of 1577. Furthermore, it was Sequera himself who took it to Spain.

The irony of what this remission meant to Fray Bernardino can be better assessed if one considers that, when he had no report of any opinion that the king or his Council of the Indies might have had about the manuscript he had submitted, he decided to write a letter on his own, indicating that he himself could send more manuscripts if the one forwarded by the viceroy had not been received. The monarch's response was swift in coming. The viceroy was once again commanded, because the friar still claimed to have other texts in his possession, to demand their immediate surrender.

Sahagún, though deprived of a goodly portion of his texts and in the midst of misadventures, from the plague to the intervention of the Holy Office of the Inquisition, continued with his work of text transcription, which so interested him. The protection of the father commissioner general would accomplish what might have seemed impossible under those circumstances. With Fray Sequers's help in preserving the necessary materials for the complete reproduction of the twelve books of the *Historia general*, Sahagún would, at long last, achieve his purpose.

THE *FLORENTINE CODEX*: ITS COMPLETION AND FORTUNATE PRESERVATION

We can make several observations about the preparation of the *Florentine Codex* by Sahagún based on a reading of the diverse prologues, notices, accounts, and other references included in the new manuscript, which is preserved at the *Medicean-Laurentian* Library in Florence, from which the codex aquired its name. Work was begun in 1575 at the College of Santa Cruz at Tlatelolco; Sahagún relied on the assistance of native scribes to accomplish this task. In reality, a great deal was achieved at that time. Among other things, perhaps for the first time the majority of the texts were translated; up to then, most had been in Nahuatl only.

It is fitting to recall, as Sahagún states himself, that the *Huehuetlahtolli*, testimonies of the *Ancient Word*, which would constitute Book VI of the *Historia general*, were rendered into Spanish in 1577, that is, toward the end of the process of transcription. Native artists also participated in the elaboration of the work, including, most probably, Agustín de la Fuente, a resident of Tlatelolco, about whom another friar, Juan Baptista, in the prologue to a *Sermonary* published in 1606, confirmed that "his whole life through, he had done nothing other than write for Fathers Fray Bernardino de Sahagún and Fray Pedro de Oroz."[13] There is evidence that this Agustín, in addition to being a scribe and printer, was also an excellent sketch artist and painter.

The work encompasses the twelve books of the *Historia general* containing the topics previously described. The left column is dedicated to the Nahuatl text, divided into books, chapters, and occasionally even paragraphs. In the right column appears the Spanish version. This translation is not literal; at times it is a summary of the content in the native language column, and at other times it is an annotated version of it. The manuscript includes many hundreds of illustrations: 1,855 in all, most of which are in color. The style of these reveals a very strong European Renaissance influence. One might say that in these paintings—as had occurred previously with the map of Mexico-Tenochtitlan, which, as we saw, was also executed at the college in 1550—the encounter of the Old World with the New World became a patent reality.

The finished work was bound together in four volumes. These, surely with great pleasure and many thanks to God, Sahagún placed in the hands of his protector, Father Rodrigo de Sequera. He dedicated the work to him in a beautiful inscription in Latin. Father Sequera left for Spain at the beginning of 1580. Bernardino might have thought that his work was finished and that it would be preserved in some great European library, where it would be widely known and studied. Nevertheless, he still had the idea floating around in his head that he would enrich and perfect it even more. It is not at all strange that in the years to come he would again take up his *magna historia*. And yet, he would write in 1585 that the person who had taken his four volumes with him, Fray Rodrigo de Sequera, "has never written me where those books came to rest . . . , nor do I know in whose possession they are."[14]

Bernardino would never discover the ultimate destination of those four books of his, which he describes as quite *historiados* (full of illustrations and interest). This was undoubtedly a source of concern and sorrow for him and yet not of discouragement because, at more than eighty years of age, as we shall see, he attempted the enrichment of some parts of the *Historia general*. At least today, we know that the books taken by Fray Rodrigo de Sequera, far from being lost, are preserved with great care (bound anew, now in three volumes) in the Medicean-Laurentian Library in Florence. In 1979 the *Archivo General de la Nación* (General Archive of the Nation) in Mexico City published a truly faithful and precious facsimile edition of these books in a printing of two thousand copies.

WERE THERE ONE OR TWO COPIES OF THE *HISTORIA GENERAL* IN NAHUATL AND SPANISH?

Several letters exist from the archbishop of Mexico City Pedro Moya de Contreras, Viceroy Martín Enríquez, and even Sahagún himself, as well as other documents, such as letters and royal orders from Philip II written around that time, that had as a topic the opus on which Sahagún was working. The study of these letters or of only some of them, carried out with meticulous care by Joaquín García Icazbalceta, Luis Nicolau D'Olwer, Howard F. Cline, and Georges Baudot, raises an issue that requires clarification.[15] This is the question of what exactly Sahagún was working on during the period between 1575 and the return to Spain of Father Sequera in January 1580.

Although the study of these letters has led García Icazbalceta, Nicolau D'Olwer, and more recently Baudot to conclude that what Sahagún accomplished with his assistants was basically the clean copy of what is today known as the *Florentine Codex*, there are others—in particular, Howard F. Cline and those who follow his view without criticism, such as John B. Glass—who postulate the preparation of two distinct manuscripts. They designate the first as the "Enríquez" manuscript, which they consider to have disappeared when it was supposedly handed over to Viceroy Enríquez, and identify the other as the one that is today called the *Florentine Codex*.

Their argument is based on what is stated in several testimonies: that there were two submissions and two remissions of texts by Sahagún to Spain. From this surely undeniable fact, Cline and those who have adopted his interpretation deduce that the manuscripts sent were two very similar transcriptions, both bilingual in Nahuatl and Spanish, of the twelve books of the *Historia general*. One of these is the one known today as the *Florentine Codex*. The other, which Cline refers to as the "Enríquez" copy, acknowledging that it is now lost, he maintains is the transcription completed somewhat earlier, which was very similar to the *Florentine Codex* and which the viceroy had forwarded after having obtained it from Sahagún.

In order to elucidate what was sent to Spain before the *Florentine Codex*, one must critically analyze the testimonies that speak of one or the other of the two remissions. It is of interest to see what can be deduced from these letters and royal orders. All of this, which might seem of little interest in a Sahagún biography, has its significance. It touches upon nothing less than his most accomplished work, that is, the one in which he organized and made a clean copy of the whole collection of Nahuatl texts and the version that, based on them, he prepared in Spanish. It is precisely this contribution, with its other documentary antecedents, that has attracted attention to this friar, who is seen as the modern initiator of anthropological research.

The first of the testimonies requiring analysis is a letter from the 28th of March, 1576, written by the archbishop of Mexico City Pedro Moya de Contreras. In it he responds to Philip II, who had ordered the preparation of a "Moral History" of the peoples of this land, their customs, beliefs, etc.; he writes,

> I came to find out that an old friar, whose name is Bernardino and [who is] the best speaker of the Mexican language there is in New Spain . . . , has completed a general history

of all the things of this New Spain having a bearing on this purpose, about which I informed President Don Juan de Ovando . . . ; and I beseeched Father Rodrigo de Sequera, Commissioner General, to have it translated into Spanish and Mexican in order to send it to Your Majesty, and he has promised me to do so.[16]

Georges Baudot, in commenting on this letter, asks himself whether it might not have been Father Sequera who moved the archbishop to write it.[17] He offers two reasons in support of this hypothesis. In the first instance, he alludes to the then deceased Juan de Ovando, who until recently had been president of the Council of the Indies. Sequera, who had maintained an amicable relationship with Ovando, would ask the archbishop to refer to him as someone who was well known for having been acquainted with and having appreciated the work of Sahagún, at least through his exposure to the *Sumario*, which had been brought to him by the Franciscans Navarro and Mendieta. In the second instance, Baudot recalls that, for some time before the archbishop wrote that letter, Father Sequera had already bestowed all of his support on Sahagún to translate and make a clean copy of his work. It was thus not the archbishop who "beseeched" Sequera to command such a task from Sahagún because the order and the support had already been given.

We can conclude from these two considerations that the archbishop wrote this letter upon the request of Sequera, precisely to preclude any suspicion or even contradiction; he must have been aware, perhaps through Sahagún, of how many Franciscans were opposed and averse to his completion of the *Historia general*. His fear was far from unfounded; a little more than a year later, the consequences of this aversion were felt. Proof of this was the already written royal order of Philip II from the 22nd of April, 1577, in which he commanded the remission of Sahagún's writings to the Council of the Indies.

The viceroy must have been cognizant of the order toward the middle of 1577. The archbishop also received a letter with similar content, dated the 13th of May of the same year.[18] An analysis of the king's communication reveals that there were many from Mexico who had denounced Sahagún's work as dangerous for having preserved the memory of idolatrous beliefs and rites. Obviously, among those denouncing Sahagún were the "opponents" from whom, he had written, he had received nothing but "great disfavor." He was referring to several of his Franciscan brothers, who were divided by internal conflicts in the province of the Holy Gospel. They were well aware of the contents of the royal order: the work was "a very copious computation . . . , divided into twelve books and in the Mexican language."

The consequence of the royal orders to the viceroy and the archbishop was that they met to consider the king's command and how to carry it out. On the 28th of October, 1577, the archbishop answered the king with the following words:

> If the Universal History about this country that Fray Bernardino has completed is not sent to Your Majesty on board this ship [the fleet that was about to set sail], I shall remind the Viceroy so that what Your Majesty has requested leaves on the next one, as you have ordered.[19]

The archbishop continued to monitor the affair; on the 30th of March, 1578, he wrote the king once again. The tone of this letter could almost be said to have been inspired by Father Sequera because it contains high praise for Sahagún and even asserts that his work could be of great help to those working for the Holy Office of the Inquisition:

> The Universal History about these natives and their rites and ceremonies, composed by Fray Bernardino de Sahagún . . . , that Your Majesty ordered remitted in the original, with no transcript remaining here . . . , the author has related to

me that he has turned it over to the Viceroy with all his original papers, in the Spanish and Mexican languages, along
with certain transcripts he had made of it.

Your Majesty would esteem the Mexican language of
this religious, who is the most elegant and proper there is in
these parts. . . . And the curiosity of this religious should be
a great emolument, and this is clear, so that the Inquisition
might have some report of their rites for when they come to
investigate the offenses of the Indians.[20]

The archbishop asserted that the author, Sahagún, had told
him that he had turned over to the viceroy "all his original papers,
in the Spanish and Mexican languages, along with certain transcripts he had made of it." This assertion is what has provided
the basis for Cline, and those who have followed him, to main-
tain that there was a manuscript in Spanish and Nahuatl that
Sahagún had turned over to Viceroy Enríquez. This manuscript
would have been prepared in a parallel manner, along with the
one that is known as the *Florentine Codex*, between the end of 1575
and the end of 1577.

We have evidence from Sahagún that counters these supposi-
tions. He also had written to Philip II just four days before, on the
26th of March, 1578. In this letter, he does not mention having
turned his papers over to Viceroy Enríquez, as he had supposedly told the archbishop, according to what the latter had said in
his letter. Sahagún asserts that he had placed them in the hands
of his protector, Father Sequera. These are his words:

Viceroy Don Martín Enríquez received a royal order from
Your Majesty, in which you commanded him to send to
Your Majesty some works that I had written in the Mexican
and Spanish languages, about which the Viceroy, as well
as the Archbishop of this city, told me; all of which works I
had finished copying cleanly this last year, and I had given
them to Fray Rodrigo de Sequera, Commissioner General
of our Order of Saint Francis, so that, if he were to depart,

he might take them to Your Majesty, and if not, he could send them on to you, for when the order came he already had them in his keeping. I understood that the Viceroy and the Commissioner would send Your Majesty these works that are divided into twelve books, in four volumes, by this fleet; if they did not send them in the ship that is reported to have left recently and if they do not send them, I humbly beseech Your Majesty be so kind as to command that I be advised so that I might transcribe them again and so that the memorable things of this New World not be lost at this juncture nor that they be left in oblivion. Your Royal Majesty may have news of me and my works through the one who conveys this to you; he is the Custodian of this Province and is on his way to the General Chapter meeting.[21]

Besides reporting that he had turned his manuscripts over to Sequera, Sahagún adds that he had done it even before the royal order had arrived. According to this, the translation and copy were completed toward the end of 1577. After stating that he does not know whether it will be Sequera himself who will hand them over to the king or, if the commissioner is detained in Mexico, whether it will be the viceroy who will send them, he says that, in case they do not arrive or in case of loss, he should be notified so that he can have a new copy made.

Another royal order issued on the 5th of July, 1578, and addressed to the archbishop offers proof that the sovereign had received nothing by the middle of that year. It reads,

If the Universal History of the Indies that Fray Bernardino de Sahagún did has not been sent, you shall request of the Viceroy that he send it at the earliest opportunity.[22]

That royal order was followed by another a short while later, an obvious consequence of what Sahagún had written, stating that he still had in his possession manuscripts from which he could make copies:

[T]he Viceroy should take whatever is left there, copies and originals, and send them all, without any copy being left behind.[23]

Aside from proving that some of Sahagún's manuscripts had been sent, what is also implied by this new order is that, in the Council of the Indies, what Sahagún had communicated was known. He had naively thought that the king and the council were interested in his papers in order to learn about "the things of this New World." A remark made by Sahagún's friend and fellow chronicler, Fray Jerónimo de Mendieta, sheds light on the matter. He declares,

> One of the former Viceroys drew them out of his control [Sahagún's papers] by a ruse in order to send them to a chronicler who had insistently been requesting writings on the Indies, and they will benefit him as much as the couplets of Gaiferos.[24]

Mendieta explains elsewhere what he meant by this, saying that these "will serve him as so much spice paper."[25] If indeed the viceroy sent the monarch some of Sahagún's papers (whether Sahagún had turned them in personally or whether the viceroy had received them from Father Sequera), these texts were not included among those contained in the copy in four volumes in Nahuatl and Spanish. If it had happened that way, it would not account for Sahagún's later comment about them as "volumes very *historiados*," that is, heavily illustrated, which Father Sequera took with him when he left Mexico. What was sent would be incomprehensible to that supposed chronicler precisely because it was mostly in Nahuatl.

GARCÍA ICAZBALCETA'S KEEN INSIGHT

It is indeed noteworthy that, at an early date (1880), Don Joaquín García Icazbalceta, without any direct access to Sahagún's manuscripts, should come to a conclusion that would be the harbinger of the one proposed here. In an attempt to clarify which manu-script the viceroy sent to Spain, García Icazbalceta, following Del Paso y Troncoso's opinion, points out,

> Don Martín Enríquez thus gathered together and remitted in 1578 a copy that was not Father Sequera's. It may have been the one made on orders from Fray Miguel Navarro in 1569; later the text was emended by the Mexicans . . . ; because the Spanish translation had yet to be completed, Mendieta thought that these papers would prove useless to a chronicler who knew no Nahuatl.[26]

What Sahagún wrote, at more than eighty-five years of age, in the last chapter of the second version of the Book of the Conquest, can be understood this way. He speaks there of two submissions:

> Which books, that were twelve in number [this number comprised the manuscripts of 1569]; the King, Our Lord, Don Philip, sent for them, and I forwarded them to him by way of Don Martín Enríquez, Viceroy of this land; and I know not what he did with them, nor do I know where they might be now.
>
> After this, Father Fray Rodrigo de Sequera took them, for he did his service here in this land as Commissioner; and he has never written me about what happened to my books, which he took in the Spanish and Mexican languages and highly illustrated; and I know not in whose hands they may be today.[27]

One can well understand what Sahagún said about sending the twelve books to the king, Don Philip, "by way of Don Martín Enríquez," in the context of what he had written to the monarch on the 26th of March, 1578. In that letter, he stated to the king that he had asked Father Sequera to turn his manuscripts over to the viceroy in case he would not be departing soon for Spain, so that the viceroy could then send them on to the sovereign in his stead. What Sahagún turned over to the viceroy was the body of the texts, most of which were untranslated into Spanish (the manuscript of 1569), and as Father Mendieta had stated, these would be incomprehensible in Spain. In the second paragraph of this letter, it is equally clear that Sequera took with him to Spain the volumes that make up the *Florentine Codex*, in Spanish and Nahuatl and "very *historiados*," that is, with many illustrations.

THE TWO DEDICATORY INSCRIPTIONS IN WHICH THE *FLORENTINE CODEX* IS DESCRIBED

The dedications that Sahagún included at the beginning of Books I and VI of his *Historia general* are quite relevant. The one in Book I is only preserved in what is known as the *Códice de Tolosa*. This manuscript, which is a copy of the *Florentine Codex*, was probably ordered by Sequera while he was in Spain and preserved the dedication that was subsequently torn out of the *Florentine Codex*, perhaps when this was bestowed on some magnate or institution.

This inscription expresses, among other things, Sahagún's great pleasure. He declares it, saying that his works "came into the hands of someone who had supported them so much." Because the inscription introduces the first volume, which in its original as well as its modern binding, encompasses the first five books of the *Historia general*, Sahagún declares,

> I beseech Your Paternity please to receive into your protection this first volume, of these your redeemed works, which contain five books and some appendices; and it is like the firstborn or eldest son, after whom the others will follow; these are being raised with the nourishment that Your Paternity has provided them.[28]

Letting it be understood that he was submitting the first volume while the others were being prepared, Sahagún wrote in the second volume another inscription in Latin, which includes valuable information for the topic that interests us. In translation, it reads,

To the most honorable Father Rodrigo de Sequera, Commissioner General of all the lands of the Western Orb, with the sole exception of Peru, Brother Bernardino de Sahagún wishes you much happiness.

You have here, most devout Father, a work worthy of the gaze of the King, which was prepared in a protracted and strenuous struggle. Of which work, this is Book VI. There are another six after this one, which together make up a dozen, divided into four volumes. This sixth one, the greatest of them all, as much for its length as for what it expresses; [I] rejoice in great jubilation for having found in you so generous a Father, both for myself as for my brothers, so that, without any shadow of a doubt whatsoever, I have come with my brothers to the maximal happiness. May you remain in good health, everywhere, may life be prosperous for you; I ardently desire it.[29]

Bernardino must have experienced great pleasure in writing these lines. Although he may not have accomplished what he set out to do (arranging his work in three columns with a Spanish version on the left, the Nahuatl text in the middle, and linguistic annotations on the right), at least what he had accomplished was no small matter. The new codex showed his Nahuatl texts in one column and his paraphrased translation in the other, in a beautiful hand, along with a wealth of colorful illustrations. Though we realize that the Spanish translation does not always literally follow what is said in Nahuatl, to date no detailed study has been carried out on the differences between the two. Their description and evaluation will prove most significant in explaining just how Sahagún understood the natives' testimonies and attempted to communicate in Spanish what was expressed in Nahuatl. At times abbreviating portions, and occasionally even suppressing them, and at other times expanding and commenting on them, Bernardino has left us an extraordinary example of a cultural-linguistic decantation in his Spanish version.

A student of Sahagún's magnum opus, Pilar Máynez Vidal, has partially undertaken this task of comparing the Nahuatl and Spanish texts. Her work has consisted of analyzing the procedures that the friar adopted to communicate in Spanish the meanings of Nahuatl lexical items related to religion and magic. Although such a contribution is of considerable interest, one has to encompass not only what refers to the Nahuatl words included in the Spanish text of the *Historia general* but also all that Sahagún tried to transfer into Spanish from what the original texts convey in Nahuatl. The complexity of such a task derives from the fact that Sahagún was dealing with beliefs, practices related to a worldview, and a religion of an Indian culture so different from his own.

In Sahagún's enterprise, two things stand out: the conceptualization of a work that would encompass the totality of Nahua culture, and the methodology used to accomplish it. Sahagún was quite concerned that his work be accessible to those who might not know Nahuatl. What he achieved is a reflection of what that culture had once been, as elucidated by the Nahua elders and sages. By means of his cultural-linguistic decantation, he sought to transmit this in his paraphrased Spanish version. Analyzing and assessing the means by which he accomplished this in the diverse and, at times, complex contexts of his work are among the tasks waiting to be addressed.

CHAPTER SEVEN

Up to the End, with Additional Works, Unpleasantness, and Hopes (1580–1590)

After Father Rodrigo de Sequera had departed for Spain, Bernardino continued working at the College of Santa Cruz at Tlatelolco. Despite the royal orders, he had kept in his possession an important portion of his "writings," some of which had served as originals for the transcription he had made, thanks to the support of the father commissioner general. After Sahagún's death, several of these papers would once again be scattered, as is confirmed by the reports of various chroniclers and other persons who had them in their possession and availed themselves of them in various forms. Among these were Fray Juan de Torquemada, Chimalpahin Cuauhtlehuanitzin, Juan Suárez de Peralta, and Francisco Hernández, all of whom were authors of important works of history. Our friar, who never felt that he had definitively completed the entire corpus of texts with which he had been occupied for so many years, would still make several contributions intimately related to his *Historia general* and other writings he had in hand.

Sahagún, who had not seen any of his own works in print (whereas others, such as Alonso de Molina, had seen many of their works published), without despairing, continued pursuing the publication of the canticles that he had long ago composed in Nahuatl. In July 1578 he managed to persuade Archbishop

Pedro Moya de Contreras to have them examined. The judgment rendered concluded that it was a book "free of all suspicion of error or heresy, quite necessary and advantageous for the erudition of these natives." A further step that was definitive for its publication was the license conceded by the viceroy, the count of La Coruña, shortly before his death on the 19th of June, 1583.

PUBLICATION OF THE *PSALMODIA CHRISTIANA*

In the midst of so many uncertainties and disturbances and because he still had no knowledge of what had become of the volumes of his *Historia general*, it gave Sahagún (who was more than eighty years old at the time) considerable satisfaction to publish at least one of his works composed many years prior. In 1583, with the press mark "House of Pedro Ocharte," this work appeared: *Psalmodia christiana y sermonario de los sanctos del año, en lengua mexicana: Compuesta por el muy reverendo padre fray Bernardino de Sahagún, de la orden de Sanct Francisco. Ordenado en cantares o psalmos para que canten los indios en los areytos que hacen en las iglesias* (Christian psalmody and sermonary of the saints of the year, in the Mexican language: Composed by the Most Reverend Father Fray Bernardino de Sahagún, of the order of Saint Francis. Arranged into songs or psalms for the Indians to sing in their feasts in the churches).[1]

In his brief "Prologue to the Reader," Sahagún recalls the importance that songs had had in the ancient Indian culture to honor the gods, evoke the feats of warriors, and other relevant events. He laments that, despite so many years of evangelization, "they insist on once again singing their ancient chants in their houses and in the *tecpas* (*tecpantli*, or communal houses or palaces).[2] By way of commentary, he expresses something that reveals a deeply rooted concern of his. The fact that such songs persist brings into "grave suspicion the sincerity of their Christian faith, because in the ancient songs mostly idolatrous things were sung about, in a style so impenetrable that there is no one who can understand them."[3]

Sahagún took pride in the publication of his "Psalmody to put an end to the ancient songs . . . and so that they might praise God and the Saints with Christian and Catholic praise." He had the same intention when he arrived in New Spain in 1529: to become acquainted with the native culture in order to cure the natives of what he considered to be the most grievous illness of idolatry, until he could attain their total conversion to Christianity.

Because of this, he expresses his gratitude, first to the viceroy Don Martín Enríquez, then to the count of La Coruña, for having granted him permission to publish his work. In concluding his prologue, he beseeches the secular authorities to consent to and favor the dissemination of this work among the natives, who are commanded under the threat of serious punishment never to sing the ancient songs, only those devoted to God and the saints.

Other contemporaries of Sahagún concur in his repeated assertion about the persistence of the old pagan songs. Fray Diego Duran warned that they ought not to be allowed:

> The songs and lamentations they sing when they see that there is no one around who can understand them. Yet, when someone appears who does understand them, they change the song and sing the ones composed for Saint Francis, with the alleluia at the end to disguise their evildoing and, in replacing the religious [Christian] one, they dedicate it to the idol.[4]

Dr. Francisco Cervantes de Salazar, former rector of the University of Mexico, expressed a like sentiment. In his *Crónica de Nueva España*, written around 1560, he stated:

> They [the Indians] are so inclined to their ancient idolatry that, if there is no one about who understands their language, in the midst of the sacred [Christian] prayers, mix in

songs from their gentile times; and, the better to cover their wicked works, they begin and end with the word God, intercalating the pagan verses while lowering their voices so that no one can understand them.[5]

What was expressed by Durán and Cervantes de Salazar surely confirms Sahagún's fears. This completely justified the dissemination of his *Psalmodia christiana* in as timely a manner as possible. It contains compositions in Nahuatl for many of the feasts throughout the liturgical year. They were distributed as chapters among the twelve months. Among the principal feasts for which there are songs, the following stand out: the Circumcision of the Lord, Epiphany, Saint Thomas Aquinas, Saint Gabriel, Saint Joseph, the Annunciation, the Resurrection of the Lord (Easter Sunday), the Ascension, Pentecost, Corpus Christi, the Apostles Peter and Paul, and many others, including one that is worth mentioning, the feast of Saint Bernard, his own patron saint.

The psalms and songs composed by him, in which the inspiration of the ancient native productions can be easily identified, including their figures of speech and metaphors, merited a special recommendation from the Third Mexican Council (of bishops), which convened in the metropolis in 1585. It is an ironic turn of events, in light of all this, that another Franciscan, Fray Francisco de la Rosa Figueroa, believed much later that he had uncovered some dangerous concepts in the *Psalmodia christiana*. His aberrant zeal led him to denounce this work before the Holy Office of the Inquisition, and acting on his own account, he burned all the copies that he could lay his hands on. In this manner Bernardino became the object of persecutions long after he was dead.[6]

SAHAGÚN EDITS HIS WORKS IN TLATELOLCO

A curious incident occurred at the College of Santa Cruz in connection with the visit of the new Franciscan commissioner, Fray Pedro Ponce, toward mid-October in 1584. He had arrived in New Spain the month before and had begun his *visita*, a tour of inspection through the central region. His mission, which would be rather lengthy, would end in a heated confrontation in the very bosom of his order. Fray Bernardino, already at an advanced age, would see himself deeply embroiled in this conflict. Without imagining that such a thing could occur to him, Sahagún took part in the welcoming reception for Fray Pedro Ponce at the College of Santa Cruz. For this purpose, a small theater production or skit had been prepared. Its theme reveals Sahagún's involvement. In his "Account by the Author Worthy of Being Read," which would be incorporated into Book X of his *Historia general*, he denounced the contradictions and attacks that several Spaniards, both secular and religious, had launched against the College of Santa Cruz. At first they had mockingly said that "no one would be competent enough to teach grammar to people as witless as these young natives."[7] Yet when they saw the great progress achieved by the students at the college,

> They were much astonished . . . and began to speak against it and to voice many objections against it in order to impede it. . . . They said that because they were not to become priests, what use was it to teach them grammar, which would only place them in danger of becoming heretics, and also that, reading the Sacred Scriptures, they might understand in them how the Patriarchs of old had had many wives, as was their wont, and would not wish to believe what we were now preaching to them about no one having more than one wife. . . . There were many other altercations that took place about the affair, which would be excessive to write down here.[8]

What seemed excessive to him to write down was transformed into a farcical one-act playlet before Father Ponce. The performance for the father commissioner began with two interlocutors speaking in Latin and Spanish. One of the actors, acknowledging his status as a student, burst out in Latin saying, in an ironic tone, that it was true that all those studying there were nothing more than magpies and parrots who would soon forget what they had been taught.

The skit proceeded with the appearance of a well-proportioned native youth dressed like a Spaniard. He spoke not in Latin but only in Spanish, the sole language the supposed Spaniard knew, and he began to criticize what, in his opinion, the College of Santa Cruz represented: educating those Indians would only serve to engender more drunkards and rogues. At the climax, another student came on stage dressed as a college master. Confronting the one dressed as a Spaniard, he chided him saying,

> The scoundrel lies! For in truth, they are good sons and careful of their virtue and their studies; yet you all know nothing more than to open your mouths to speak ill of them; and whatever thing they may prosper in, you take much to heart. For you would like nothing better than to see them burdened with a load on their backs, busy about your service.[9]

The jest, as is obvious, addressed the realities that were concerns to set before Father Ponce. A traveling companion, Fray Antonio de Ciudad Real, was so impressed with what was in the performance that he wrote down the entire episode in the journal he was keeping of the commissioner general's tour. Sahagún, the probable covert author of the farce, must have taken great pleasure in it and the lesson it imparted to Father Ponce.

Sahagún, with the aid of his native scribes, proceeded with the work he was anxious to bring to closure. This included four different matters, which was an extraordinary thing, considering his age of more than eighty-four years. The topics were these: a new *kalendar in Mexican, Spanish, and Latin; a* revised exposition of *The Art of Divination That the Mexicans Employed in the Times of Their Idolatry, Called* Tonalamatl, *Which Means Book Dealing with the Fates and Fortunes of Those Born, According to the Signs and Characters into Which They Are Born*; a new account of the Spanish Conquest; and his project for a grammar and trilingual vocabulary in Nahuatl, Latin, and Spanish.

NEW TREATISE ON THE CALENDAR

With regard to the calendar, a copy of which is preserved in the National Library of Mexico, it is worth noting that Sahagún prepared it in keeping with the Gregorian calendar reform of 1582, which went into effect in Mexico in 1584. His purpose was to present a native calendar that was also "reformed"; instead of the eighteen twenty-day periods with five unlucky days at the end ([18 × 20] + 5 = 365), he distributed those five ill-fated days among five twenty-day periods. In a rather strange manner, he also altered the date that he had fixed in his *Historia general* for the start of the new year, from the 2nd to the 1st of February. He also included a summary of all the rituals and sacrifices throughout each of the twenty-day periods.

He then included twenty tables with the hieroglyphic sign for each day within a twenty-day period and the symbol corresponding to the name of each "month," or twenty-day period. Bernardino's ultimate purpose was to provide a practical application for his queries on calendrical matters in his *Historia general*. He thought that, because the native calendar was "reformed" and correlated with the Gregorian reformed calendar, it would prove more useful to the forewarned missionaries in being able to identify, throughout the feasts of the year, any possible pagan survivals. In fact, another friar, Fray Martín de León, copied what Sahagún had published on the native calendar and included it in a work that he published in Mexico in 1611, entitled *Camino del cielo* (Road to heaven).[10]

THE *ARTE ADIVINATORIO* (ART OF DIVINATION)

The same preoccupation with exposing idolatry apparently became exacerbated in Fray Bernardino with the passage of time; it led him to prepare a new version of what he called the *Arte adivinatorio* (Art of divination). In it, probably working from a Nahuatl text (because he mentions rendering it "in Romance"), he offers a version quite similar to the one he had presented in the first twenty chapters of Book IV of his *Historia general*. Of particular

interest in this work is the prologue. As was mentioned about his
first impressions upon arriving in Mexico, he levels an acid criticism of the method of evangelizing the Indians and of its results.
Since first joining the Franciscans of the province of San Gabriel,
he had shared the ideals that motivated men such as Fray Martín
de Valencia; now—in 1585—more than ever, he felt a profound
disappointment. The ideal of implanting within the Indians the
seed that would sprout and develop vigorously into a Christianity like that of the primitive church had not become a reality.
Among other things, he writes this in his prologue:

> The absence of the wisdom of the serpent in the founding
> of the Church became quite evident after a few years [New
> Testament counsel: "be as wise as the serpent"], due to ig-
> norance of the conspiracy among the leaders and satraps to
> receive Jesus Christ as one among their many gods. . . . In
> this way, they took as yet another god the God of the Span-
> iards without, however, relinquishing their ancient gods;
> and this they concealed during their catechesis for Baptism.
> . . . Thus, this new Church came to be founded on false-
> hood, and even though it has been reined in somewhat, it is
> still rather injured and ruinous.[11]

He follows this immediately with the statement "this twisted
perversity has been emended, the calendar has been elaborat-
ed, and now this *Art of Divination* has been written." According
to Bernardino, the same thing occurred among the Indians as
among the followers of Mohammed: namely, many false conversions. It follows that it is absolutely indispensable for one to be
fully informed about the ancient beliefs in order to expose them
and strip away all their disguises. In drawing up a summary of
the attributes of the gods worshipped by the ancient Mexicans,
he states that the treatise he has written on divination "can well
be called a refutation of idolatry."[12] In light of all this, one can
better understand what he had written less than ten years before
on the equally suspect devotion to Our Lady of Guadalupe on

the hill of Tepeyacac, where the Indians had had a temple dedicated to the mother of the gods, whom they called Tonantzin, which means "Our Mother."[13]

THE NEW *BOOK OF THE CONQUEST*, THE *GRAMMAR*, AND THE *VOCABULARY*

As he had many years before, between 1553 and 1554 (Sahagún stated it thus: "now more than thirty years ago"), he once again undertook research with the help of certain elders, who spoke to him at the College of Santa Cruz so he could listen to their accounts of the Conquest. According to Sahagún, he undertook this research because in the former book of his *Historia general*,

> [w]herein is treated the Conquest, there were several defects, and it was that things were placed in the narrative of this Conquest that were ill-placed; and others that were kept silent, which ought not have been. For this reason, this year of fifteen hundred eighty-five, I have emended this book.[14]

In what follows, the way he decided to present it is described. His deeply rooted idea of offering his texts "in columns" reappears here. The same can be stated about its historical as well as linguistic interest. Fray Bernardino remained the same person, indefatigable, a perfectionist, and, let us acknowledge it at once, a bit ambivalent: he felt that he must uncover and pursue idolatries, yet he was also deeply interested in native antiquities, their "divine, human, and natural things." The Conquest, which, as he said on several occasions, had altered everything radically, was also a matter of vital interest. This book tells us,

> It is written in three columns. The first is in the native language, thus unrefined, as they uttered it and was written in the other books [of the *Historia general*]. The second column is an emendation of the first, thus as much in words as in sentences. The third column is in Romance, written with the corrections from the second column.[15]

The first account of the Conquest was in an "unrefined" language; the new one contained emendations, as much in the linguistic structures (that is, words and constructions) as in the content of the sentences. Because it is not credible that he proceeded in an arbitrary manner in these emendations, that is, at his whim, most probably he once again harkened to the testimonies of his elderly consultants. Bernardino's intention is stated in the following:

> Those who possess this treatise in the Mexican language only [as did Fray Juan de Torquemada, who had it along with several others], let them be aware that many things have been emended in this one that is in three columns in each sheet.[16]

It is indeed a misfortune that this treatise in three columns has not reached us either in the original or in any copy. Only the text "in Romance" is known, that is, the version in Spanish "as emended." Although it may seem strange, for quite a long time only one complete edition existed of that Spanish version of the new book on the Conquest by Sahagún. That edition was published in 1840 by the Mexican statesman and prolific editor of old texts, Carlos María de Bustamante. So curious, not to say extravagant, was that publication that, for reasons that would have perplexed Sahagún, it appeared with the strange title of *La aparición de Nuestra Señora de Guadalupe de México, comprobada con la refutación del argumento negativo que presenta don Juan Bautista Muñoz (cronista español del siglo XVIII), fundándose en el testimonio del padre fray Bernardino de Sahagún, o sea, la* Historia *original de ese escritor, que altera la publicada en 1829* (Apparition of Our Lady of Guadalupe of Mexico, proven with the refutation of the negative argument that Don Juan Bautista Muñoz [Spanish chronicler of the eighteenth century] presents, basing itself on the testimony of Father Fray Bernardino de Sahagún, i.e., the original *History* by that writer, which alters the one published in 1829).[17]

In 1829 Bustamante had the honor, along with Lord Kingsborough in London, of being the first to rescue and edit the Spanish text of the *Historia general,* based on the copy preserved in the monastery at Tolosa. Shortly thereafter he developed the picturesque idea of using the new version of the Conquest to demonstrate that the text published earlier by the same author (in which Sahagún suspects the cult of the Virgin of Guadalupe at Tepeyacac) was an erroneous transcription, or that (at least in the book on the Conquest) there might be another version that emended the errors. Thus, so many years after Sahagún's death, due to nationalistic motives (the Virgin of Guadalupe was a symbol that the insurgents appropriated in Mexico's War of Independence), his work was, if not an object of persecution, at least one of manipulation.

In 1989 a critical edition of this second version of the Conquest (now preserved in the Boston Public Library) was published, comparing it with the one from 1840 published by Bustamante; we owe this edition to Susan L. Cline, who provided an ample introduction as well as annotation. As she notes, she profited from what her father, Howard F. Cline, had left when he was unable to conclude the project.

The comparison between what Bustamante had published and what is included in the manuscript preserved in Boston allows one to see differences worthy of attention. These probably originate from transcription errors in Bustamante's copy or from his intention to present a somewhat freer version. Another form of comparison (this one with the Spanish version in the *Florentine Codex*) allows one to see which changes Sahagún introduced in his 1585 presentation. A very important change consisted in highlighting some positive attributes in Hernán Cortés's personality. In this, Bernardino acted in harmony with the stance adopted by the majority of the Franciscans in Mexico, who saw in Cortés a providential figure, thanks to whom it had been possible to preach the gospel in Mexican lands. Let us consider an example of this. This consists of the words that Cortés supposedly addressed to the Mexicas just before the final assault on Tenochtitlan. Cortés recriminates the natives, saying that it was they who had provoked Pedro de Alvarado to attack them in the precinct of the

PSALMODIA

CHRISTIANA, Y SERMONA-
rio delos Sanctos del Año, en lengua Mexicana:
cópuesta por el muy. R. Padre Fray Bernardino
de Sahagun, de la orden de sant Francisco.
Ordenada en cantares ò Psalmos: paraque canten los
Indios en los areytos, que hazen en las Iglesias.

EN MEXICO.
Con licencia, en casa de Pedro Ocharte.
M.D.LXXXIII. Años.

Frontispiece to the *Psalmodia christiana*, the only book of his that Sahagún would see in print.

PRIMERO
Pſalmo.

Omnipoten-
cia.

Yioiauc, in ti Dios, in titeuth, in mo
techtzinco cenquiztoc inifquich tla
matiliztli, in vel moncifcauiltzi, in cem
anca tlamatiliztli, ma iccuel, ma xiual
mouica, xtecchmopaleuiliqui.

In

Page from the *Psalmodia christiana* pertaining to the feast of the Annunciation.

Historia universal delas Cosas
dela Nueva España, en doce libros
y quatro Volumenes en lengua Española.
Compuesta y Copilada Por el M.R.P.e
Fr. Bernardino de Sahagun, de la
orden delos Frayles menores de Observancia.

Nota.

Este Libro se hallava en el Convento de Frayles
Franciscos de la Villa de tolosa de Guipuzcoa,
de donde lo recojió en virtud de Rl. órn de 6. de Abril
de 1783. por el ex.mo S.r D.n Jph de Galvez, y D.n Juan Baup-
tista Muñoz Cosmografo mayor de Yndias Comisiona-
do por S.M. para escribir la Historia Real de aquellos
Dominios, por cuyo fallecimto. se traxo con otros papeles
suyos á esta Secra. del Despacho de Gracia y Justicia de Yndias.
Habiendolo reclamado dhos Religiosos, se les intimó que
Su ex.a tendria gusto de tenerlo; en cuya virtud lo cedie-
ron voluntariamte. dandoles una Copia integra de
dho Libro en el año de 1804. como consta del expediente
causado sobre el particular y existe en esta Secre-
taria. Este Libro aunque se llama Original, no es
sino Copia ni tiene otra recomendacion que el estar
escrito en letra antigua de la epoca de la conquista
de Nueva España, y á pocos años despues de ella.
Madrid 4. Julio de 1804.

First page of the copy of the new version of the history of the Conquest, prepared by Sahagún in 1585 (Boston Public Library).

LA

APARICION

DE

N.ᵗᵃ SEÑORA DE GUADALUPE

DE MEXICO,

Comprobada con la refutacion del argumento negativo que presenta
D. Juan Bautista Muñoz, fundandose en el testimonio del P. Fr. Bernardino Sahagun;

ó sea:

HISTORIA ORIGINAL

DE ESTE ESCRITOR,

QUE ALTERA LA PUBLICADA EN 1829

EN EL EQUIVOCADO CONCEPTO

DE SER LA UNICA Y ORIGINAL DE DICHO AUTOR.

PUBLÍCALA,

Precediendo una disertacion sobre la
Aparicion Guadalupana, y con notas sobre la conquista de Mexico,

Cárlos M. de Bustamante,

INDIVIDUO DEL SUPREMO PODER CONSERVADOR.

⤛⤜⤛⤜

Mexico. [IMPRESO POR IGNACIO CUMPLIDO,] 1840.

CALLE DE LOS REBELDES nº 2.

393

Cover to the extravagant edition of Book XII of the *Historia general* published by Carlos María de Bustamante in Mexico in 1840.

Fray Bernardino de Sahagún

Historia general de las cosas de Nueva España

TOMO PRIMERO

PRIMERA VERSIÓN ÍNTEGRA DEL TEXTO CASTELLANO
DEL MANUSCRITO CONOCIDO COMO
CÓDICE FLORENTINO

INTRODUCCIÓN, PALEOGRAFÍA, GLOSARIO Y NOTAS DE
ALFREDO LÓPEZ AUSTIN Y JOSEFINA GARCÍA QUINTANA

Fomento Cultural Banamex

MÉXICO 1982

Cover to the first edition of the *Historia general*. The transcription of the
Spanish text is included in the *Florentine Codex*.

Monument erected to Fray Bernardino in his native town in Spain on 11 June 1966.

Monument erected to Fray Bernardino in the town of Sahagún, state of Hidalgo.

Templo Mayor in order to prevent a treacherous uprising, and that they were also responsible for the death of Motecuhzoma:

> After I left here in a few days, you say that the Captain I left, who is Pedro de Alvarado, who is here, treacherously and without any cause whatsoever, attacked you in a war-like manner during a feast that you were celebrating in honor of your god Huitzilopochtli, and that he killed and annihilated the flower of the Mexicans; and then, before the Spaniards regrouped, so many Mexican warriors attacked them that it became necessary for them to gain their fort and enclose themselves therein, where I had left them (and this was the signal that this war had truly begun); to impute the blame for this affair on my Captain and my Spaniards, you began to publicize that they had treacherously attacked you without any cause whatsoever for doing what they did.
>
> Yet this is not so, for when I returned and inquired then about this affair, how it had come to pass, [I] discovered that during the feast you had all conspired to kill all whom I had left behind, Spaniards and Indians; when they learned of this, they preempted you most certainly in doing what they—the Captain and the Spaniards—did, which they did well in doing.
>
> You also blame us for the death of Motecuhzoma, and that is untrue, because from before I arrived from the Coast, by order of Don Pedro de Alvarado, he came out onto the roof to command the Mexicans to cease fighting (though the Spaniards were surrounding and sheltering him); not only did you not wish to obey him, but you dishonored him and us, the Spaniards, and you cast stones at him, by which he was struck, and he died at your hands. Not only did you not desist from fighting, as you were commanded to by your lord, rather you went on struggling even harder against the Spaniards and you took away from them all their supplies, and when I arrived they were starving; and knowing I was

coming and seeing me enter into your city, there was no man who did speak to me and wish to see me.

When I came to where the mistreated Spaniards were, neither your lord nor any of you wished to see me nor greet me, and I commanded you to cease your fighting and to give us provisions; you refused and more diligently fought on to take away and kill anyone who might give us provisions clandestinely. Thus we were obliged to flee by night from where we were and to get out as well as we could with our fallen Spaniards and the friendly Indians; and you robbed us of all we had and chased us up to the borders of Otumba, where you attacked us in such a way from every side that, had it not been for a miracle of God, you would have killed us then, just as you wished to.

All these things and many more that I pass in silence you did against us as an idolatrous and cruel people ignorant of any justice or humanity.[18]

Having introduced passages such as this, which seems implausible as a testimony provided by the Mexicas, Bernardino gave as a reason for his changes that the friars and students could use the new text as a complement to his other projects involving the comprehension and teaching of the Nahuatl language:

I also emended this treatise because I intend, upon concluding the grammar and the dictionary of the Mexican language, which I am now undertaking, to lecture our religious on the grammar of this Mexican language and also its vocabulary and this conquest, reading it in their own Nahuatl language as it is written there.[19]

The topic of the grammar and the vocabulary, which we know would be trilingual (Nahuatl, Latin, and Spanish), so often alluded to by Sahagún throughout his life, reappears here. At the age of eighty-five or a little more, he was "undertaking" it, quite busily actually. His only motive in all of this was that he wished "to lecture our religious," on it, that is, to train them so that with the grammar, the vocabulary, and new texts on the Conquest, they might further penetrate the secrets of their own language and of the native culture that was so damaged by the triumph-at-arms of Hernán Cortés.

It seems strange that Sahagún, who had collected the dramatic native testimonies that make up the "Vision of the Vanquished," in his old age would attempt to alter what he had written back then; however, there is at least a double consideration to entertain. On the one hand, his never suppressed concerns about the persistence of idolatry must be taken into account. The native testimonies about the Conquest might seem so powerful that they could be construed as an explanation for the rejection of a definitive evangelization. This would justify (as Sahagún might have thought) their revision and emendation. On the other hand, in what appears to be his ambivalent attitude of rejection and admiration, he did not wish to suppress the original version and preserved, in the now lost manuscript, "the Indian language, crude, as they spoke it." In this way he preserved the original version in one column; in the other he made additions and alterations such as the one cited here. After all, his critical sense moved him to do it.

We know very little about the other frequently fondled projects that Sahagún said he wished to finish. I refer to the completion of a grammar and trilingual vocabulary in Nahuatl, Latin, and Spanish. Nothing can be said about the grammar because no manuscript is known to contain it nor even to relate to it. As far as the vocabulary is concerned, one can mention the manuscript preserved in the Ayer Collection at the Newberry Library in Chicago. It consists of a volume with 158 folios on both sides, in which, following Nebrija's format, Sahagún has added Nahuatl equivalents.

Although there are some who doubt that this vocabulary was actually prepared by Sahagún or that it was a first draft or an early attempt, there are others, such as Luis Nicolau D'Olwer and John Frederick Schwaller, who are inclined to identify it as such. Schwaller would also credit Bernardino with the Latin-Nahuatl glossary accompanying the already cited *Evangelarium, Epistolar-*

ium et Lectionarium Aztecum (Of the Gospels, Epistles, and readings of the Aztecs), published in 1858 by Bernardino Biondelli. Although this attribution is not easily demonstrable, it is appropriate at least to be cognizant of it.[20]

The works with which Sahagún was involved at that time were certainly related to the great motivators throughout his life. These were to unmask idolatries, to establish Christianity, and to accomplish it completely through a knowledge of the language in which one must preach and the assessment of the ancient culture. These continued to be at the heart of Bernardino's activities. He had already dedicated fifty-six years of his life to these purposes, from 1529 to 1585.

LAST STORM IN WHICH FRAY
BERNARDINO BECAME EMBROILED

As we have seen, in September 1584, Commissioner General Fray Pedro Ponce was in Mexico City. Sahagún had met him during his visit to the College of Santa Cruz. Father Ponce's actions were in no way unobtrusive. One alteration was felt by several members of the province of the Holy Gospel in Mexico City, when they noted the acquiescence of Fray Pedro before Archbishop Moya de Contreras's attitude of turning parishes over to secular priests; as missions and catechetical centers, these had, up till then, been in the control of the Franciscans.

In the midst of these circumstances, it became known that a new minister general had been elected by the order in Rome. This event was adduced as an argument by the provincial of the Holy Gospel, Fray Pedro de San Sebastián. In his judgment, the change of minister general nullified the authority under which Father Ponce had been acting. Father Ponce, for his part, supported the validity of his nomination as commissioner general in a brief to Pius V and in other legal dispositions of the order.

The conflict grew worse until it erupted as an open storm among the Franciscans of the Holy Gospel. Provincial Fray Pedro de San Sebastián openly confronted Father Ponce and obtained the backing of Viceroy Don Alvaro Manríquez de Zúñiga, Marquis of Villamanrique. His wife, Doña Blanca Velasco, also intervened in the episode; she was a devotee of the Franciscan provincial. The viceroy's decision on this occasion was extremely grave. The commissioner was detained and then expelled. He had to depart for Guatemala in 1586.

The tempest soon affected Fray Bernardino in a very direct manner. While he was immersed in his labors of revising and editing the *Art of Divination* and the new version of the *Book of the Conquest*, he had to take on the charge of *primer definidor* (president or chair of the order chapter), which came as a result of the provincial chapter election held on the 20th of June, 1585. Fray Pedro Ponce, on leaving Mexico City as an exile heading for Guatemala, stated that it fell to Fray Bernardino de Sahagún, precisely in his capacity as *primer definidor*, to take on the position of commissioner general of the province of the Holy Gospel. Bernardino, at more than eighty-five years of age, who must have already felt quite uncomfortable with his election as *primer definidor*, became very perturbed with the difficult task of acting as commissioner general of the province of the Holy Gospel in such circumstances. This position could lead him to a confrontation with Provincial Pedro de San Sebastian and with other members of his order.

Father Ponce, revealing little skill as a conciliator, charged two Franciscans with the task of carrying out a kind of survey to ascertain who in the order accepted and who rejected Fray Bernardino as commissioner general. As might have been expected, this decision did little to defuse the conflict. Because several friars declared that they were prepared to acquiesce to the decision made by the former commissioner, the viceroy, being a partisan of Provincial Pedro de San Sebastián, had these friars apprehended. The detained were sent to the fortress of San Juan de Ulúa in Veracruz to be shipped off to Spain.

While awaiting their deportation, they lodged a series of accusations and denunciations of some gravity before representatives of the Holy Office of the Inquisition. According to these Franciscan friars, Fray Juan Cancino and Fray Andrés Vélez, they had been apprehended unjustly because the only reason was that they had not bent to the will of the provincial. According to their statements, the provincial and other friars had mocked the decision of Father Ponce, who had enforced his orders under threat of excommunication. Furthermore, they declared that the provincial and his followers had stated that the viceroy should be obeyed as "the head of these kingdoms in spiritual and temporal matters."[21] This, according to the plaintiffs, was nothing other than a Lutheran heresy, "such as the one existing in England at that time."[22] These occurrences must have left Fray Bernardino quite perplexed; he was then obliged to separate himself from his studies in order to deal with this thorny issue that had befallen him so suddenly after receiving his charge as *primer definidor* of the province.

There are few scholars who have worked on unraveling what was at the heart of this tempest that so affected the Franciscans of Mexico in 1585 and the following years. Smaller still is the number of those who have attempted to explain what soon became Fray Bernardino's firm attitude under these circumstances. The Spanish expatriate scholar living in Mexico, Luis Nicolau D'Olwer, in the biography he wrote on Bernardino de Sahagún, interpreted the events in terms of a confrontation between the Franciscans with a peninsular origin and those born in New Spain. According to this theory, Ponce represented the peninsulars, whereas Provincial Pedro de San Sebastián unfurled the flag of the native-born. It is not that simple, however. Sahagún would have sided with the peninsulars from the first, upon receiving the order from Ponce to take up the office of commissioner general. Nevertheless, his situation grew complicated when in April 1586, he declared that the true superior continued to be Provincial Pedro de San Sebastián.[23]

The appointment that he held as commissioner general Sahagún surrendered to the viceroy. He likewise declared that the penalty of excommunication that Father Ponce was attempting

to impose was null and void because he lacked the authority. Standing firm on this position—with his authority as *primer
definidor* (first definer) and with the participation of the others,
fellow definers (superiors) of the province of the Holy Gospel—
he signed a letter on the 16th of May, 1587, addressed to Father
Ponce, in which he was advised that Sahagún had renounced his
appointment as commissioner general. In response, on the 19th
of December of the same year, Ponce fulminated with an excommunication against Sahagún and the other definers. Fray Bernardino's change in attitude, having sided with Provincial Pedro de
San Sebastián's faction, has been seen, in this manner of interpretation, as a sign of senility.

Another interpretation, however, has been developed that is
perhaps more suitable to this whole series of events, which must
have affected Bernardino very strongly at his more than eighty-
seven years of age. We owe this theory to Georges Baudot, a
well-known Sahagún specialist. Taking into account several communications addressed to none other than Philip II from the four
definers of the province (among whom was Bernardino de Sahagún), Provincial Pedro de San Sebastián, and the celebrated chronicler Pedro de Oroz, Baudot comes to a very different conclusion.

These communications, which had remained forgotten in the
General Archive of the Indies at Seville, were signed by those
who identified themselves as defenders of the natives. They insist before the king that they have lived in strict religious observance with no property whatsoever and that their sole purpose
has been to impede the wayward schemes of Commissioner
Ponce. He, because of his friendship with Archbishop Moya de
Contreras, has been attempting to have the Franciscans of the
province of the Holy Gospel turn their monasteries and catechetical centers over to the secular clergy. In the opinion of Sahagún
and of those who signed the letters with him, if such a measure
were to be implemented, it would negatively affect, and very se-
riously so, the great enterprise of evangelization of the natives of
New Spain. They have thus turned to the king so that he might

free them from the dangers that have arisen from the presence of Father Ponce.[24]

Taking into account this documentation, one may interpret these events in a different way. The opposition of the Franciscans, led by Provincial Pedro de San Sebastián, to the measures that Father Ponce was attempting to implement, and the attitude that Fray Bernardino soon assumed quite resolutely, were nothing more than a ratification of the ancient ideals that had flourished since their beginnings, first in the *custodia* and then in the province of the Holy Gospel.

Father Ponce's proposal implied incorporating the natives into secular parishes, obliging them to participate in the same way of life as the Spaniards and mestizos. Were such a proposition to triumph, the possibility would disappear forever of establishing in the New World the ideals of a purer Christianity in its original form, about which the founders of the province of San Gabriel in Extremadura had dreamed. Many threats had already been leveled against these ideals, but this last one, if victorious, would bring down the total ruin of everything for which the first twelve friars—led by Fray Martín de Valencia—had worked. Sahagún must have felt overwhelmed and, at certain junctures, rather perplexed by all of this.

In fact, toward 1585, in the last pages of his second version of the *Libro de la Conquista* (Book of the Conquest), he would once again ponder what had been and continued to be the process of Christianization of the Mexican natives. He recalled how the task of evangelizing the many native peoples who lived in the great expanse of New Spain had been commended to the Franciscans:

> Captain Hernán Cortés was made Governor of this country [on triumphing over the Mexicas], and then he and all the other captains and leaders of these lands wrote letters to the most invincible Charles V . . . , in which they beseeched him to send to these parts preachers of the Catholic faith and devout Recollect friars of Saint Francis, so that they might

preach to this Indian and idolatrous people the law of God
. . . , [a]bout which the Emperor wrote the Supreme Pontiff.
Pope Hadrian VI, who had been a tutor of the Emperor,
took care of this matter by sending to this land twelve friars
of Saint Francis, Recollects, Spaniards, of the Province of
San Gabriel of Extremadura, with all his authority, to found
and rule over all those Indians who converted.[25]

Recalling this reinforced in Fray Bernardino the decision that
he had taken in the conflict. The Franciscans, heirs to the ideals of
the province of San Gabriel of Extremadura, could not turn over
the souls of so many natives whom they had had in their care
since the emperor and Pope Hadrian VI had entrusted them. Yet
at the same time that such recollections came to his mind, it is very
probable that Sahagún continued to meditate, also toward 1585,
on what he had written about the great risk that the new church
was founded on falsehood. The Franciscans themselves had frequently acted without the necessary prudence, being ignorant of
the ancient culture and precipitously baptizing Indians.

This would become even more serious with the intention of
Father Ponce to comply with Archbishop Moya de Contreras in
his plans to secularize missions and catechetical centers. As Sahagún had written in 1576 while preparing the clean copy of his
Historia general, there was a danger that in New Spain an ancient
process might repeat itself: the decadence of Christianity. Fray
Bernardino, by the way in which he alludes to this, shows himself to be deeply concerned and, in a certain way, pessimistic.
This type of burden would strain the fabric of his last years of
life. We shall attempt at least an approach to the last phase of his
existence on earth.

BERNARDINO'S LAST YEARS

What he was to write around the year 1585—in the preface to
his *Art of Divination* and elsewhere in his new book on the Conquest—allows us to perceive a Sahagún who reflects worriedly
on what had been the principal concern of his life, after hav-

ing been confronted by realities that were in no way pleasant for him. Of prime importance to him was the establishment of the Christian faith. That was the reason for his coming to Mexican soil. History, however, offered a somber lesson. Attempts to cause Christianity to take root had failed in many parts of the world. This is what he thought and even wrote about:

> The Church Militant began in the Kingdom of Palestine, and from there it marched into many parts of the world. . . . The Church departed Palestine, and now it is ruled by infidels; from there it went to Asia, where there are no longer any Christians, in which there are nothing but Turks and Moors; it also went to Africa, where there are no longer any Christians; it went to Germany, where there are nothing but heretics; it went to Europe, where in most places there is no obedience to the Church.
>
> Where it enjoys the greatest stability are Spain and Italy, from whence, crossing the Ocean Sea, it has reached these parts of the Western Indies, where there are a variety of peoples and tongues, of which many have already disappeared, and those which are left are on the same road to extinction; the most populous and most advanced of these Western Indies has been and is this New Spain. . . .
>
> It seems to me that the Catholic Faith will endure but a short time in these parts; one reason is because the populace is fast disappearing . . . and everything is coming to an end, for bread is very expensive and difficult to obtain, and the religious fall ill and become exhausted.[26]

As if in the midst of such a bitter reflection he were seeking some hope, Fray Bernardino alludes to what he has heard about the kingdom of China, where it is said, "there are very able people endowed with high culture and knowledge."[27] One who had worked for years in New Spain and had gathered such valuable testimonies must have felt afflicted by the contradictions by which he was assaulted time and time again. He had been denied the assistance of scribes and access to ink and paper. His writings had been dispersed and, since Father Rodrigo de Sequera had taken them with him, he had lost track of them. Now in his most advanced years, he had had to confront the storm that Father Ponce had stirred up. If the Indians of New Spain were on the path to extinction and if the Christian faith had not taken root, why then had he been so zealous in collecting so many testimonies and in digging so deeply into the divine, human, and natural things of these people?

A world of uncertainty and woe must have burdened Fray Bernardino. Nevertheless, he had also written a phrase around the year 1576 that sounds almost epigraphic. It was the bearer of a very different pronouncement: "It is my feeling that there will always be a great number of Indians in these lands."[28]

It is a very difficult thing to penetrate into the secrets of a mind. It becomes impossible when it is the mind of someone who has departed forever. One road at least is open to us for forming an opinion about what Fray Bernardino experienced in his mind during the last years of his life, especially what he thought about himself, his work as a researcher and missionary, and the destiny he glimpsed as the fate of the Indians. This road is offered by those who knew him, dealt with him close at hand, and left their testimony about him and his last years. What Fray Jerónimo de Mendieta has left us about him stands out above all else. Mendieta particularly highlights Bernardino's perseverance in fulfilling up to the very end what he understood to be his duty: "[W]ith all his years, he was never known to have missed matins nor any of the other hour [of communal prayer]." About his personality, Mendieta adds that he was consistently meek, humble, poor, and in his conversation, judicious and affable with everyone.

As if Father Mendieta wished to explain to us what would account for Fray Bernardino reaching such an advanced age, after so much work and so many misadventures, he adds,

In his life, he was very orderly and concerted, and so he lived longer than any other of the elders because, full of good works, he was the last to die of all of them, ending his days at the venerable old age of more than ninety years.[29]

Of Fray Bernardino's death, the same Father Mendieta and also several of the native chroniclers have something to say. According to Mendieta, in 1590 Bernardino caught a cold that was afflicting many others about that time. The other friars who lived with him in Tlatelolco feared that he might "slip away out of their hands" and insisted on taking him to the infirmary at the monastery of San Francisco in Mexico City. To this Bernardino responded, "Silence, little fools, leave me, because my hour has yet to come." [30]

They importuned him to such an extent that he finally acquiesced to being transferred to the infirmary of San Francisco. There, according to his words, recorded by Mendieta, he said this to the attending nurse brother:

> "Those little fools of my brothers have made me come here needlessly." He was then able to return for a short time to his beloved Tlatelolco, until a few days later he had a relapse, and then he said, "Now the hour has come." And he had his children brought before him, the Indians he had raised at the College and, bidding them farewell, he was taken to Mexico City, where, after having devoutly received the sacraments at that Monastery of San Francisco of the City, he died blissfully in the Lord and is buried there.[31]

From the several native testimonies in Nahuatl on his death, I shall relate only two. One comes from the manuscript known as *Anales mexicanos, número 4*, which is preserved, unpublished, in the archive adjoining the National Library of Anthropology and History in Mexico City. It reads as follows:

> On the fifth day of the month of February, 1590, was when our beloved Father Bernardino de Sahagún died. He had been at Tlatelolco, and he was buried here at San Francisco. The lords of Tlatelolco came to his funeral.[32]

The other testimony, fuller and with more feeling, we owe to the native chronicler Domingo de San Antón Muñón Chimalpahin Cuauhtlehuanitzin. In his *Memorial breve de la fundación de Culhuacan* (Brief memorandum on the founding of Culhuacan), he recalls what was at the heart of Sahagún's work:

> He wrote according to his interrogation of those who were elders in older times, those who preserved books of paintings, in accord to what was painted in them, those who in ancient times were elders.
>
> Thanks to them he spoke about all the things that happened in antiquity.[33]

In addition to this succinct description of the work to which Fray Bernardino dedicated his life, the same native chronicler described his death on the first page of his journal, in words that were almost identical to those written in the already cited *Anales mexicanos*:

> And on the 5th of February, our beloved Father Fray Bernardino de Sahagún died. He had resided at Tlatelolco. He was buried here at San Francisco.[34]

The negligence, if not stupidity, of many of the rulers that Mexico has had to suffer has permitted mercenary interests to erase invaluable testimonies of its historic being. It was thus that the monastery and church of San Francisco in Mexico City were sold to a circus in the mid-nineteenth century. On the site where the Franciscan cemetery of that monastery lay now rises the Torre Latinoamericana. There, due to official indifference, is the spot where Fray Bernardino de Sahagún and other remarkable Franciscans are buried. At least History knows how to avenge herself. Before those who would ignore her, the present argues for her survival in the future. Bernardino de Sahagún lies today in the very heart of Mexico.

As in the case of other worthy Franciscans (among them Fray Peter of Ghent, Toribio de Benavente Motolinía, and Alonso de

Molina), the memory of the life and death of Fray Bernardino was preserved not only in the chronicles of his order, but also in the annals of the Indians. They were well acquainted with the friars who had come to their land to struggle on their behalf and to inform the world of the testimony of their *Ancient Word* and their culture.

CHAPTER EIGHT

THE LEGACY OF
BERNARDINO DE SAHAGÚN

Throughout this book, we have drawn close to the life and work of this Franciscan who labored in Mexico for more than sixty years. We know what composed his great research enterprise on the human, divine, and natural things of the peoples in what was called New Spain. He brought with him as part of his own spiritual baggage a rich humanistic formation acquired for the most part in Salamanca. His apostolic ideals were nurtured in the doctrine and way of conceiving the world of that group of friars who had founded the Franciscan province of San Gabriel of Extremadura. As they did, Bernardino believed that a pure and holy Christianity, like that of the primitive church, could be recreated in the New World. In order to achieve this, an indispensable precondition would be to learn about the soul and culture of those people among whom Christianity would be sown.

Sahagún, as did others among his Franciscan brothers, experienced many adversities. He observed how the Indians grew fewer in number, he saw himself deprived of assistance in his work and despoiled of his "writings," and, at his most advanced age, he became embroiled in a heart-rending conflict among his own Franciscans. It seems likely that a deep bitterness and a mountain of doubts weighed heavily on his soul. But the fact that, up to the end, he always returned to what had been the deepest interest of his life—as an obstinate perfectionist, time and time again to enrich his various works—reveals to us, above all else, a Sahagún fully convinced of the transcendent significance of his work. He must have known that it would endure, like a torch passed from hand to hand to light the way for those willing to tread the same path.

Sahagún's legacy encompasses a great body of folios in which are preserved his written works. As much in the works that were his own personal creation as in those that were the fruit of his research, he gathered the testimonies of the oldest and wisest natives. We have already discussed the great bulk of his texts, thus there would be no sense in recapitulating that here. Briefly stated, it is fitting to note that they constitute the richest trove of testimonies, in what was the lingua franca of ancient Mexico, that allow us to penetrate the secrets of the culture. Thanks to Bernardino, we are familiar with examples of the pre-Hispanic literary tradition, such as the *Huehuetlahtolli*, the 'Ancient Word,' as well as the sacred hymns to the gods. We are also indebted to him for the accounts of those who lived through the violent clash of the invasion and conquest perpetrated by the men of Castile. By virtue of Sahagún's efforts, we have been able to salvage the point of view of the "Other," what we have called the "Vision of the Vanquished."

ON THE METHODOLOGY ADOPTED BY SAHAGÚN IN HIS RESEARCH

As that treasure trove of texts was important, so was the methodology itself, created and implemented by Bernardino during his many years as a researcher. In order to describe in a few words what the method consisted of, it will suffice to highlight some key aspects:

1. The consistent use of the native language in the research. He and his collaborators (former students at Tlatelolco) were profoundly knowledgeable about it, the latter as

native speakers. They also had a deep familiarity with grammar.

2. The preparation of a questionnaire, or "agenda," that facilitated the inquiry into the culture of the Nahua peoples, not in a fragmentary manner but rather with an integrated focus. This agenda had, as an important complement, the formulation of further questionnaires, which, in many cases, allowed for the systematic inquiry into diverse aspects and institutions of the ancient culture.

3. The adaptation to the native method of transmitting knowledge, via dialogues and "speeches" with the elderly consultants, chosen from among the most knowledgeable about "all the religious, military, political, and even idolatrous things." This adaptation consisted of receiving what the elders communicated via "pictures," which were then commented upon, as if the words sprang from them.

4. Having these paintings copied and the corresponding words transcribed in an alphabetic script that represented the phonemes of Nahuatl, a task carried out by his former students.

5. Proceeding with flexibility, on many occasions setting aside the questionnaires and allowing the consultants to express freely whatever they considered pertinent. This was how he obtained, among other things, what I have called the "canonical texts of the ancient tradition."

6. Submitting to various critical reviews—"a triple sifting," always in consultation with experienced natives—whatever had been communicated to him.

7. After a long process of analysis, without altering or doing any violence whatsoever to the texts, structuring all that had been collected in the manner of an encyclopedia or "history." In such a conceptualization, the word *history* was understood by Sahagún not merely as the "exposition of past events" but also as Sebastián de Cobarrubias

noted in 1611 in his *Tesoro de la lengua castellana o española* (Treasury of the Castilian or Spanish language): "*Largo modo* [in a broad sense] it is called history, the history of animals, the history of plants, etc., etc. Pliny entitled his work . . . *Natural History*."[1] History, therefore, is understood as a work that encompasses what is most notable about the culture of a people and the environment that it inhabits.

8. Joining together two purposes in what is achieved: On the one hand, to gather together and preserve the native testimonies in Nahuatl with copies of the paintings, and on the other hand, to make accessible to those who are unfamiliar with the language the content of everything contained in the work. This was accomplished by preparing a version, not literal but paraphrased, at times abbreviating what the native text expresses, at other times, expanding on it. In accomplishing this, Bernardino bore in mind not only his brother missionaries, who needed to know the native culture in order to proceed appropriately in their tasks of evangelization, but also others, who in Mexico, Spain, and Europe in general might wish to assess the "character of the Mexican people."

Sahagún made several commentaries intimately related to the methodology and goals of his work. One goal he had in mind was "to bring to light all of the words of the language [Nahuatl], with their proper and metaphorical meanings, and all manner of speech, and most of their antiquities."[2] This can be seen in several of the Nahuatl texts he had copied: for example, in describing a ceremony, a specific profession, or a custom in the protocol observed by rulers in various circumstances; or in describing the field of natural things, the aspects of a plant, tree, or animal. Quite frequently such procedures gave rise to diverse manners of speech to express—with certain figures and nuanced

expressions characteristic of the language—what was intended
to be communicated.

THE LINGUISTIC INTEREST

Sahagún insists on his linguistic interest in various prologues to
the different books of the *Historia general*. Thus, in the one that
precedes Book VII, he notes,

> For one thing, there are many synonyms, and one expres-
> sion or a thought has many different forms of being ex-
> pressed. This was done intentionally: to learn and write
> down all of the words for each thing and all the ways to
> express one thought. And this [is true] not only in this book,
> but throughout the work.[3]

In Book X, in treating "the vices and virtues of this people,
and of the parts of the body . . . , and of the illnesses and medicines to combat them, and of the nations who have come to inhabit this land," he states that everything is described

> with a bounty of nouns, adjectives, and verbs, where there
> is great abundance in the language, very proper and com-
> mon among them.[4]

A further example of the effort to contribute linguistic information can be read in the following:

> There is a great bounty of words, and much very proper and
> common language, and very tasteful matter. . . . Thus the
> present volume can be held or esteemed to be a treasury of
> language and words of this Mexican language.[5]

The insistence on putting into relief the linguistic achievements of his work, which is reflected effectively in the abundance
of synonyms and in the great variety of ways of expressing the
same thing, has seemed to some to be a redundancy or a com-
pulsion for repetition. In reality, aside from reflecting the genius

of Nahuatl, it addresses the issue of, as Sahagún would have it, "bringing to light all the words of this language, with their proper and metaphorical meanings," revealing at the same time its rich resources: lexical and, more broadly, morphological and syntactic. Sahagún's contribution (even when he managed to include only a small portion of the "linguistic glosses" that should have accompanied the texts in another column), maintained an interest in the study of the language per se.

SAHAGÚN'S *INDIGENISMO*

Another contribution, also linked to his work, can be classified as "indigenist" (pro-native). In addition to his goals as a missionary, intent on learning about the culture of those he sought to evangelize, he attempted to open the eyes of those who disparaged the Indians and had caused them grievous harm. He speaks extensively of this in his "Account by the Author Worthy of Being Noted," which he intercalated in Book X of his *Historia general*. He ponders and praises there the manner in which the Nahuas raised their children and laments that the Conquest and the Spanish presence had reversed this and, more generally, the political and social life of the Nahuas:

> With regard to the fact that they were greater in times past, as much in the ruling of the republic as in the cult of the gods, it is because they held the business of education in conformity with the capacity of the people; and for this reason, the boys and girls were raised very strictly into adulthood . . . , and for this reason, they raised them with the aid of very solicitous and rigorous teachers, the men on their side and the women on theirs. There they were taught how to honor their gods and how they were to be attentive and obedient to the republic and its rulers. . . .
>
> Because this ceased due to the coming of the Spaniards, and because they toppled and cast down to the ground all the customs and ways of ruling that the natives had had,

and they wished to reduce them to the way of life in Spain in divine as well as in human things, with the understanding that they were idolaters and barbarous, their entire form of government was lost.[6]

In attempting to account for why (seeking their conversion to Christianity) it seemed necessary to topple and "cast down to the ground" the ancient native customs and style of government, he adds this, giving expression to what might be considered his obsession with idolatry:

> It was necessary to destroy the idolatrous things, and all the idolatrous buildings, and even the customs of the republic that were intertwined with idolatrous rites and accompanied by idolatrous ceremonies, which was in virtually everything concerning the republic with which it ruled; and for that reason it was necessary to dismantle it all and place it in another manner of governance that would have no trace of idolatrous practices.[7]

Despite the fact that, to put an end to idolatry, it seemed to him necessary to "dismantle it all," he soon recognized the harm that had been done to what he called the "republic" of the Indians, that is, to their form of government and social organization, which there and in other sections of his *Historia general* he acknowledges as having been admirable. As he thought and said,

> No semblance of what they had formerly been remained. Thus they are held to be barbarians and a people of little worth, yet in truth, in matters of culture, they are a step ahead of many nations that presume to be civilized.[8]

Turning once again to matters of education and lamenting the chaos brought on by the Conquest, he adds,

> It is to our great shame that the native Indians, rational and prudent, knew how to remedy the harm that this land

imposes on those who live in it, obviating the things of nature with contrary exercises; yet we sink to the bottom with
our evil inclinations.[9]

Beyond characterizing as failed the form imposed by those
who had come to rule over the Indians, he asserts, in following this train of thought, that if it were possible to free it from
any trace of idolatry, the native manner of education and governance of the republic would be superior to that which the Spaniards wished to impose:

> And if that manner of governing had not been so infested
> with idolatrous rites and superstitions, it seems to me that
> it was quite good; and when purified of all the idolatrous
> matter it had and thoroughly Christianized, were it to be
> introduced into this republic [the entire community and its
> organization], Indian and Spanish, it would certainly be a
> great boon and a cause thus to free the one and the other
> republics from great evils and great travails for those who
> rule.[10]

To evaluate more thoroughly what Sahagún's thinking was in
this regard, we can recall what he maintained when he said that
the *Huehuetlahtolli*, the counsels of parents to their sons and daughters, would be of greater benefit than many a sermon preached
from the pulpits. It is also worth recalling this once more:

> Among the Mexicans, the wise rhetoricians, the virtuous,
> and the courageous were much esteemed. From these they
> elected their high priests [pontiffs], lords and rulers, and
> their principal captains, however lowly their rank might be.
> These ruled the republics and led the armies and presided
> in the temples. They were, to be sure, extreme in these things,
> most devoted to their gods, most zealous of their republic,
> among themselves quite urbane and proper . . . ; and now
> all of that is lost, as the reader of this book can ascertain by

comparing what it contains with the life they now have. I
say nothing of the cause because it is so obvious.[11]

The cause Sahagún had quite clearly in his mind: those who
had conquered Anahuac had "toppled and cast down to the
ground all the customs and ways of ruling that the natives had
had." Sahagún's *indigenismo* comes to the surface in this, as in
many other places in his *Historia general.* He bears witness to the
fact that, in his zeal to learn about the culture of the "Other," he
came to appreciate and even admire it in and of itself.

PIONEER OF ANTHROPOLOGICAL RESEARCH

If *anthropology* in its broadest sense means research into the culture, language, and antiquities of a people, it is with good reason
that Sahagún has been referred to as "the Father of Anthropology in the New World." Indeed, his schema, methodology, and
achievements in research justify such a title given to him by Mexicans and Spaniards as well as other European and North American scholars.[12] No attempt is made here to disguise Sahagún's
goals in undertaking his research. This was intimately linked to
his profession as a missionary friar who had come to Mexico to
evangelize the natives. It was in that sense that he wrote at the
beginning of his *Historia general* that he as well as the other friars needed to act as physicians who, in order to cure the patient,
must learn about his ailments. He reiterated many times, almost
obsessively, that in the native culture idolatry was the most serious sickness that impeded the implanting of Christianity.

To some, Bernardino's activities might seem ambivalent. It
is true that, as he uncovered the "carat," as he called the cultural worth of the Indians and in particular of their spiritual creations, including the *Huehuetlahtolli,* he perceived the existence
of a deep moral wisdom. He set one limit only in his inescapable
condition as Christian and evangelizer. He understood, admired,
and described the native culture in all that was not contrary (or
seemed to him as not contrary) to his faith as a Catholic and as a

Franciscan missionary. In his zeal to understand the "Other," he was unable to remain calm and objective before what he characterized as "other innumerable insanities and gods without number that your ancestors had invented": idolatry. His schema, methodology, and achievements are not invalidated because of this.

In speaking about Sahagún's legacy, one must mention his activity as a teacher at the College of Santa Cruz at Tlatelolco and in his research activities, training, as he did, the young native scholars. He also managed to motivate diverse groups of collaborators, working with them as a member of a team and seeing to it that the interests of people with radically different backgrounds converged on one goal. On the one hand, he had with him his "trilinguals"—his former students—as consultants and commentators, as well as others educated at the same College of Santa Cruz, who worked as scribes and copyists of glyphs and paintings. On the other hand, he managed to enlist the interest of native elders, nobles, learned men, and groups of Nahua physicians to provide him with, over the course of many years, invaluable data on pre-Hispanic antiquity.

With regard to his trilinguals, whose names he gave on various occasions, it must be added that Fray Bernardino proposed to turn them into new researchers, who might then be able to work on their own. As we would say today, he knew how to found a school. To that group of his former students we owe the collection of other testimonies of the pre-Hispanic tradition, such as collections of songs and poems, ancient annals, and other genres, almost all in Nahuatl, either original creations or the fruit of historical investigation. The list of works that were produced in this manner and that have come down to us is rather long. The transcriptions of Mexican songs stand out as do those of diverse annals, such as those of Cuauhtitlan, and many personal works, among which are the ones by those who in one way or another were influenced by him: Nazareo of Xaltocan, Antonio Valeriano, Martín Jacobita, Hernando Alvarado Tezozomoc, and Chimalpahin Cuauhtlehuanitzin.

PROSECUTION OF THE STUDY AND
PUBLICATION OF FRAY BERNARDINO'S WORKS

Of Sahagún's works themselves (copious as they are), much remains to be studied and made known. Important contributions have been made in the last decades. A succinct recapitulation will have to do for the ones concerned with the culmination of his ethnographic enterprise, the *Florentine Codex*.

The facsimile edition of this codex has proven to have great significance; produced by the Mexican government by means of the General Archive of the Nation, it appeared in 1979 in three meticulously printed volumes. It placed within reach of scholars the final form in which Sahagún distributed his Nahua texts and, for the first time, his Spanish version of these. Up to that time, all the editions of the *Historia general de las cosas de la Nueva España* had been based for the most part on the *Tolosa Codex*. This is a copy prepared in Spain of the Spanish portion of the *Historia general*. Although we do not know with certainty who was responsible for that copy, it is clear that it includes numerous deviations from to the original in the *Florentine Codex*.

The first edition of the whole Spanish text of the *Florentine Codex* was facilitated by this facsimile reproduction. The paleography and presentation of the same are due to Alfredo López Austin and Josefina García Quintana. This first edition appeared in a most luxurious format, sponsored by the National Bank of Mexico in 1982. This was followed by other more affordable reprintings, which were published in Madrid in 1988 and in Mexico in 1989.[13] It is now possible to approach both the Spanish paraphrased version and the Nahuatl original version of what was the culmination of Sahagún's work.

Although we do not have at our disposal a complete translation into Spanish of the Nahuatl text, there is one in English under the title *Florentine Codex: General History of the Things of New Spain*. This great undertaking of paleography, English translation, notes, and introduction is owed to Arthur J. O. Anderson and Charles E. Dibble. Their meritorious achievement—in twelve volumes, which appeared between 1950 and 1982—is an example worthy of imitation in a parallel version in Spanish.

With regard to the texts of the *Códices matritenses*, there are the editions, all of them partial, by Eduard Seler, Walter Lehmann, Angel María Garibay Kintana, Leonhard Schultze-Jena, Miguel León-Portilla, Wigberto Jiménez Moreno, and Alfredo López Austin.

The facsimile publication of the *Primeros memoriales* (1993) deserves particular mention, followed by its paleography, English translation, and notes (1997) done by Thelma Sullivan with the collaboration of other scholars.[14] Although there are Spanish translations of several portions of the *Primeros memoriales*, we continue to lack, as is the case with the Nahuatl text of the *Florentine Codex*, a direct and complete Spanish version of these.[15]

In the last decades, other Sahagún works have also been the object of attention and of publication. One of these, of considerable interest, is the *Coloquios y doctrina christiana*, which has already been described in this book. There were previously only one transcription of its text in Spanish and partial versions of the one preserved in Nahuatl. J. Jorge Klor de Alva published an English translation (1980). Miguel León-Portilla published a facsimile reproduction of the manuscript, with an ample introduction and translation into Spanish of the original in Nahuatl (1986).

The *Breve compendio de los ritos idolátricos que los indios de esta Nueva España usaban en tiempos de su infidelidad* (Brief compendium of the idolatrous rites that the Indians of this New Spain practiced in the times of their infidelity) is the text, also described above, that Sahagún sent to Pope Pius V, and of which only the edition by Livario Oliger (1942), which was difficult to access, existed. It has since been published in a facsimile edition, with paleography and introduction by María Guadalupe Bosch de Souza (1990).

The eminent scholar Arthur J. O. Anderson deserves credit for two publications of other works by Fray Bernardino. One is the

English version, annotated and with an adequate introduction, of the *Psalmodia christiana* (1993), the only one of Sahagún's works that he was able to see in print while he was still alive. Mention has already been made of the Spanish version of the *Psalmodia christiana* by José Luis Suárez Roca, published in León, Spain, in 1999.

The other work, with a similar Christian content, is the one entitled *Adiciones, apéndice a la postilla y ejercicio cotidiano* (Additions, appendix to the commentary, and daily exercise) (1993), which had remained unedited until then. The introduction, paleography, and Spanish translation of the Nahuatl text, all valuable contributions by Anderson, are preceded by a prologue by Miguel León-Portilla, in which he describes the attributes of this edition and notes the significance of the doctrinal texts by Fray Bernardino.

As can be seen, in the last decades a considerable salvage operation has been carried out on a significant portion of the great Sahagún corpus. Nevertheless, there still remains much to be done. In particular, it is urgent to bring the paleography and translation into Spanish and other languages of the collection of all the texts included in the *Códices matritenses*, especially of those that were prepared at Tlatelolco and revised at the monastery of San Francisco in Mexico City.

Someone should study and compare the contents of the *Códice de Tolosa* with that of the *Florentine Codex*. Though the *Códice de Tolosa* is a copy of the latter, because the editions of the *Historia general* cannot be considered critical ones, and because they contain omissions and some poor transcriptions, the proposed study and even a facsimile edition of the *Códice de Tolosa* can offer more than a few surprises.

There is similarly a need for an analysis and comparison of the Nahuatl text of the *Florentine Codex* with the Spanish paraphrased version prepared by Sahagún. Such a study would reveal not only how Bernardino understood and translated the Nahuatl texts, but also the effort he made in decanting an entire worldview as distinct as that of the Nahuas into a European medium. In this attempt, Sahagún added information in several places that he had obtained from various sources and that shed light on what his consultants communicated to him. It can be stated that from the proposed comparative work one would derive important conclusions that would contribute to understanding and assessing more completely the significance of Sahagún's great contribution. The Spanish paraphrased version, which constitutes the final link in Sahagún's enterprise, requires attention that, up till now, has not been received, above all in light of its relation with the Nahuatl texts obtained from his consultants.

As already mentioned, a contribution by Pilar Máynez Vidal touches directly on what I am proposing. She focuses on an identification and description of the procedures adopted by Sahagún to elucidate the meanings of the Nahuatl words that he was obliged to employ in the Spanish text of the *Historia general*. The reason for this was that Bernardino did not find word equivalents that could designate the concepts, institutions, or objects that were characteristic of the Nahuatl culture but had no equivalent in the Spanish culture.

Limiting her investigation to the semantic domains of "religion and magic," she undertook it as " a problem of linguistic transculturation."[16] Various procedures that Sahagún conceived and applied are brought to light. In some cases, Sahagún employed comparisons, such as relating the attributes of the native gods to those of the Greco-Roman pantheon. Thus he states, "Tezcatlipoca is another Jupiter," and "Chicomecoatl is another Ceres." He used the predicate adjective *like* in some comparisons, for example, "this *mexica teohuatzin* was like a patriarch"; "these *tamales* are like round breads made of corn, neither plump nor round"; "the house called *calmecac* was like a monastery."

Sahagún also relied on paraphrases by way of explanation. In order to elucidate the name of the feast of *Atamalcualiztli*, he wrote, "These natives would celebrate a feast every eight years, which they called *Atamalcualiztli*, which means a fast of bread and water; for eight days, they ate nothing but tamales made without salt, neither did they drink anything but clear water."

In explaining the meanings of Nahuatl words he had to introduce into his Spanish text, Sahagún relied on appositions and interpretations, in some cases, interpreting the Nahuatl as onomatopoetic. Thus he said, "little birds in this land that they call *cocotli,* because when the little turtledoves sing, they say *coco, coco.*" He similarly turned on occasion to his own religious thought to explain certain Nahuatl words that denote concepts somehow connected to his own religious beliefs. Thus he noted that "*Cihuacoatl* is our Mother Eve" and that "the lapidaries who carve precious stones worshipped four gods, or better said, devils, in their pagan times."

The many hundreds of Nahuatl words related to religion and magic are only one part of the many more words that appear in the *Historia general.* That Sahagún had to include them, and that he saw himself compelled to adopt various procedures to render their meaning comprehensible to his readers, constitute but one part of the multiple problems that he had to confront in his paraphrased version of the Nahuatl texts.

The comparative study that I have proposed between the Nahuatl and Spanish texts of the *Florentine Codex* will bring us to an understanding of the many complexities that Sahagún confronted and of what he was obliged to accomplish in transposing them into a cultural and linguistic medium that was so different from what was expressed in the Nahuatl texts. They were, in and of themselves, a decantation into an alphabetic script, and their representation in paintings from their oral state were, in their own right, a revelation of the natural, human, and divine things of the Nahua world.

As can be seen, Sahagún's contributions continue to be open to investigations that, as in the case of the *Códices matritenses,* must culminate in critical editions. This is also true for his other writings that remain unpublished. Though they are mostly works of a doctrinal bent, they are nevertheless not lacking in interest. They may reveal a parallel process, though in the opposite direction from the one with which we have been dealing. There the problem would be to see how Bernardino transposed Judeo-Christian thought into Nahuatl.

I shall mention only the principal writings that await study: the sermons preserved in the National Library of Mexico and in the Ayer Collection of the Newberry Library in Chicago; the lives of the saints; the trilingual vocabulary in the latter library; and the collection of the Gospels and Epistles in Nahuatl, taking into account the edition by Bernardino Biondelli. Another task would be to edit and duly annotate Sahagún's letters, which have been preserved in the Archivo General de Indias, Audiencia de Mexico, Branch 287.

Bearing this in mind, we must repeat that much remains to be done in broadening the study and research into the great Sahagún corpus. Only when we have in hand in critical editions the totality of Fray Bernardino's contribution will we be truly able to take advantage of it as a source for the production of further works on a great variety of topics related to "the divine, human, and natural things" of the ancient Mexicans.

Teacher, indefatigable researcher, poor in worldly goods, by nature meek and humble, yet more than once, he would make his voice the clamor of the prophets in defense of the Indians— Bernardino de Sahagún has left Mexico and the world a rich cultural legacy. His presence and his work on Mexican soil are a perennial testament of the best in Spanish Renaissance humanism. Through him and through the lives and works of other great men, such as Toribio de Benavente Motolinía, Sebastián Ramírez de Fuenleal, Alonso de la Veracruz, Vasco de Quiroga, and Bartolomé de las Casas—not by dint of arms and conquest—Mexico and Spain draw close and are sisters.

From the four corners of the world, many have come to rely on Sahagún; they are those who wish to know about one of the great original civilizations that grew up in the course of history, that of the Mesoamericans. Today, thanks to archaeology, we can admire the temples, palaces, sculptures, and many other monuments in the lands of the Mayas, Oaxaca, the Gulf Coast, and the Pacific, as well as in the Central Plateau. Long before this, Bernardino demonstrated the close ties between "the paintings with characters" and their oral expression among the Nahua peoples and left us an immense treasure trove of testimonies in the native language. Like a thick torch that does not smoke, they shed light, allowing us to draw near to the ancient Mexicans' thoughts, the institutions they created, their way of life, and an infinitude of other things. These testimonies, as he perceived and reiterated them, being bearers of wisdom and beauty, intertwined in a humanism distinct from that of Europe, enrich today the universal legacy of culture.

NOTES

INTRODUCTION

1. Bernardino de Sahagún, *Historia general de las cosas de la Nueva España* (*General history of the things of New Spain*); introduction, paleography, glossary, and notes by Josefina García Quintana and Alfredo López Austin, 2 vols. (México: National Council for Culture and the Arts and Alianza Editorial Mexicana [Mexican Publishers' Alliance], 1989), I, 33.

2. Ibid., I, 31.

3. Ibid., I, 71.

4. Ibib.

5. Ibid., I, 106–107.

6. Prologue to Bernardino de Sahagún, *Arte adivinatorio* . . . (Art of divination that the Mexicans employed in the times of their idolatry, called *tonalámatl*), written in a second version in 1585. Joaquín García Icazbalceta, *Bibliografía mexicana del siglo XVI* (México: Fondo de Cultura Económica, 1954), 382.

7. Ibid. 384.

8. Ibid., 386.

9. Sahagún, *Historia general*, I, 305–306.

10. Ibid., I, 307.

11. Ibid., I, 316.

12. Ibid., I, 370.

13. Walden Browne, *Sahagún and the Transition to Modernity* (Norman: University of Oklahoma Press, 2000), 208.

14. Sahagún, *Historia general*, I, 79.

15. Browne, *Sahagún*, 203.

16. Ibid.

17. Angel María Garibay Kintana, *Historia de la literatura náhuatl*, 2 vols. (México: Editorial Porrúa, 1953–1954), II, 63–88.

18. Luis Nicolau D'Olwer, *Fray Bernardino de Sahagún (1499–1590)* (México: Instituto Panamericano de Geografía e Historia, 1952), 13.

19. Ibid., 142–143.

20. Manuel Ballesteros Gaibrois, *Vida y obra de fray Bernardino de Sahagún* (León, España: Institución fray Bernardino de Sahagún, Consejo Superior de Investigaciones Científicas, 1973), 11.

21. Ibid., 12.

22. Florencio Vicente Castro and J. Luis Rodríguez Molinero, *Bernardino de Sahagún, primer antropólogo en Nueva España (siglo XVI)*, (Salamanca: Universidad de Salamanca, Institucíon fray Bernardino de Sahagún, Consejo Superior de Investigaciones Científicas, 1986).

23. Miguel León-Portilla, *Bernardino de Sahagún* (Madrid: Historia 16, Quorum, 1987).

24. Sahagún, *Historia general*, I, 32.

25. Ibid., I, 305.

CHAPTER 1: ROOTS AND EDUCATION

1. Antonio de Herrera, *Historia de los hechos de los castellanos en las islas y tierra firme del mar océano* (History of the deeds of the Castilians among the islands and the mainland of the ocean sea) (Madrid: Real Academia de la Historia, Decade IV, Book VI, 1948), VIII, 361.

2. The royal orders as well as the report on the gifts are to be found in various folders of the *Contratación* (Contracts) section, no. 4675B, fols. 126v–127r: *An Account of the Support Provided for the Indians Whom Fray Antonio de Ciudad Rodrigo Presented in This House . . .* , and in the *Contaduría* (Accounts) 269 of the *Archivo General de Indias*.

3. There is additional information on the Indians whom Cortés took to Spain in: *Historia de las conquistas de Hernando Cortés* (History of the conquests of Hernando Cortés], written in Spanish by Francisco López de Gómara, translated from the Nahuatl according to the version and addenda by Chimalpahin Cuauhtlehuanitzin, in an edition by Carlos María de Bustamante, 2 vols. (México: Imprenta del Gobierno, 1826), II, 163–164.

4. Juan de Torquemada, *Monarquía indiana*, edited by Miguel León-Portilla et al., 7 vols. (México: UNAM, Instituto de Investigaciones Históricas, 1975–1983), VI, 262.

5. Ibid.

6. Sahagún, *Historia general*, I, 32.

7. Georges Baudot, "Fray Toribio de Motolinía denunciado ante la Inquisición por fray Bernardino de Sahagún," *Estudios de Cultura Náhuatl* (México: UNAM, Instituto de Investigaciones Históricas) 21 (1991): 129.

8. Jerónimo de Mendieta, *Historia eclesiástica indiana* (Ecclesiastical history of the Indies), edited by Joaquín García Icazbalceta (México: Antigua Librería, 1870), 663.

9. *Le guide du pèlerin de Saint Jacques de Compostelle*, texte latin du XIIème Siècle, edited by Jean Viellard (Paris: Librairie de Philosophie, J. Vrien, 1984), 6–7.

10. Ibid.

11. *De Origine Seraphicae Religionis Franciscanae eiusque Progressibus de Regularis Observantiae Institutione, Forma Adminstrationis ac Legibus, Admirabilique eius Propagatione*, F. Francisci Gonzagae eiusdem Religionis Ministri Generalis ad S.D.N. Sixtum V opus quattuor partes divisum (Romae: 1587), 864–865.

12. F. Francisco Ruizio Vallisoletano, S. Facundi ordinis S. Benedict Abbate. *Index Locupletissimus, Duobus Tomis Digestus, in Totius Aristotelis Stagiritae Operae. In quo tam Multa Exposita Sunt in Quibus Plurimis et Obscuris apud Aristotelem Locis quae aut Perperam Integellecta Hactenus aut Ommino Omissa Fuerunt, ut Vice Commentari Attento Lectori Esse Possint.* Apud inclitum Sanctorum martyrum facundi et Primitivi Coenobium. Anno Domini MDXL. Mense Februarii. Cum privilegio Caroli V Imperatoris semper Augusti ad decennium.

13. Marcial Solana, *Historia de la filosofía española* (Madrid: Espasa, 1941), II, 78–79.

14. Angel María Garibay Kintana, "Proemio general," in *Historia general de las cosas de la Nueva España*, 4 vols. (México: Editorial Porrúa, 1956), I, 21.

15. Bernardino Biondelli, ed., *Evangelarium, Epistolarium et Lectionarium Aztecum sive Mexicanum, ex Antiquo Codice Mexicano nuper Reperto* (Mediolani [Milan]: Typis Jos. Bernardoni, Qm. Johannis, 1858).

16. Arthur J. O. Anderson, "Sahagún's Career and Character," in *Florentine Codex. Introductions and Indices*, preface by Miguel León-Portilla (Santa Fe, N. Mex.: The School of American Research and the University of Utah, 1982), 30.

17. Mendieta, *Historia eclesiástica indiana*, 662.

18. Sahagún, *Historia general*, I, 33.

19. Bernardino de Sahagún, *Coloquios y doctrina christiana*, edited and translated by Miguel León-Portilla (México: UNAM, Instituto de Investigaciones Históricas and Fundación de Investigaciones Sociales, 1986), 72.

20. Mendieta, *Historia eclesiástica indiana*, 662.

21. Toribio de Benavente Motolinía *Memoriales o Libro de las cosas de la Nueva España y de los naturales de ella* (Memoranda or Book of the things of New Spain and of its natives), edited by Edmundo O'Gorman (México: UNAM, Instituto de Investigaciones Históricas, 1971), 180. The establishments in the province of San Gabriel in Extremadura are amply dealt with by Fray Juan Bautista Moles, in *Memoria de la provincia de San Gabriel, de la orden de los Frailes Menores de la Observancia* (Memory of the province of San Gabriel, of the order of Minor Friars of the Observance) (Madrid: 1612). Further information on the monastery at Belvís de Monroy is furnished by Fray Angel Ortega, "The Monastery of Saint Francis of Belvís of the Province of San Gabriel in Extremadura," *Archivo Ibero-Americano* 8 (1917): 18–34.

22. Motolinía, *Memoriales*, 180.

23. Ibid., 181–182.

24. Diego Valadés, *Retórica christiana* (1579), facsimile edition, with an introduction by Esteban J. Palomera (México: Fondo de Cultura Económica, 1989), 505.

25. Sahagún, *Coloquios y doctrina christiana*, 123 ff.

26. Ibid., 121 ff.

27. Ibid., 137 ff.

28. *Doctrina breve muy provechosa de las cosas que pertenecen a la fe católica y a nuestra cristiandad en estilo llano para común inteligencia* (Brief and very advantageous doctrine of the things that relate to the Catholic faith and our Christianity in a plain style for the common intelligence). Composed by the Most Reverend Señor Don Juan de Zumárraga, first Bishop of Mexico, of His Majesty's Council. Printed in this same Mexico City by his command and at his expense. The year MDXLIII. The citation comes from "Conclusión exhortatoria de la obra, sin folio" (Hortatory conclusion of the work, without folio).

CHAPTER 2: ENCOUNTER WITH THE NEW WORLD

1. This quote comes from the prologue to Book XII, signed by Sahagún, in the revision he did in 1585 of this text about the Conquest. It has been reproduced in the 1938, 1946, and 1956 editions of the *Historia general* and also in the publication devoted to that book by Carlos María de Bustamante in 1840. See the edition by Angel María Garibay Kintana, *Historia general de las cosas de la Nueva España*, 4 vols. (México: Editorial Porrúa, 1956), IV, 17. This is also available in an English version: *Conquest of New Spain, 1585 Revision*. Translated by Howard F. Cline, edited

with an introduction and notes by S. L. Cline (Salt Lake City: University of Utah Press, 1989), 27.

2. Sahagún, *Historia general*, II, 807.

3. Motolinía, *Memoriales*, 27.

4. Ibid., 22.

5. Ibid.

6. Ibid. 26.

7. Ibid., 28.

8. Torquemada, *Monarquía indiana*, III, 219.

9. Sahagún, in García Icazbalceta, *Bibliografía mexicana*, 361.

10. Motolinía, *Memoriales*, 29.

11. On the letter and the denunciation by Juan de Paredes, see Joaquín García Icazbalceta, *Don fray Juan de Zumárraga, primer obispo y arzobispo de México* (Fray Juan de Zumárraga, first bishop and archbishop of Mexico), 4 vols. (México: Editorial Porrúa, 1947, II, 167–168.

12. "Letter of Jerónimo López to the Emperor," undated but probably from 1529, in Francisco del Paso y Troncoso, ed., *Epistolario de la Nueva España*, 16 vols. (México: Antigua Librería Robredo, 1940), XV, 189.

13. Ibid., XV, 190.

14. "Letter to His Majesty from the Bishop-Elect of Mexico Fray Juan de Zumárraga, 27 August 1529," in García Icazbalceta, *Don fray Juan de Zumárraga*, II, 232–233.

15. Ibid.

16. Ibid., II, 237.

17. Justo Sierra, *Evolución política del pueblo mexicano* (Political evolution of the Mexican people) (México: Fondo de Cultura Económica, 1950), 62.

18. "Information at the Behest of Nuño Beltrán de Guzmán," 23 August 1529, in *Colección de documentos inéditos relativos al descubrimiento, conquista y organización de las antiguas posesiones de América y Oceanía, sacados en su mayor parte del Archivo de Indias* (Collection of unedited documents on the discovery, conquest, and organization of the former possessions in America and Oceania, taken principally from the Archive of the Indies), 42 vols. (Madrid: Sucesores de Rivademeyna, 1864–1884), XL, 549–552.

19. "Information requested by Bishop Don Fray Juan de Zumárraga, 11 July 1531" (Seville: General Archive of the Indies, Justice, 1006).

20. Ibid.

21. Ibid.

22. Ibid.

23. Ibid.

24. Ibid.

25. "Letter of Fray Peter of Ghent to the Fathers and Brothers of the Province of Flanders, 27 June 1529," in Ernesto de la Torre Villar, *Fray Peter of Ghent* (México: Seminar on Mexican Culture, 1973), 71–75.

26. Sahagún, *Historia general*, I, 33.

27. Ibid.

28. Mendieta, *Historia eclesiástica indiana*, 664.

29. Ibid., 594.

30. Sahagún, *Historia general*, II, 806.

31. Ibid., II, 808.

32. On this work, see García Icazbalceta, *Bibliografía mexicana*, 336.

33. Sahagún, *Historia general*, II, 626-627.

34. Ibid., II, 627.

35. Ibid., II, 633–635.

36. "Letter of Jerónimo López to the Emperor, 25 February 1545," in Paso y Troncoso, ed., *Epistolario de la Nueva España*, IV, 168–169.

37. Sahagún, *Historia general*, I, 70.

38. Motolinía, *Memoriales*, 122.

39. Sahagún, in García Icazbalceta, *Bibliografía mexicana*, 383.

40. *Proceso criminal del Santo Oficio de la Inquisición y del fiscal en su nombre contra Carlos indio principal de Tetzcoco* (Criminal trial of the Holy Office of the Inquisition and the judge in his name against Carlos, a noble Indian of Tetzcoco), preliminary preface by Luis González Obregón (Mexico: Publicaciones del Archivo General de la Nación, 1910), 40.

41. Ibid., 40-41.

42. Ibid.

43. On this other case, see Luis González Obregón, *Procesos de indios idólatras y hechiceros* (Trials of Indian witches and idolaters) (México: Archivo General de la Nación, 1912), 115–140.

CHAPTER 3: PLAN FOR EVANGELIZATION

1. Sahagún, *Historia general*, II, 634.

2. Manuscript preserved in the Ayer Collection of the Newberry Library, Chicago, Ill., Ms. 1485, fol. 1 of 98, written on both sides.

3. Sahagún, *Historia general*, II, 630.

4. Mendieta, *Historia eclisiástica indiana*, 442–443.

5. Sahagún, *Historia general*, II, 494.

6. Ibid., II, 672.

7. Ibid., II, 801.

312312312

8. Ibid.
9. Ibid., II, 807.
10. Ibid.
11. Ibid., II, 809.
12. Ibid., II, 635.
13. Alonso de Zorita, *Historia de la Nueva España* (Madrid: Librería General de Victoriano Suárez, 1909), 9.
14. Sahagún, *Historia general*, II, 811.
15. Ibid., II, 635.
16. Juan de Grijalva, *Crónica de la orden de Nuestro Padre San Agustín en las provincias de la Nueva España* (Chronicle of the order of Our Father St. Augustine in the provinces of New Spain) (México: Editorial Porrúa, 1985), 152
17. "Letter of Jerónimo López to Prince Don Philip, 10 September 1545," in Paso y Troncoso, ed., *Epistolario de la Nueva España*, II, 371.
18. Torquemada, *Monarchía indiana*, II, 371.
19. Bernardino de Sahagún, *Códice florentino*, facsimile reproduction, 3 vols., prepared by the Government of Mexico, 1979, II, fol. 215v.
20. Sahagún, *Historia general*, I, 305.
21. Ibid.
22. Ibid., I, 305–306.
23. See *Huehuetlahtolli, Testimonies of the Ancient Word*, introduction by Miguel León-Portilla, transcription of the Nahuatl text and Spanish version by Librado Silva Galeano (México: Ministry of Public Education and the Fondo de Cultura Económica, 1991).
24. Sahagún, *Historia general*, II, 307.
25. Ibid., II, 370.
26. Sahagún, *Florentine Codex*, II, fols. 74v ff.
27. Sahagún, *Historia general*, II, 307 ff.
28. On this war, see Miguel León-Portilla, *La flecha en el blanco. Francisco Tenamaztle y Bartolomé de las Casas en la lucha por los derechos de los indígenas, 1541–1556* (The arrow on target. Francisco Tenamaztle and Bartolomé de las Casas in the struggle for the rights of the Indians, 1541–1556) (México: Editorial Diana and Colegio de Jalisco, 1995).
29. See the most recent edition of this manuscript: Francis F. Berdan and Patricia Rieff Anawalt, *The Codex Mendoza*, 4 vols. (Berkeley: University of California Press, 1992).
30. See Miguel León-Portilla and Carmen Aguilera, *Mapa de México-Tenochtitlan y sus contornos hacia 1550* (Mexico-Tenochtitlan and its environs circa 1550), facsimile edition (México: Celanese, 1986).

31. Emily W. Emmart, *The Badianus Manuscript* (Baltimore: Johns Hopkins Press, 1940).

32. Martín de la Cruz, *Libellus de Medicinalibus Indorum Herbis,* facsimile reproduction, Spanish version, with commentaries by various authors (México: Instituto Mexicano del Seguro Social, 1964; rev. ed., México: Fondo de Cultura Económica, Instituto Mexicano del Seguro Social, 1991).

33. Sahagún, *Historia general,* II, 636.

34. "Letter of Fray Juan de San Francisco and Others to the Emperor, 20 October 1552," in *Cartas de Indias,* 2 vols. (Madrid: Ministerio de Fomento, 1877), I, document 21, 120.

35. Mendieta, *Historia eclesiástica indiana,* 664.

36. Bernardino de Sahagún, *Conquest of New Spain, 1585 Revision,* reproductions of the Boston Public Library manuscript and Carlos María de Bustamante 1840 edition, translated by Howard F. Cline, edited with an introduction and notes by S. L. Cline (Salt Lake City: University of Utah Press, 1989), 417–418.

37. Sahagún, *Historia general,* II, 817.

38. Ibid., II, 538.

39. Ibid., II, 817.

40. Alonso de Molina, *Aqui comienza un vocabulario en la lengua castellana y mexicana compuesto por el muy reverendo padre fray Alonso de Molina* (Here begins a vocabulary in the Castilian and Mexican languages composed by the Most Reverend Fray Alonso de Molina) (México: House of Juan Pablos, 1555). See preliminary pages.

CHAPTER 4: BEGINNING OF RESEARCH

1. Sahagún, *Historia general,* I, 77.
2. Ibid., I, 32.
3. Ibid., I, 31.
4. Ibid.
5. Ibid., I, 33.
6. Ibid., I, 35–36.
7. Ibid., I, 36.
8. Ibid., I, 33.
9. Ibid., I, 34.
10. Ibid., I, 306.
11. Ibid., I, 77.
12. Ibid.

13. See what Donald Robertson has to say about this in "The Sixteenth-Century Mexican Encyclopedia of Fray Bernardino de Sahagún," *Cahiers d'Histoire Mondiale* (Paris) 9, no. 3 (1966): 617–628.

14. Motolinía, *Memoriales* 119.

15. On the monastery at Tepepulco, see José Gorbea Trueba, *Tepepulco* (México: Instituto Naciónal de Antropología e Historia, Dirección de Monumentos Coloniales, 1957), and John McAndrews, *The Open-Air Churches of Sixteenth-Century Mexico* (Cambridge, Mass.: Harvard University Press, 1965), 244–245.

16. García Icazbalceta, *Bibliografía mexicana,* 345.

17. Sahagún, *Historia general,* I, 77.

18. Fernando de Alva Ixtlilxochitl, *Obras históricas,* edited with an introduction by Edmundo O'Gorman and preface by Miguel León-Portilla, 2 vols. (México, UNAM, Instituto de Investigaciones Históricas, 1975), I, 84.

19. Tepeapulco parish archive, "Libro de matrimonios, 1590." The first entry, which I cited here, appears after several folios that contain edicts and documents addressed to the "regular, temporary, and coadjutant priests."

20. Sahagún, *Historia general,* I, 78.

21. Ibid.

22. *Diccionario de autoridades: Diccionario de la lengua castellana en que se explica el verdadero sentido de las voces, su naturaleza y calidad con las frases o modos de hablar* (Dictionary of authorities: Dictionary of the Spanish language in which the true meaning of words is explained, their nature and quality with sentences or manner of speech), 6 vols. (Madrid: Spanish Royal Academy, 1737), V, 338.

23. Sahagún, *Historia general,* I, 78.

24. Ibid., I, 79.

25. Bernardino de Sahagún, *Historia general de las cosas de la Nueva España,* publication funded by the Ministry of Justice and Public Education of Mexico, edited by Francisco del Paso y Troncoso, vol. 6, *Códices matritenses in the Mexican Language,* notebook 2, *Primeros memoriales* and *Memoriales con escolios* (Madrid: Photocopy by Hauser and Menet, 1905).

26. Primeros memoriales *by Fray Bernardino de Sahagún,* facsimile edition, photographed by Ferdinand Anders (Norman: University of Oklahoma Press, in cooperation with the Patrimonio Nacional and Real Academia de la Historia, Madrid, 1993).

27. Primeros memoriales *by Fray Bernardino de Sahagún,* paleography of Nahuatl and English translation by Thelma D. Sullivan, completed and revised with additions by H. B. Nicholson, Arthur J. O. Anderson, Charles

E. Dibble, Eloise Quiñones Keber, and Wayne Ruwet (Norman: University of Oklahoma Press, in cooperation with the Patrimonio Nacional and Real Academia de la Historia, Madrid, 1997).

28. See the corresponding references in the bibliography at the end of this book.

CHAPTER 5: EDITING AND EXPANSION OF MATERIAL

1. Sahagún, *Historia general*, I, 78.

2. *Códice de la Real Academia, Historia general*, facsimile edition prepared by Francisco del Paso y Troncoso, VIII, fol. 172.

3. Ibid., II, 781.

4. *Códice del Real Palacio*, VI, fol. 160r.

5. Sahagún, *Coloquios y doctrina christiana*, 75.

6. Ibid.

7. Sahagún, *Historia general*, I, 78.

8. See the aforementioned edition of these texts in *Huehuetlahtolli*, with a transcription by Silva Galeano and introduction by León-Portilla.

9. Hernando Alvarado Tezozomoc, *Crónica mexicana*, annotated by Manuel Orozco y Berra (México: Editorial Porrúa, 1975) and Diego Durán, *Historia de las Indias e islas de tierra firme de la Nueva España* (History of the Indies and islands of terra firme of New Spain), edited by Angel María Garibay, 2 vols. (México: Editorial Porrúa, 1967–1968).

10. Miguel León-Portilla, *El tonalámatl de los pochtecas* (*Códice Fejérváry-Meyer*) (México: Celanese, 1985).

11. See Alfredo López Austin, "Estudio acerca del método de la investigación de fray Bernardino de Sahagún" (Study about Fray Bernardino de Sahagún's research methodology), in Jorge Martínez Ríos, comp., *La investigación social de campo en México* (Social anthropological fieldwork in Mexico) (México: UNAM, Instituto de Investigaciones Sociales, 1976), 9–56.

12. See Miguel León-Portilla, "Los huaxtecos según los informantes de Sahagún" (The Huaxtecs according to the informants of Sahagún), *Estudios de Cultura Náhuatl* (México: UNAM, Instituto de Investigaciones Históricas) 5 (1965): 15–30.

13. Sahagún, *Historia general*, I, 78–79.

14. "Relación y descripción de la provincia del Santo Evangelio de México," in *Códice franciscano: Nueva colección de documentos para la historia de México* (Franciscan codex: New collection of documents for the history of Mexico), edited by Joaquín García Icazbalceta (México: Editorial Salvador Chávez, Hayhoe, 1941), II, 41.

15. Sahagún, *Historia general*, I, 79.

16. Ibid.

17. Ibid.

18. Ibid.

19. See Jean-Pierre Berthe, "Les franciscains de la province mexicaine du Saint-Evangile en 1570: Un catalogue de fray Jerónimo de Mendieta" (The Franciscans of the Mexican province of the Holy Gospel in 1570: A catalogue by Fray Jerónimo de Mendieta), in *Enquètes sur l'Amérique Moyenne*, Mélanges offerts a Guy Stresser-Péan (México: INAH and the Centre d'Etudes Mexicaines et Centroaméricaines, 1989), 222.

20. Ibid., 223.

21. Ibid.

22. Sahagún, *Historia general*, I, 79.

23. Ibid.

24. It appeared published by Livario Oliger, *Breve compendio de los ritos idolátricos que los indios de esta Nueva España* (Brief compendium of the idolatrous rites of the Indians of this New Spain), by Bernardino de Sahagún, O.F.M., Pio V dicatum (Romae: Ex Schola Typographica Pio X, 1942).

25. See Francisco Hernández, *Antigüedades de la Nueva España* (Antiquities of New Spain), edited by Ascensión Hernández de León-Portilla (Madrid: Historia 16, 1986).

26. Georges Baudot published this denunciation, "Fray Toribio Motolinía denunciado ante la Inquisición por fray Bernardino de Sahagún" (Fray Toribio Motolinía denounced before the Inquisition by Fray Bernardino de Sahagún), *Estudios de Cultura Náhuatl* (México: UNAM, Instituto de Investigaciones Históricas) 21 (1991): 127–132.

27. Sahagún, *Historia general*, I, 277.

28. Ibid., I, 277–278.

29. "Carta del fray Cristóbal de Briviesca; Tlalmanalco, 12 Febrero 1573" (Letter from Fray Cristóbal of Briviesca; Tlalmanalco, 12 February 1573) in Alfonso Toro, "Ethnographic and Linguistic Significance of Fray Bernardino de Sahagún's Works," in *Anales del Museo Nacional de Arqueología, Historia y Etnografía* (México: 1924), 4th epoch, nos. 2, 3.

CHAPTER 6: COMPOSITION OF THE *HISTORIA GENERAL*

1. Sahagún, *Historia general*, I, 79–80.

2. Ibid., I, 80.

3. Ibid.

4. Francisco Hernández, *Obras completas, Escritos varios* (Complete works, Various writings), edited by Efrén C. del Pozo et al. (México: UNAM, 1959–1984), VI, 481–482.

5. Sahagún, *Historia general*, I, 635–636.

6. Ibid.

7. Ibid.

8. Torquemada, *Monarquía indiana*, V, 178.

9. See the edition prepared by Arthur J. O. Anderson: Bernardino de Sahagún, *Adiciones y apéndice a la postilla y ejercicio cotidiano*, prologue by Miguel León-Portilla, Facsimiles de Lingüística y Filología Nahuas, vol. 6 (México: UNAM, Instituto de Investigaciones Históricas, 1993).

10. Bernardino de Sahagún, "Parecer de fray Bernardino de Sahagún sobre cuales libros religiosos hay traducidos en lenguas indígenas y si los pueden tener los indios" (Fray Bernardino de Sahagún's opinion on which religious books in native languages there are and whether the Indians should have them), in Francisco Fernández del Castillo, comp., *Libros y libreros en el siglo XVI* (México: Archivo General de la Nación and Fondo de Cultura Económica, 1982), 82.

11. *Sermones en mexicano*, Biblioteca Nacional de México, Ms. 1482; and *Síguense unos sermones . . .*, Newberry Library, Ayer Collection, Ms. 1485; such as *Evangelarium, Epistolarium et Lectionarium Aztecum sive Mexicanum ex Antiquo Codice Mexicano nuper Reperto*, edited by Bernardino Biondelli (Mediolani [Milan]: Typis Joséph Bernardoni, 1858).

12. "Royal Order of Philip II, 22 April 1577," in *Códice franciscano*, edited by Joaquín García Icazbalceta, in *Nueva colección de documentos para la historia de México* (México: Editorial Salvador Chávez, Hayhoe, 1944), 267.

13. Fray Juan Baptista, *Sermonario en lengua mexicana*, pt. 1 (México: Casa de Diego López Dávalos, 1606), preliminary pages. Cited in García Icazbalceta, *Bibliografía mexicana*, 476.

14. Bernardino de Sahagún, *La aparición de Nuestra Señora de Guadelupe de México*, edited by Carlos María de Bustamante (México: Ignacio Cumplido, 1840), 234.

15. Howard F. Cline and Luis Nicolau D'Olwer, "Bernardino de Sahagún, 1499–1590, and His Works," in *Handbook of Middle American Indians* (Austin: University of Texas Press, 1952), vol. 13, 186–207.

16. *Copias de documentos del Archivo General de Indias*, Biblioteca Nacional de Antropología, carpeta XII, documento 689.

17. Georges Baudot, "Fray Rodrigo de Sequera, avocat du diable pour une histoire interdite" (Fray Rodrigo de Sequera, devil's advocate for a

forbidden history), *Caravelle, Cahiers du Monde Hispanique et Luso-Brésilien* (Toulouse: Université de Toulouse-Le Mirail) 12 (1969): 47–52.

18. "Carta del arzobispo Pedro Moya de Contreras a Felipe II, del 28 de octubre, 1577" (Letter from Archbishop Pedro Moya de Contreras to Philip II, 28 October 1577), in Albert María Carreño, *Un cedulario desconocido del siglo XVI perteneciente a la catedral de México*, Doc. 697. (México: Ediciones Victoria, 1944).

19. Letter included in García Icazbalceta, *Bibliografía mexicana*, 347.

20. Ibid., 348.

21. Ibid., 350.

22. "Real cédula dirigida al arzobispo con fecha en San Lorenzo el Real, a 5 de julio de 1578" (Royal order addressed to the archbishop dated at San Lorenzo el Real on 5 July 1578), cited by García Icazbalceta, *Bibliografía mexicana*, 348.

23. Ibid.

24. Mendieta, *Historia eclesiástica indiana*, 551.

25. Ibid., 663.

26. García Icazbalceta, *Bibliografía mexicana*, 350.

27. Sahagún, *La aparición*, edited by Bustamante, 350.

28. See Sahagún, *Historia general*, edited by Angel María Garibay, 21.

29. Sahagún, *Historia general*, (1989 edition), I, 306.

CHAPTER 7: UP TO THE END

1. On this work, Arthur J. O. Anderson published an article entitled "*La psalmodia* de Sahagún," with a translation of part of it, in *Estudios de Cultura Náhuatl* (México: UNAM, Instituto de Investigaciones Históricas) 20 (1990): 17–38. The same distinguished scholar has translated the same work into English, with a transcript of the Nahuatl text: *Bernardino de Sahagún's Psalmodia christiana* (*Christian Psalmody*) (Salt Lake City: University of Utah Press, 1993). Recently (1997) the Spanish scholar José Luis Suárez Roca also translated the *Psalmodia christiana* into Spanish (León, España: Instituto Leonés de Cultura, 1999).

2. Sahagún, *Psalmodia christiana*, 1583 edition, preliminary pages.

3. Ibid.

4. Durán, *Historia de las Indias*, I, 122.

5. Francisco Cervantes de Salazar, *Crónica de Nueva España*, edited by Francisco del Paso y Troncoso, 3 vols. (Madrid: Hauser and Menet, 1914–1936), II, 46.

6. See Fray Francisco de la Rosa Figueroa's comments in this regard, in García Icazbalceta, *Bibliografía mexicana*, 326.

7. Sahagún, *Historia general*, II, 634.

8. Ibid.

9. Antonio de Ciudad Real, *Tratado curioso y docto de las grandezas de la Nueva España. Relación breve y verdadera de algunas cosas que sucedieron al padre fray Alonso Ponce* . . . (Curious and learned treatise on the great things of New Spain. A brief and true account of the many things that happened to Father Alonso Ponce . . .), edited by Josefina García Quintana and Víctor M. Castillo Farreras, 2 vols. (México: UNAM, Instituto de Investigaciones Históricas, 1976), I, 16–17.

10. Fray Martín de León, *Camino del cielo, con todos los requisitos necesarios para conseguir este fin* (Road to heaven, with all the requisites necessary to achieve this goal) (México: Diego López Dávalos, 1611), fol. 95r–104v.

11. Quoted by García Icazbalceta, *Bibliografía mexicana*, 382–383.

12. Ibid., 386.

13. Sahagún, *Historia general*, II, 808. He also insists on this in the text addressed "To the Reader" on the calendar. See García Icazbalceta, *Bibliografía mexicana*, 381.

14. Sahagún, *Conquest of New Spain, 1585 Revision*, 147.

15. Ibid., 147–148.

16. Ibid., 148.

17. As I have already noted, this document of Sahagún is to be found tucked away in the edition cited in note 14.

18. Ibid., 211–212.

19. Ibid., 148.

20. John Frederick Schwaller, "Nahuatl Manuscripts in the Newberry Library (Chicago)," *Estudios de Cultura Náhuatl* (México: UNAM, Instituto de Investigaciones Históricas) 18 (1986): 326–327.

21. "Proceso contra fray Pedro de San Sebastián, provincial de la orden de San Francisco" (Trial of Fray Pedro de San Sebastián, provincial of the Franciscan Order) (México: Archivo General de la Nación), Inquisición, vol. 120, documento 12, cited by Georges Baudot in "Los últimos años de fray Bernardino de Sahagún o la esperanza de lo inaplazable" (The last years of Fray Bernardino de Sahagún or the hope for what cannot be postponed), in *La pugna franciscana por México* (The Franciscan struggle for Mexico) (México: Consejo Nacional para la Cultura y las Artes y Alianza Editorial Mexicana, 1990), 247.

22. Ibid.

23. Ibid., 244.

24. Georges Baudot reproduces these letters in *Utopía e historia en México*, 249, 253.

25. Sahagún, *Conquest of New Spain, 1585 Revision*, 238–239.

26. Sahagún, *Historia general*, II, 811.

27. Ibid., II, 813.

28. Ibid., II, 816.

29. Mendieta, *Historia eclesiástica indiana*, 664.

30. Ibid.

31. Ibid.

32. "Anales mexicanos, número 4," in *Anales antiguos de México y sus contornos* (Ancient annals of Mexico and its environs) (México: Biblioteca Nacional de Antropología e Historia, Colección Antigua), vol. 273, 495.

33. Domingo de San Antón Muñón Chimalpahin Cuauhtlehuanitzin, *Memorial breve de la fundación de Culhuacan* (Brief memorandum on the founding of Culhuacan) (Paris: Bibliothèque Nationale), Ms. Mexicain 74, fol. 40v.

34. Chimalpahin Cuauhtlehuanitzin, *Diario* (Paris: Bibliothèque Nationale), Ms. Mexicain 220, fol. 1.

CHAPTER 8: LEGACY OF BERNARDINO DE SAHAGÚN

1. Sebastián de Cobarrubias, *Tesoro de la lengua castellana o española* (1611) (Treasury of Castilian or Spanish) (Madrid: Ediciones Turner, 1984), 692.

2. Sahagún, *Historia general*, I, 33.

3. Ibid., II, 478.

4. Ibid., II, 583.

5. Ibid., II, 677–678.

6. Ibid., II, 627.

7. Ibid., II, 627–628.

8. Ibid., I, 33.

9. Ibid., II, 629.

10. Ibid., II, 629.

11. Ibid., I, 305.

12. Among other scholars who have expressed this are those who participated with F. S. C. Northrop as coordinator of a symposium that convened in Burg Wartenstein, Austria, in September 1962. The eighteen anthropologists, historians, and other scholars from different disciplines—hailing from North America, Germany, France, Italy, Austria, Israel, Japan, and Mexico—in the dedication to the book resulting from

the symposium, referred to Sahagún as the "Father of Anthropology in the New World," followed by an ample justification. See F. S. C. Northrop and Helen H. Livingston (eds.), *Cross-Cultural Understanding: Epistemology in Anthropology* (New York: Harper and Row Publishers, 1964).

13. Besides these editions, there exists another, also based on the Spanish text of the *Florentine Codex*, by Juan Carlos Temprano, in *Crónicas de América* 55, 2 vols. (Madrid: Historia 16, 1990). Of the edition by López Austin and García Quintana, a reprint in three volumes has appeared, published in 2000 by the Consejo Nacional para la Cultura y las Artes in Mexico City and enriched with a copious analytical index.

14. These editions have already been described in Chapter 5 of this book.

15. In the bibliography are listed the Spanish versions of parts of the *Primeros memoriales*.

16. Pilar Máynez Vidal, *Religión y magia. Un problema de transculturación lingüística en la obra de Bernardino de Sahagún* (Religion and magic. A problem of linguistic transculturation in the work of Bernardino de Sahagún), prologue by Miguel León-Portilla (México: UNAM, Escuela Nacional de Estudios Profesionales Acatlán, 1989).

BIBLIOGRAPHY

PUBLISHED WORKS BY BERNARDINO DE SAHAGÚN

Sahagún, fray Bernardino, *Psalmodia christiana y sermonario de los sanctos del año en lengua mexicano*. México: Casa de Pedro Ocharte, 1583.

———. *Historia general de las cosas de la Nueva España*. En doce libros y dos volúmenes escribió el R.P. Fr. Bernardino de Sahagún, dada a luz con notas y suplementos Carlos María de Bustamante, 3 vols. México: Imprenta del Ciudadano Alexandro Valdés, 1829–1830.

———. "Historia universal de las cosas de la Nueva España." In Edward King, Lord Kingsborough, *Antiquities of Mexico: Comprehending Facsimiles of Ancient Mexican Paintings and Hieroglyphs*. 9 vols. London: 1830–1848.

———. *La aparición de Nuestra Señora de Guadalupe de México, comprobada con la refutación del argumento negativo que presenta D. Juan Bautista Muñoz (cronista español del siglo XVIII), fundándose en el testimonio del P. Fr. Bernardino de Sahagún, o sea, la* Historia *original de ese escritor, que altera la publicada en 1829. (Relación de la Conquista de 1585)*. Carlos Ma. de Bustamante, ed. México: Ignacio Cumplido, 1840.

———. *Evangelarium Epistolarium et Lectionarium Aztecum sive Mexicanum ex Antiquo Codice Mexicano nuper Reperto Depromptum*. Cum praefatione, interpretatione, adnotationibus, glossario. Edidit Bernardinus Biondelli. Mediolani (Milan): Typis Jos. Bernardoni, Qm. Johannis, 1858.

———. *Histoire générale des choses de la Nouvelle Espagne*. Traduction et edition de Edouard Jourdanet et Rémi Siméon. Paris: G. Masson, 1880.

———. *Ein Kapitel aus den aztekischer Sprache geschriebenen, ungedruckten Materialien zu dem Geschichtswerk des Padre Sahagún (Göttertrachte und Attribute).* Eduard Seler, ed., trans. Bd. I, Heft IV, 5, 117–174. Berlin: Veröpffentlichungen aus dem Königlichen Museum fur Völkerkunde, 1890.

———. *Historia general de las cosas de la Nueva España.* Carlos Ma. de Bustamante, ed. 4 vol. México: Imprenta, Litografía y Encuadernación de Ireneo Paz, 1890–1895.

———. "Die religiösen Gesänge der alten Mexikaner." Edición y traducción de Eduard Seler. *Gesammelte Abhandlungen* (Berlin) 2 (1904): 959–1107.

———. *Historia general de las cosas de la Nueva España. Códices matrienses.* Edición de Francisco del Paso y Troncoso. 4 vols. Publícase con fondos de la Secretaría de Instrucción Pública y Bellas Artes de México. Madrid: Fototipia de Hauser y Menet, 1905–1908.

———. "Fray Bernardino de Sahagún, O.F.M. *Un breve compendio de los ritos idolátricos que los indios desta Nueva España usaban en el tiempo de su infidelidad.*" Nach dem vatikanischen Geheimarchiv aufbewahrten Original zum ersten Mal herausgegeben von Wilhelm Schmidt. *Anthropos, Ephemers Internationalis Ethnologia et Linguistica* (Salzburg) 1 (1906): 320–338.

———. "Calendario mexicano atribuido a fray Bernardino de Sahagún." Juan B. Iguíniz, ed. *Boletín de la Biblioteca Nacional* (México: UNAM, 1918) 12 (1918): 189–222 + 11 lám.

———. "El libro perdido de las *Pláticas* o *Coloquios* de los doce primeros misioneros de México." José Ma. Pou y Martí, ed. *Miscellanea Francisco Ehrle Dicata.* (Roma: Biblioteca Vaticana) 3 (1924): 281–333.

———. *Einige Kapitel aus dem Geschichtswerk des Fray Bernardino de Sahagún aus dem Aztekischen.* Übersetzt von Eduard Seler, Herausgegeben von Cäcilie Seler Sachs, Walter Lehmann und Walter Krickeberg. Stuttgart: Strecker und Schröder, 1927.

———. "El libro perdido de las *Pláticas* y *Coloquios* de los doce primeros misioneros en México." Edición de Zelia Nuttall. *Revista Mexicana de Estudios Históricos* (reproducción xilográfica) (México) 1 (1927): 101–141 y apéndice.

———. *A History of Ancient Mexico.* Based on the edition by Carlos Ma. de Bustamante. Translated by Fanny R. Bandelier. Nashville, Tenn.: Fisk University Press, 1932.

———. *Historia general de las cosas de la Nueva España.* Introducción de Wigberto Jiménez Moreno. Edición de Joaquín Ramírez Cabañas. 5 vols. México, Pedro Robredo, 1938.

———. "Breve compendio de los ritos idolátricos de Nueva España." Edición notas y comentarios del P. Livario Oliger. *Antonianum*, 17 (1942): 3–38, 133–174.

———. *Breve compendio de los ritos idolátricos de Nueva España*. Pío V dicatum. Edidit notisque illustravit P. P. Livario Oliger, O.F.M. Romae: Via Merulana, 1942.

———. "Paralipómenos de Sahagún." Primer estudio. Lista de augurios y sueños de los *Primeros memoriales*. Paleografía y traducción de Angel María Garibay K. *Tlalocan* (México) 1 (1944): 307–313.

———. *Historia general de las cosas de la Nueva España*. 3 vols. Edición de Miguel Acosta Saignes. México: Editorial Nueva España, 1946.

———. "Paralipómenos de Sahagún." 2o. estudio. Nómina de hombres y mujeres malos de los *Primeros memoriales*. Paleografía y traducción de Angel María Garibay K. *Tlalocan* (México) 2, no. 2 (1946), no. 3 (1947): 235–254.

———. "Paralipómenos de Sahagún." 3er. estudio. Relación breve de las fiestas de los dioses. Paleografía y traducción de Angel María Garibay K. *Tlalocan* (México) 2, no. 4 (1948): 289–320.

———. *Sterbender Götter und Christliche Heilsbotschaft. Wechselreden Indianischer Vornehmer und Spanischer Glaubensapostel in Mexiko 1524, "Coloquios y Doctrina Christiana" des Fray Bernardino de Sahagún aus dem Jahr 1564*. Spanisches und mexikanischer Text mit deutscher Übersetzung von Walter Lehmann. Aus dem nachlass herausgegeben von Gert Kutscher. Quellenwerke zur alten Geschichte Amerikas aufgezeichnet in der Sprachen der Eingeborenen. Herausgegeben von der Lateinamerikanischen Bibliothek, Berlin. Stuttgart: W. Kohlhammes Verlag, 1949.

———. *Wahrsagerei, Himmelskunde und Kalender der Alten Azteken*. Leonhard Schultze-Jena, ed., trans. Quellenwerke zur alten Geschichte Amerikas aufgezeichnet in der Sprachen der Eingeborenen. Herausgegeben von der Lateinamerikanischen Bibliothek, Berlin. Stuttgart: W. Kohlhammes Verlag, 1950.

———. *Florentine Codex. General History of the Things of New Spain*. Arthur J. O. Anderson and Charles E. Dibble, eds. and trans. 12 vols. Santa Fe, N. Mex.: School of American Research and University of Utah Press, 1950–1982.

———. *Gliederung des Alt-Aztekischen Volks in Familie, Stand und Beruf* Leonhard Schultze-Jena, ed., trans. Quellenwerke zur alten Geschichte Amerikas aufgezeichnet in der Sprachen der Eingeborenen. Herausgegeben von der Lateinamerikanischen Bibliothek, Berlin. Stuttgart: W. Kohlhammes Verlag, 1952.

————. *Historia general de las cosas de la Nueva España*. Edición y estudios de Angel Ma. Garibay K. 4 vols. México: Editorial Porrúa, 1956 (Biblioteca Porrúa 8–11).

————. *Ritos, sacerdotes y atavíos de los dioses*. Textos de los informantes de Sahagún. I. Introducción, paleografía, versión y notas por Miguel León-Portilla. México: UNAM, Instituto de Investigaciones Históricas, 1958 (Fuentes Indígenas de la Cultura Náhuatl 1).

————. *Veinte himnos sacros de los nahuas*. Textos de los informantes de Sahagún. II. Introducción, paleografía, versión y notas de Angel Ma. Garibay K. México: UNAM, Instituto de Investigaciones Históricas, 1958 (Fuentes Indígenas de la Cultura Náhuatl 2).

————. *Vida económica de Tenochtitlan. Pochtecáyotl, arte de traficar*. Textos de los informantes de Sahagún. III. Paleografía, versión y notas de Angel Ma. Garibay K. México: UNAM, Instituto de Investigaciones Históricas, 1961 (Fuentes Indígenas de la Cultura Náhuatl 3).

————. *Códices matritenses de la Historia general de las cosas de la Nueva España*. Edición de Manuel Ballesteros Gaibrois et al. 2 vols. Madrid: José Porrúa Turanzas, 1964.

————. *Augurios y abusiones*. Textos de los informantes de Sahagún. IV. Introducción, versión y notas de Alfredo López Austin. México: UNAM, Instituto de Investigaciones Históricas, 1969 (Fuentes Indígenas de la Cultura Náhuatl 7).

————. "De las enfermedades del cuerpo humano y de las medicinas contra ellas." Edición de Alfredo López Austin. *Estudios de Cultura Náhuatl* (México: UNAM, Instituto de Investigaciones Históricas) 8 (1969): 51–122.

————. "De las plantas medicinales y de otras cosas medicinales." Paleografía y traducción de Alfredo López Austin. *Estudios de Cultura Náhuatl* (México: UNAM, Instituto de Investigaciones Históricas) 9 (1971): 125–230.

————. "Textos acerca de las partes del cuerpo humano y de las enfermedades y medicinas en los *Primeros memoriales* de Sahagún." Paleografía y traducción de Alfredo López Austin. *Estudios de Cultura Náhuatl* (México: UNAM, Instituto de Investigaciones Históricas) 10 (1972): 129–154.

————. "The Arms and Insignia of the Mexica." Version of Thelma D. Sullivan. *Estudios de Cultura Náhuatl* (México: UNAM, Instituto de Investigaciones Históricas) 10 (1972): 155–193.

————. "Descripción de medicinas en textos dispersos del Libro X de los *Códices matritenses y florentino*." Paleografía y traducción de Alfredo

López Austin. *Estudios de Cultura Náhuatl* (México: UNAM, Instituto de Investigaciones Históricas) 11 (1974): 45–136.

———. "Relación tepepulca de los señores de México-Tenochtitlan y de Acolhuacán." Paleografía y traducción de Víctor M. Castillo F. *Estudios de Cultura Náhuatl* (México: UNAM, Instituto de Investigaciones Históricas) 11 (1974): 183–225.

———. *Primeros memoriales de fray Bernardino de Sahagún. Relación breve de las fiestas.* Textos en náhuatl. Traducción directa, prólogo y comentarios por Wigberto Jiménez Moreno. México: SEP-INAH, 1974 (Colección Científica, Historia, 16).

———. *1547–1577: A History of Ancient Mexico by Fray Bernardino de Sahagún.* Translation of the Spanish version of Carlos Ma. de Bustamante. Reprint of the 1932 edition, Fisk University, Nashville, comprising Books I–IV of the *Historia General*. Translated by Fanny R. Bandelier. Introductory essay by John Greenway. Glorieta, N. Mex.: Rio Grande Press, 1976.

———. *War of Conquest: How It Was Waged Here in Mexico. The Aztecs' Own Story, as Given by.* . . . Rendered into modern English by Arthur J. O. Anderson and Charles E. Dibble. Salt Lake City: University of Utah Press, 1978.

———. *Códice florentino. Historia general de las cosas de la Nueva España.* Manuscrito 218-20 de la Colección Palatina de la Biblioteca Medicea-Laurenziana. Edición facsimilar. 3 vols. Florencia: Casa Editorial Giunti Barbera. México: Archivo General de la Nación, 1979.

———. "The Aztec-Spanish Dialogues of 1524." Traducción y estudio preliminar del libro de los *Coloquios* de fr. Bernardino de Sahagún (traducción sólo de la versión náhuatl) por J. Jorge Klor de Alva. *Alcheringa: Ethnopoetics* 4 (1980): 52–193.

———. "O Precious Necklace, O Quetzal Feather!: Aztec Pregnancy and Childbirth Orations." Edited and translated by Thelma D. Sullivan. *Alcheringa: Ethnopoetics* 4, no. 2 (1980): 38–52.

———. "Salutación y súplica que hacía un principal al 'tlatoani' recién electo." Traducción y estudio de Josefina García Quintana. *Estudios de Cultura Náhuatl* (México: UNAM, Instituto de Investigaciones Históricas) 14 (1980): 65–94.

———. *Historia general de las cosas de la Nueva España.* Primera versión íntegra del texto castellano del manuscrito conocido como *Códice florentino*. Introducción, paleografía, glosario y notas de Alfredo López Austin y Josefina García Quintana. 2 vols. México: Fondo Cultural Banamex, 1982.

————. "Carta de Pedro de San Buenaventura a fray Bernardino de Sahagún acerca del calendario solar mexicano." Edición y traducción de Elena Díaz Rubio y Jesús Bustamenate García. *Revista Española de Antropología Americana* (Madrid: Universidad Complutense) 13 (1983): 109–120.

————. Coloquios y doctrina christiana con *que los doce frailes de San Francisco, enviados por el papa Adriano VI y por el emperador Carlos V, convirtieron a los indios de la Nueva España*. En lengua mexicana y española. Los diálogos de 1524, dispuestos por fray Bernardino de Sahagún y sus colaboradores Antonio Valeriano de Azcapotzalco, Alonso Vegerano de Cuauhtitlan, Martín Jacobita y Andrés Leonardo de Tlatelolco y otros cuatro ancianos muy entendidos en todas sus antigüedades. Edición facsimilar, introducción, paleografía, versión del náhuatl y notas de Miguel León-Portilla. México: UNAM, Fundación de Investigaciones Sociales A.C., 1986 (Colección de Facsímiles de Lingüística y Filosofía Nahuas 4).

————. *Historia general de las cosas de la Nueva España*. Primera versión íntegra del texto castellano del manuscrito conocido como *Códice florentino*. Introducción, paleografía, glosario y notas de Alfredo López Austin y Josefina García Quintana. 2 vols. Madrid: Alianza Quinto Centenario, 1988–1989 (Colección Alianza Universidad, 560–561).

————. *Conquest of New Spain, 1585 Revision*. Reproductions of the Boston Public Library manuscript and Carlos María de Bustamante 1840 edition. Translated by Howard F. Cline. Edited with an introduction and notes by S. L. Cline. Salt Lake City: University of Utah Press, 1989.

————. *Historia de las cosas de la Nueva Espana*. Edición de Juan Carlos Temprano, 2 vols. Madrid: Historia 16, 1990 (Crónicas de América 55).

————. *De Azteken: Kroniek van een verdwenen cultuur*. Edition by Rudolf van Zantwijk. Amsterdam: Meuleuhoff, 1991.

————. Primeros Memoriales *by Bernardino de Sahagún*. Facsimile edition, photographed by Ferdinand Anders. Norman: University of Oklahoma Press, in cooperation with the Patrimonio Nacional and Real Academia de la Historia, 1993.

————. *Veinte himnos sacros de los nahuas*. Textos de los informantes de Sahagún. II. Introducción, versión, notas y apéndices de Angel María Garibay K. 2a. ed. México: UNAM, Instituto de Investigaciones Históricas, 1995 (Fuentes Indígenas de la Cultura Náhuatl 2).

————. Primeros Memoriales *by Fray Bernardino de Sahagún*. Paleography of Nahuatl text and English translation by Thelma D. Sullivan,

completed and revised with additions by Henry Nicholson, Arthur J. O. Anderson, Charles E. Dibble, Eloise Quiñones Keber, and Wayne Ruwet. Norman: University of Oklahoma Press, in cooperation with the Patrimonio Nacional and Real Academia de la Historia, 1997.
———. See also the citations listed under the "Other Documents" subheading in the bibliography.

OTHER DOCUMENTS

Archivo de la parroquia de Tepeapulco (Hidalgo). Libro de matrimonios en náhuatl) de los años 1590 a 1617.
Archivo General de Indias (Sevilla). Información promovida por el obispo don fray Juan de Zumárraga, 11 de julio de 1531, Justicia, 1906.
Archivo General de la Nación (México). Proceso del Santo Oficio de la Inquisición contra Puchteca Tlailotla por haber ocultado ídolos, 1539, Inquisición, tomo 37, exp.2. Proceso del Santo Oficio de la Inquisición contra don Carlos, indio principal de Tetzcoco por idolatría, 1539, tomo 2, exp. 2. Tomo de justificaciones que abarca el año de 1572, tomo 224, 67 r.
Biblioteca Nacional (México). Fray Bernardino de Sahagún. Sermones en mexicano. Ms. 1482.
———. Fray Bernardino de Sahagún. Cantares mexicanos, "Aquí comienza el arte adivinatorio que usaban los mexicanos en tiempo de su ydolotría llamado tonalámatl." Ms. 1628 bis, fols. 101r–125r.
Biblioteca Nacional de Antropología Historia (México). Anales antiguos de México y sus contornos. Colección antigua, vol. 273. Copias de documentos del Archivo General de Indias, s.f., carpeta 12, documento 689.
Bibliothèque Nationale (Paris). Chimalpahin Cuauhtlehuanitzin, Domingo de San Antón Muñón. Diario. Ms. Mexicain 220.
———. Chimalpahin Cuauhtlehuanitzin, Domingo de San Antón Muñón. Memorial breve de la fundación de Culhuacan. Ms. Mexicain 74, fol. 40v.
Cartas de Indias. Edición de Justo Zaragoza. Madrid: 1877. Reproducción facsimilar. México: Miguel Angel Porrúa, 1980.
Colicción de documentos para la historia de México. Edición de Joaquín García Icazbalceta. 2 vols. México: Librería de J. M. Andrade, 1858–1866.
Epistolario de la Nueva Expaña. Compilación de Francisco del Paso y Troncoso. 16 vols. México: Editorial Pedro Robredo, 1939–1942.
Newberry Library (Chicago). Fray Bernardino de Sahagún. Sermonario y santoral. Copy of the manuscript of 1540. Ayer Collection, Ms. 1485.
———. Fray Bernardino de Sahagún. Vocabulario en tres lenguas. Ayer Collection, Ms. 1478.

Nueva colección de documentos para la historia de México. Vol. I, *Cartas de religiosos de Nueva España, 1539–1594*. México: 1886. Vol. II, *Códice franciscano. Siglo XVI*. México: 1889. Vol. III, Pomar-Zurita, *Relaciones antiguas (siglo XVI)*; Vol. IV y V, *Códice Mendieta*, Documentos franciscanos, siglos XVI y XVII, edición de Joaquín García Icazbalceta. México: 1886–1892.

OTHER BOOKS AND ARTICLES

Alva Ixtlilxóchitl, Fernando de. *Obras históricas*. Estudio introductorio por Edmundo O'Gorman, prefacio de Miguel León-Portilla. 2 vols. México: UNAM, Instituto de Investigaciones Históricas, 1975.

Alvarado, Tezozómoc, Hernando. Crónica mexicana. Anotada por Manuel Orozco y Berra. México: Editorial Porrúa, 1975.

Anderson, Arthur J. O., "Sahagún's Nahuatl Texts as Indigenist Documents." *Estudios de Cultura Náhuatl* (México: UNAM, Instituto de Investigaciones Históricas) 2 (1960): 31–42.

———. "Sahagún's Sources for Book II." *Estudios de Cultura Náhuatl*, (México: UNAM, Instituto de Investigaciones Históricas) 15 (1982): 73–88.

———. "Sahagún's 'Doctrinal Encyclopaedia." *Estudios de Cultura Náhuatl* (México: UNAM, Instituto de Investigaciones Históricas): 16 (1983): 109–122.

———. "La psalmodia de Sahagún." *Estudios de Cultura Náhuatl*, (México: UNAM, Instituto de Investigaciones Históricas) 20 (1990): 17–38.

———. Adiciones, y Apéndice a la postilla y ejercicio cotidiano *de Bernardino de Sahagún*, prólogo de Miguel León-Portilla. Facsímiles de Lingüística y Filología Nahuas, 6. México: UNAM, Instituto de Investigaciones Históricas, 1993.

———. Psalmodia christiana *(Christian psalmody)*. Salt Lake City: University of Utah Press, 1993.

———. "'Los primeros memoriales' y *El códice florentino*." *Estudios de Cultura Náhuatl* (México: UNAM, Instituto de Investigaciones Históricas) 24 (1994): 49–91.

Anderson, Arthur J. O., and Charles E. Dibble, eds. and trans. *Florentine Codex. General History of the Things of New Spain*. 12 vols. Santa Fe, N. Mex.: School of American Research and University of Utah Press, 1950–1982.

Anderson, Arthur J. O., and Wayne Ruwet. Sahagun's *Manual del Cristiano*." *Estudios de Cultura Náhuatl* (México: UNAM, Instituto de Investigaciones Históricas) 23 (1993): 17–45.

Antonio, Nicolás. *Biblioteca Hispana Nova sive Hispaniorum Scriptorum qui ab Anno MD, ad MDCLXXXIV, Fluoruere Notitia.* 2 vols. Edición facsimilar de la impresa en Madrid, por Joaquín de Ibarra, en 1783 y 1788. Primera edición impresa en Roma, por Nicolás Tinassii, en 1672. Torino: Botega d'Erasmo, 1963.

Asensio, Eugenio. "El erasmismo y las corrientes espirituales afines (conversos, franciscanos, italianizantes)." *Revista de Filología Española* (Madrid: Consejo Superior de Investigaciones Científicas) 36 (1952): 31–90.

Baird, Ellen Taylor. "Text and Image in Sahagun's 'Primeros Memoriales.'" In *Text and Image in Pre-Columbian Art*, edited by Janet C. Berlo. Series 180, 155–179. Oxford: BAR International, 1983.

———. "Sahagun's 'Primeros Memoriales' and *Codex Florentino.*" In *European Elements in the Illustrations. Smoke and Mist.* Mesoamerican Studies in Memory of Thelma D. Sullivan, edited by J. Kathryn Josserand and Karen Dakin, 15–40. Oxford: BAR International, 1988.

Ballesteros Gaibrois, Manuel. *Vida y obra de fray Bernardino de Sahagún.* León, España: Institución fray Bernardino de Sahagún, Consejo Superior de Investigaciones Científicas, 1973.

———. et al. "Los manuscritos matritenses de Sahagún." En *Akten des 34. Internationalen Amerikanisten Kongresses* (Wien, 18 bis 25 juli 1962), 226–243. Wien (Vienna): Horn Wien Verlag Ferdinand Berger, 1962.

Baptista, fray Juan. *Advertencias para los confesores de los naturales. Primera parte.* México: En el convento de Santiago Tlatelolco, por M. Ocharte, 1600.

———. *Sermonario en lengua mexicana.* México: En casa de Diego López Dávalos, 1606.

Bataillon, Marcel. *Erasmo y España. Estudios sobre la historia espiritual del siglo XVI.* Traducción de Antonio Alatorre. México-Madrid-Buenos Aires: Fondo de Cultura Económica, 1983.

Baudot, Georges. "Fray Rodrigo de Sequera, avocat du diable pour une histoire interdite." *Caravelle, Cahiers du Monde Hispanique et Luso-Brésilien* (Toulouse: Université de Toulouse-Le Mirail) 12 (1969): 47–82.

———. "Los últimos años de fray Bernardino de Sahagún o la esperanza de lo inaplazable." *Caravelle, Cahiers du Monde Hispanique et Luso-Brésilien* (Toulouse: Université de Toulouse-Le Mirail) 23 (1974): 23–45.

———. "Los Huehuetlahtolli en la cristianización de México: Dos sermones en lengua náhuatl de fray Bernardino de Sahagún." *Estudios de Cultura Náhuatl* (México: UNAM, Instituto de Investigaciones Históricas) 15 (1982): 125–145.

———. *Utopía e historia en México. Los primeros cronistas de la civilización mexicana (1520–1569)*. Madrid: Espasa-Calpe, 1983.

———. *La pugna franciscana por México*. México: Consejo Nacional para la Cultura y las Artes y Alianza Editorial Mexicana, 1990.

———. "Fray Toribio Motolinía denunciado ante la Inquisición por fray Bernardino de Sahagún." *Estudios de Cultura Náhuatl* (México: UNAM, Instituto de Investigaciones Históricas) 21 (1991): 127–132.

Beltrami, Jules-César. *Le mexique*. 2 vols. Paris: Delanay Librairie, 1830.

Bernal, Ignacio. "Vida y obra de Sahagún, tema de dos cartas inéditas de Francisco del Paso y Troncoso a don Joaquín García Icazbalceta," con notas de Miguel León-Portilla. *Estudios de Cultura Náhuatl* (México: UNAM, Instituto de Investigaciones Históricas) 15 (1982): 247–290.

———. "La obra de Sahagún, otra carta inédita de Francisco del Paso y Troncoso." *Estudios de Cultura Náhuatl* (México: UNAM, Instituto de Investigaciones Históricas) 16 (1983): 265–325.

Berthe, Jean-Pierre. "Les franciscains de la province mexicaine du Saint-Evangile en 1570: Un catalogue de fray Jerónimo de Mendieta." En *Enquètes sur l'Amérique Moyenne*, 222–228. México: INAH y Centre d'Etudes Mexicaines et Centroamericaines, 1989.

Biondelli, Bernardino, ed. *Evangelarium, Epistolarium et Lectionarium Aztecum sive Mexicanum, ex Antiquo Codice Mexicano nuper Reperto*. Mediolani (Milan): Typis Jos. Bernardoni, Qm. Johannis, 1858.

Bosch de Souza, María Guadalupe. *Bernardino de Sahagún. Breve compendio de los ritos idolátricos que los indios de esta Nueva España usaban en tiempos de su infidelidad*. México: Lince Editores, 1990.

Brinton, Daniel G. *Rig Veda Americanus: Sacred Songs of the Ancient Mexicans*. Philadelphia: 1890 (Library of Aboriginal American Literature 8).

Browne, Walden. *Sahagún and the Transition to Modernity*. Norman: University of Oklahoma Press, 2000.

Burkhart, Louise M. "Sahagún's 'Tlauculcuicatl,' a Nahuatl Lament." *Estudios de Cultura Náhuatl* (México: UNAM, Instituto de Investigaciones Históricas) 18 (1986): 181–218.

———. "Doctrinal Aspects of Sahagún's 'Coloquios,'" In *The Work of Bernardino de Sahagún, Pioneer Ethnographer of Sixteenth-Century Aztec Mexico*, edited by J. Jorge Klor de Alva et al., Studies on Culture and Society, vol. 2, 65–82. Albany: Institute for Mesoamerican Studies, University of Albany, and State University of New York, 1988.

Bustamante García, Jesús, "Fray Bernardino de Sahagún o la necesidad de actuar desde el conocimiento." En *Ciencia, vida y espacio en*

Iberoamérica, coordinación de José Luis Peset, vol. 1, 179–181. Madrid: Consejo Superior de Investigaciones Científicas, 1989.

———. *Fray Bernardino de Sahagún: Una revisión crítica de los manuscritos y de su proceso de composición*. México: UNAM, Instituto de Investigaciones Bibliográficas, Biblioteca Nacional y Hemeroteca Nacional, 1990.

Campbell, R. Joe, and Mary L. Clayton. "Fray Bernardino de Sahagún's Contribution to the Lexicon of Classical Nahuatl." In *The Work of Bernardino de Sahagún, Pioneer Ethnographer of Sixteenth-Century Aztec Mexico*, edited by J. Jorge Klor de Alva, et al. Studies on Culture and Society, vol. 2, 295–314. Albany: Institute for Mesoamerican Studies, University of Albany, and State University of New York, 1988.

Carochi, Haracio. *Arte de la lengua mexicana*. México: Juan Ruiz, 1645.

Carreño, Alberto María. *Un cedulario desconocido del siglo XVI perteneciente a la catedral de México*. Doc. 697. México: Ediciones Victoria, 1944.

Castro, Florencio Vicente, and J. Luis Rodríguez Molinero. *Bernardino de Sahagún, primer antropólogo en Nueva España (siglo XVI)*. Salamanca: Universidad de Salamanca, Institución fray Bernardino de Sahagún, Consejo Superior de Investigaciones Científicas, 1986.

Castro Seoane, José. Aviamiento y catálogo de los misioneros que en el siglo XVI pasaron de España a Indias y Filipinas, según los libros de la contratación." En *Missionalia hispanica*, vols. 13–14. Contiene: I. "Franciscanos y Dominicos a la Española, 1505 a 1525," vol. 13 (1956), 83-140. II. "Expediciones franciscanas, 1526 a 1545," vol. 14 (1957), 105–173. Madrid.

Cervantes de Salazar, Francisco. *Crónica de la Nueva España*. Prólogo de Juan Miralles Ostos. Colección Biblioteca Porrúa, 84. México: Editorial Porrúa, 1985.

Chavero, Alfredo. *Sahagún*. México: Imprenta de José Ma. Sandoval, 1877. Sobretiro del artículo publicado en *Boletín de la Sociedad Mexicana de Geografía y Estadística de la República Mexicana* (México) vol. 6 (1877).

———. "Apuntes sobre bibliografía mexicana. Sahagún." *Boletín de la Sociedad Mexicana de Geografía y Estadística de la República Mexicana* (México) 3a. época, 6 (1882): 5–42.

Chimalpahin Cuauhtlehuanitzin, Domingo de San Antón Muñón. *Sixième et septième relations (1258–1612)*. Traducidas por Rémi Siméon. Paris: Maisonneuve et Ch. LeClerq Editeurs, 1889.

———. *Relaciones originales de Chalco Amaquemecan*. Trad. de Silvia Rendón. México: Fondo de Cultura Económica, 1965.

———. See also Bibliothèque Nationale (Paris) under the "Other Documents" subheading in the bibliography.

Ciudad Real, Antonio de. *Tratado curioso y docto de las grandezas de la Nueva España. Relación breve y verdadera de algunas cosas que sucedieron al padre fray Alonso Ponce en las provincias de la Nueva España siendo comisario general de aquellas partes.* 2 vols. Edited by Josefina García Quintana and Víctor M. Castillo Farreras, vol. 1, 16–17. México: UNAM, Instituto de Investigaciones Históricas, 1976.

Clavijero, Francisco Javier. *Historia antigua de México.* Colección de Escritores Mexicanos, 4 vols. México: Editorial Porrúa, 1945.

Cline, Howard F. "Notas sobre la historia de la conquista de Sahagún." En *Historia y sociedad en el mundo de habla española.* Homenaje a José Miranda, editado por Bernardo García Martínez et al., 121–140. México: El Colegio de México, 1970.

———. "Missing and Variant Prologues and Dedications in Sahagún's *Historia General*: Texts and English Translations." *Estudios de Cultura Náhuatl* (México: UNAM, Instituto de Investigaciones Históricas) 9 (1971): 137–251.

———. "Evolution of the *Historia General.*" In *Handbook of Middle American Indians,* vol. 13, 189–207. Austin: University of Texas Press, 1973.

———. "Sahagún's Materials and Studies, 1948–1971." In *Handbook of Middle American Indians,* vol. 13, 218–232. Austin: University of Texas Press, 1973.

Cline, Howard F., and Luis Nicolau D'Olwer. "Bernardino de Sahagún, 1499–1590, and His Works." In *Handbook of Middle American Indians,* vol. 13, 186–207. Austin: University of Texas Press, 1973.

Cline, Sue L. "Revisionist Conquest History: Sahagún's Revised Book XII." In *The Work of Bernardino de Sahagún, Pioneer Ethnographer of Sixteenth-Century Aztec Mexico,* edited by J. Jorge Klor de Alva et al. Studies on Culture and Society, vol. 2, 169–177. Albany: Institute for Mesoamerican Studies, University of Albany, and State University of New York, 1988.

Cobarrubias, Sebastián de. *Tesoro de la lengua castellana o española.* Primer diccionario de lengua (1611). Madrid: Ediciones Turner, 1984.

Códices matritenses de la Real Academia de la Historia y del Real Palacio. Edición facsimilar preparada por Francisco del Paso y Troncoso, 3 vols. Madrid: Fototipia de Hauser y Menet, 1905–1907.

Cruz, Martín de la. *Libellus de Medicinalibus Indorum Herbis.* Versión en español, con comentarios de varios autores. México: Fondo de Cultura Económica, Instituto Mexicano del Seguro Social, 1991.

Davies, Nigel. "The Mexican Military Hierarchy as Described by Sahagún." In *The Work of Bernardino de Sahagún, Pioneer Ethnographer of*

Sixteenth-Century Aztec Mexico, edited by J. Jorge Klor de Alva et al. Studies on Culture and Society, vol. 2, 161–168. Albany: Institute for Mesoamerican Studies, University of Albany, and State University of New York, 1988.

Diaz Rubio, Elena, and Jesús Bustamante García. "Carta de Pedro de San Buenaventura a fray Bernardino de Sahagún acerca del calendario solar mexicano." *Revista Española de Antropología Americana* (Madrid: Universidad Complutense) 13 (1983): 109–120.

Dibble, Charles E. "Spanish Influence on Nahuatl Texts of Sahagún's *Historia.*" In *Akten des 34. Internationalen Amerikanisten Kongresses* (Wien, 18 bis 25 juli 1962), 244–247. Vienna: Horn Wein Verlag Ferdinand Berger, 1962.

———. "Glifos fonéticos del *Códice florentino.*" *Estudios de Cultura Náhuatl* (México: UNAM, Instituto de Investigaciones Históricas) 4 (1963): 55–60.

———. "Sahagún's *Historia.*" In *Florentine Codex. General History of the Things of New Spain,* edited and translated by Arthur J. O. Anderson and Charles E. Dibble, vol. 1, 9–23. Santa Fe, N. Mex.: School of American Research and University of Utah Press, 1950–1982.

———. "The Watermarks in the Florentine Codex." In *Florentine Codex. General History of the Things of New Spain,* edited and translated by Arthur J. O. Anderson and Charles E. Dibble, vol. 1, 25–28. Santa Fe, N. Mex.: School of American Research and University of Utah Press, 1950–1982.

———. "The *Breve Compendio* and the Subsequent Sahagún Manuscripts." In *De la historia. Homenaje a Jorge Gurría Lacroix,* 69–74. México: UNAM, Instituto de Investigaciones Históricas, 1985.

———. "Molina and Sahagún." In *European Elements in the Illustrations. Smoke and Mist.* Mesoamerican Studies in Memory of Thelma D. Sullivan, 2 vols., edited by J. Kathryn Josserand and Karen Dakin, vol. 1, 69–97. Oxford: BAR International, 1988.

Dibble, Charles E., and Arthur J. O. Anderson. See Sahagún, *Florentine Codex. General History of the Things of New Spain.*

Dibble, Charles E., and Norma B. Mikkelsen. "La olografía de fray Bernardino de Sahagún." *Estudios de Cultura Náhuatl* (México: UNAM, Instituto de Investigaciones Históricas) 9 (1971): 231–236.

Diccionario de autoridades: Diccionario de la lengua castellana en que se explica el verdadero sentido de las voces, su naturaleza y calidad con las frases o modos de hablar. . . . 6 vols. Madrid: Real Academia Española, 1737. Reproducción facsimilar. Madrid: Editorial Gredos, 1963.

Durán, fray Diego. *Historia de las Indias e islas de tierra firme de la Nueva España*. Edición de Angel María Garibay, 2 vols. México: Editorial Porrúa, 1967–1968.

Edmonson, Munro, ed. *Sixteenth-Century Mexico: The Work of Sahagún*. Albuquerque: University of New Mexico Press, 1974.

Eguiara, Juan José de. *Biblioteca mexicana*. México: Fondo de Cultura Económica, 1944.

Eisinger, Marc. "Valores numéricos de frecuencia de letras y dígrafos en el texto náhuatl del Libro I del *Códice florentino*." *Estudios de Cultura Náhuatl* (México: UNAM, Instituto de Investigaciones Históricas) 14 (1980): 379–417.

Emmart, Emily W. *The Badianus Manuscript*. Baltimore: Johns Hopkins Press, 1940.

Fernández del Castillo, Francisco. *Libros y libreros en el siglo XVI*. Edición facsimilar de la de 1914. México: Archivo General de la Nación y Fondo de Cultura Económica, 1982.

García Icazbalceta, Joaquín. *Don fray Juan de Zumárraga, primer obispo y arzobispo de México*. Edición adicionada de Rafael Aguayo Spencer y Antonio Castro Leal. 1a. edición, México, 1881. México: Editorial Porrúa, 1947 (Colección Escritores Mexicanos 41–44).

———. *Bibliografía mexicana del siglo XVI*. Nueva edición por Agustín Millares Carlo. México: Fondo de Cultura Económica, 1954 (Colección Biblioteca Americana).

———. See also *Colección de documentos para la historia de México* and *Nueva colección de documentos para la historia de México* under the "Other Documents" subheading in the bibliography.

Garibay Kintana, Angel María. "Versiones discutibles del texto náhuatl de Sahagún." *Tlalocan* (México) 3, no. 2 (1952): 187–190.

———. *Fray Bernardino de Sahagún: Relación de los textos que no aprovechó en su obra. Su método de investigación*. México: UNAM, Sociedad Folklórica de México, 1953.

———. *Historia de la literatura náhuatl*. 2 vols., 2a. ed. México: Editorial Porrúa, 1953–54.

———. *Veinte himnos sacros de los nahuas*. Los recogió de los nativos fray Bernardino de Sahagún, paleografía, versión, introducción y comentarios. México: UNAM, Instituto de Investigaciones Históricas, 1958 (Informantes de Sahagún 2).

———. *Vida económica de Tenochtitlan. Pochtecáyotl, arte de traficar*. Paleografía, versión, introducción y notas. México: UNAM, Instituto de Investigaciones Históricas, 1961 (Informantes de Sahagún 3).

―――. *Historia de los mexicanos. Tres opúsculos del siglo XVI.* 2a. ed. México: Editorial Porrúa, 1973 (Colección "Sepan Cuantos" 37).

―――. See also his edition of Sahagún, *Historia general.*

Giménez, Iris. "L'elaboration de la *Historia general de las cosas de la Nueva España* de Fray Bernardino de Sahagún. Un exemple: Les folios 82, 88 et 104 de l'Académie de l'Histoire de Madrid." *Caravelle, Cahiers du Monde Hispanique et Luso-Brésilien* (Toulouse: Université de Toulouse-Le Mirail) 27 (1976): 171–187.

Glass, John B. *Sahagún: Reorganization of the Manuscript of Tlatelolco, 1566–1569.* Contributions to the Ethnohistory of Mexico 7. Lincoln Center, Mass.: Conemex Associates, 1978.

Grijalva, Juan de. *Crónica de la orden de nuestro padre San Agustín en las provincias de la Nueva España.* México: Editorial Porrúa, 1985.

Hernández, Francisco. *Antigüedades de la Nueva España.* Traducción del latín y notas de Joaquín García Pimentel. México: Editorial Pedro Robredo, 1946.

―――. *Obras completas, Escritos varios.* 7 vols. México: UNAM, 1959–1984.

Hernández de León-Portilla, Ascención, ed. *Antigüedades de la Nueva España de Francisco Hernández.* Madrid: Historia 16, 1986.

―――. *Tepuztlahcuilolli, impresos nahuas.* Historia y bibliografía, 2 vols. México: UNAM, Instituto de Investigaciones Históricas y Filológicas, 1988.

―――. *Bernardino de Sahagún. Diez ensayos acerca de su historia, edición e introducción.* México: Fondo de Cultura Económica, 1990, 1997.

Herrera, Antonio de. *Décadas del Nuevo Mundo.* 10 vols. Buenos Aires: Editorial Guarania, 1943–1947.

―――. *Historia de los hechos de los castellanos en las islas y tierra firme del mar océano,* vol. 8. Madrid: Real Academia de la Historia, 1948.

Hinz, Eike. *Analyse aztekischer Gedan Kensysteme. Wahrsageglaube und Erziehungsnomen als Alltagstheorie Sozialen Handelsn. Auf Grund des 4. und 6. Buches der "Historia General" Fray Bernardino de Sahagún aus der Mitte des 16. Jahrhunderts.* Acta Humboldtiana. Series Geographica et Ethnographica. Nr. 6. Wiesbaden: Franz Steiner Verlag, GMH, 1978.

Huehuetlahtolli. Testimonios de la Antigua Palabra. Reproducción facsimilar. Estudio introductorio por Miguel León-Portilla. Versión de los textos nahuas por Librado Silva Galeana. México: Comisión Nacional Conmemorativa del V Centenario del Encuentro de Dos Mundos, 1988.

Iguíniz, Juan B. "Calendario mexicano atribuido a fray Bernardino de Sahagún." *Boletín de la Biblioteca Nacional de México* (México: UNAM) 121 (1918): 189–222.

Jiménez Moreno, Wigberto. "Fray Bernardino de Sahagún y su obra." Introducción en Sahagún, *Historia general de las cosas de la Nueva España*, 5 vols. México: Pedro Robredo, 1938.

————, ed. Primeros meemoriales *de fray Bernardino de Sahagún*. México: Instituto Nacional de Antropología e Historia, 1974.

Klor de Alva, J. Jorge. "La historicidad de los *Coloquios* de Sahagún." *Estudios de Cultura Náhuatl* (México: UNAM, Instituto de Investigaciones Históricas) 15 (1982): 142–184.

————. "Sahagún and the Birth of Modern Ethnography: Representing, Confessing, and Inscribing the Other." In *The Work of Bernardino de Sahagún, Pioneer Ethnographer of Sixteenth-Century Aztec Mexico*, edited by J. Jorge Klor de Alva et al. Studies on Culture and Society, vol. 2, 31–52. Albany: Institute for Mesoamerican Studies, University of Albany, and State University of New York, 1988.

————. "Sahagún's Misguided Introduction to Ethnography and the Failure of the 'Coloquios' Project." In *The Work of Bernardino de Sahagún, Pioneer Ethnographer of Sixteenth-Century Aztec Mexico*, edited by J. Jorge Klor de Alva et al. Studies on Culture and Society, vol. 2, 83–92. Albany: Institute for Mesoamerican Studies, University of Albany, and State University of New York, 1988.

Klor de Alva, J. Jorge, Henry B. Nicholson, and Eloise Quiñones Keber, eds. *The Work of Bernardino de Sahagún, and Pioneer Ethnographer of Sixteenth-Century Aztec Mexico*. Studies on Culture and Society, 2 vols. Albany: Institute for Mesoamerican Studies, University of Albany, and University of New York, 1988.

Leal, Luis. "El Libro XII de Sahagún." *Historia Mexicana* (México: El Colegio de México) 2 (1955): 184–210.

León, Martín de. *Camino del cielo en lengua mexicana*. . . . México: Diego López Dávila, 1611.

León-Portilla, Miguel. *La filosofía náhuatl estudiada en sus fuentes* (1a. edición, 1956). 8a. ed. México: Instituto de Investigaciones Históricas, 1996.

————. *Antiquos mexicanos a través de sus crónicas y cantares*. México: Fondo de Cultura Económica, 1961.

————. "Los huaxtecos según los informantes de Sahagún." *Estudios de Cultura Náhuatl* (México: UNAM, Instituto de Investigaciones Históricas) 5 (1965): 15–30.

————. "Significado de la obra de fray Bernardino de Sahagún." *Estudios de Historia Novohispana* (México: UNAM, Instituto de Investigaciones Históricas) 1 (1966): 13–26.

———. *Significado de la obra de fray Bernardino de Sahagún. Alumno de Salamanca, padre de la antropología en el Nuevo Mundo.* Salamanca: Publicaciones de la Asociación de Antiguos Alumnos y Amigos de la Universidad de Salamanca, España, 1966.

———. "Ramírez de Fuenleal y las antigüedades mexicanas." *Estudios de Cultura Náhuatl* (México: UNAM, Instituto de Investigaciones Históricas) 18 (1969): 9–49.

———. "The Problematics of Sahagún: Certain Topics Needing Investigation." In *Sixteenth-Century Mexico: The Work of Sahagún*, edited by Munro S. Edmonson 235–255. Albuquerque: School of American Research and University of New Mexico Press, 1974.

———. "La investigación integral de Sahagún y la problemática acerca de ella." En *Toltecáyotl, aspectos de la cultura náhuatl*, 101–135. México: Fondo de Cultura Económica, 1983.

———. "Los franciscanos vistos por el hombre náhuatl. Testimonios indígenas del siglo XVI." *Estudios de Cultura Náhuatl* (México: UNAM, Instituto de Investigaciones Históricas) 17 (1984): 260–339.

———. *Bernardino de Sahagún.* Madrid: Historia 16 y Quorum, 1987 (Colección Protagonistas de América).

———. "Chimalpahin's Use of a Testimony by Sahagún; the Olmecs in Chalco-Amaquemecan." In *The Work of Bernardino de Sahagún, Pioneer Ethnographer of Sixteenth-Century Aztec Mexico*, edited by J. Jorge Klor de Alva et al. Studies on Culture and Society, vol. 2, 179–198. Albany: Institute for Mesoamerican Studies, University of Albany, and State University of New York, 1988.

———. *La flecha en el blanco. Francisco Tenamaztle y Bartolomé de las Casas en la lucha por los derechos de los indígenas 1541–1556.* México: Editorial Diana y El Colegio de Jalisco, 1995.

———. See also his edition of Sahagún, *Coloquios y doctrina christiana.*

León-Portilla, Miguel, and Carmen Aguilera. *Mapa de México-Tenochtitlan y sus contornos hacia 1550.* México: Celanese, 1986.

López Austin, Alfredo. "De las enfermedades del cuerpo humano y de las medicinas contra ellas." *Estudios de Cultura Náhuatl* (México: UNAM, Instituto de Investigaciones Históricas) 8 (1969): 51–121.

———. "De las plantas medicinales y de otras cosas medicinales." *Estudios de Cultura Náhuatl* (México: UNAM, Instituto de Investigaciones Históricas) 9 (1971): 125–130.

———. "Textos acerca de las partes del cuerpo humano y de las enfermedades y medicinas en los *Primeros memoriales* de Sahagún." *Estudios de Cultura Náhuatl* (México: UNAM, Instituto de Investigaciones Históricas) 10 (1972): 129–153.

———. "Descripción de medicinas en textos dispersos del Libro XI de los *Códices matritenses* y *florentino.*" *Estudios de Cultura Náhuatl* (México: UNAM, Instituto de Investigaciones Históricas) 11 (1974): 45–135.

———. "The Research Method of Bernardino de Sahagún: The Questionnaires." In *Sixteenth-Century Mexico: The Work of Sahagún*, edited by Munro S. Edmonson, 111–149. Albuquerque: School of American Research and University of New Mexico Press, 1974.

———. "Sahagún's Work and the Medicine of the Ancient Nahuas: Possibilities for Study." In *Sixteenth-Century Mexico: The Work of Sahagún*, edited by Munro S. Edmonson, 205–224. Albuquerque: School of American Research and University of New Mexico Press, 1974.

———. *Textos de medicina náhuatl*. México: UNAM, 1975.

———. "Estudio acerca del método de la investigación de fray Bernardino de Sahagún." In *La investigación social de campo en México*, compiled by Jorge Martínez Ríos, 9–56. México: UNAM, Instituto de Investigaciones Sociales, 1976.

———. "El Xiuhpohualli y el Tonalpohualli de los memoriales de Tepepulco." In *Mesoamérica: Homenaje al Doctor Paul Kirchhoff*. Coordinated by Barbro Dahlgren, 41–57. México: INAH, 1979.

———. *Educación mexica. Antología de documentos sahaguntinos*. Selección, paleografía, traducción, introducción, notas y glosario. México: UNAM, 1985.

———. See also his edition of Sahagún, *Historia general*.

López de Gómara, Francisco. *Historia de las conquistas de Hernando Cortés*. 2 vols. Escrita en español por Francisco López de Gómara. Traducida al mexicano y aprobada por verdadera por D. Juan Bautista de Domingo de San Antón Muñón Chimalpahin Cuauhtlehuanitzin, indio mexicano. México: Imprenta de la Testimentaria de Ontiveros, 1826.

Marchetti, Magda [*sic* por Giovanni]. "Hacia la edición crítica de la 'Historia' de Sahagún." *Cuadernos Hispanoamericanos*, 396 (1983): 505–540.

Martínez, José Luis. "Fray Bernardino de Sahagún y sus informantes indígenas, vida y obra." En *El México Antiguo*. Selección y reordenación de la *Historia general de las cosas de la Nueva España* de fray Bernardino de Sahagún y de los informantes indígenas. Edición, prólogos y cronología. Caracas: 1981 (Biblioteca Ayacucho 80).

———. *El Códice florentino y la* Historia general *de Sahagún*. México: Archivo General de la Nación, 1982 (Colección Documentos para la Historia 2).

Máynez Vidal, Pilar. *Religión y magia. Un problema de transculturación lingüística en la obra de Bernardino de Sahagún*. México: UNAM, Escuela Nacional de Estudios Profesionales Acatlán, 1989.

McAndrews, John. *The Open Air Churches of Sixteenth-Century Mexico*. Cambridge, Mass.: Harvard University Press, 1965.

Mendieta, Jerónimo de. *Historia eclesiástica indiana*. Edición de Joaquín García Icazbalceta. México: Antigua Librería, 1870.

Moles, fray Juan Bautista. *Memoria de la provincia de San Gabriel de la orden de Frailes Menores de la Observancia*. Madrid: 1612.

Molina, Alonso de. "Doctrina christiana breue traduzida en lengua mexicana." México: 1546. There is only a manuscript copy published in *Códice franciscano*, edited by Joaquín García Icazbalceta, 1886–1892. Reprinted in México, 1941, II, 34–61.

————. *Vocabulario en la lengua castellana y mexicana*. México: Casa de Juan Pablos, 1555.

————. *Arte de la lengua mexicana y castellana*. Edición facsimilar de la de México, 1571. Reproducción facsimilar, Madrid, 1945 (Colección de Incunables Americanos, siglo XVI, no. 6).

————. *Vocabulario en lengua castellana y mexicana y mexicana y castellana*. Estudio preliminar de Miguel León-Portilla. Reproducción de la facsimilaria de Julius Platzman, Leipzig, 1880, de la original de México, 1571. México: Editorial Porrúa, 1977 (Colección Biblioteca Porrúa 44).

Moreno de los Arcos, Roberto. "Guía de las obras en lenguas indígenas existentes en la Biblioteca Nacional." *Boletín de la Biblioteca Nacional* (México: UNAM) 17 (1966): 21–210.

Motolinía, fray Toribio de Benavente. *Memoriales o Libro de las cosas de la Nueva España y de los naturales de ella*. Edición de Edmundo O'Gorman. México: UNAM, Instituto de Investigaciones Históricas, 1971.

————. "La vida de fray Martín de Valencia." En *Memoriales o Libro de las cosas de la Nueva España y de los naturales de ella*, 175–186. México: UNAM, Instituto de Investigaciones Históricas, 1971.

Nebrija, Elio Antonio de. *Diccionario latino-español*. Salamanca: 1491. Facsimile reproduction edited by Germán Colón and Amadeus J. Soberanes. Barcelona: Puvill Editor, 1979.

————. *Gramática de la lengua castellana*. Edited by Antonio Quilis. Madrid: Editorial Nacional, 1980.

————. *Introductiones Latinae*. Edición facsimilar de la de 1481, a cargo de un colectivo editorial bajo la dirección de la Universidad de Salamanca. Salamanticae: 1981.

Nicholson, H. B. "Sahagún's 'Primeros memoriales,' Tepepulco 1559–1561." In *Handbook of Middle American Indians*, vol. 13, 207–218. Austin: University of Texas Press, 1973.

————. "Tepepulco, the Locale of the First Stage of Fray Bernardino de Sahagún's Great Ethnographic Project, Historical and Cultural Notes." In *Mesoamerican Archeology: New Approaches,* edited by Norman Hammond, 145–154. London: Duckworth, 1974.

————. "Recent Sahaguntine Studies: A Review." In *The Work of Bernardino de Sahagún, Pioneer Ethnographer of Sixteenth-Century Aztec Mexico,* edited by J. Jorge Klor de Alva et al. Studies on Culture and Society, vol. 2, 229–253. Albany: Institute for Mesoamerican Studies, University of Albany, and State University of New York, 1988.

Nicolau D'Olwer, Luis. *Fray Bernardino de Sahagún (1499–1590).* México: Instituto Panamericano de Geografía e Historia, 1952 (Colección Historiadores de América 9).

————. *Fray Bernardino de Sahagún (1499–1590).* Translated by Mauricio J. Mixco. Foreward by Miguel León-Portilla. Salt Lake City: University of Utah Press, 1987.

Nicolau D'Olwer, Luis, and Howard F. Cline. "Sahagún and His Work." In *Handbook of Middle American Indians,* vol. 13, 186–189. Austin: University of Texas Press, 1973,.

Nieremberg, Juan Eusebio. *Historia Naturae Maximae Peregrinae.* Amberes: Baltasar Moreto, 1635.

Northrop, F. S. C., and Helen H. Livingston, eds. *Cross-Cultural Understanding: Epistemology in Anthropology.* New York: Harper and Row Publishers, 1964.

Ocaranza, Fernando. *El Imperial Colegio de Indios de Santa Cruz de Santiago de Tlatelolco.* México: 1934.

Oliger, Livario. "Sahagún OFM e una sua visita di S. Bernardino in lingua nahuatl." *Bulletino di Studi Bernardiniani* (Siena) 2 (1936): 207– 212.

————. "Breve compendio de los ritos idolátricos de Nueva España." Edición, notas y comentarios del P. Livario Oliger. *Antonianum* 17 (1942): 3–38, 133–174. Hay tambien edición separada: *Breve compendio de los ritos idolátricos de Nueva España,* auctore B. de Sahagún, O. F. M. Pio V dicatum. Edidit notisque illustravit P. Livarius Oliger, O. F. M. Romae: Via Merulana, 1942.

Oroz, fray Pedro de, fray Gerónimo de Mendieta y fray Francisco Suárez. "Relación de la descripción de la provincia del Santo Evangelio que es en las Indias Occidentales que llaman la Nueva España. Hecha el año de 1585." Introducción y notas por fray Fidel de J. Chauvet. *Anales de la Provincia Franciscana del Santo Evangelio de México* (México) año 4, no. 2 (abril-junio 1947): 1–203.

————. *The Oroz Codex* (The Oroz Relation, or Relation of the description of the Holy Gospel Province in New Spain, and the lives of the founders and other noteworthy men of said province). Composed by fray Pedro de Oroz, 1584–1586. Translated and edited by Angélico Chávez. Washington, D.C.: Academy of American Franciscan History, 1972.

————. *Relación de la descripción de la provincia del Santo Evangelio que es en las Indias Occidentales que llaman la Nueva España. Hecha el año de 1585.* Introducción y notas por fray Fidel de J. Chauvet. Nueva edición. México: Editorial Junípero Serra, 1975.

Paso y Troncoso, Francisco del. "Estudios sobre el códice mexicano del padre Sahagún conservado en la Biblioteca Mediceo-Laurenziana de Florencia." *Anales del Museo Nacional de Arqueología, Historia y Etnología* (Mexico), 4a. época, 4 (1926): 316–320.

————. "Carta a Joaquín García Icazbalceta, dada en Amecameca a 17 de octubre de 1884." Editada por Ignacio Bernal y notas de Miguel León-Portilla. *Estudios de Cultura Náhuatl* (México: UNAM, Instituto de Investigaciones Históricas) 15 (1982): 247–290.

————. "La obra de Sahagún, otra carta inédita de Francisco del Paso y Troncoso." Editada por Ignacio Bernal. *Estudios de Cultura Náhuatl* (México: UNAM, Instituto de Investigaciones Históricas) 16 (1983): 265–325.

————. See also his edition of Sahagún, *Historia general.*

Peset, José Luis. "Fray Bernardino de Sahagún o la necesidad de actuar desde el conocimiento." En *Ciencia, vida y espacio en Iberoamérica,* vol. 1, 179–191. Madrid: Consejo Superior de Investigaciones Científicas, 1989.

Peterson, Jeanette Favrot. "The 'Florentine Codex.' Imagery and the Colonial 'Tlacuilo.'" In *The Work of Bernardino de Sahagún, Pioneer Ethnographer of Sixteenth-Century Aztec Mexico,* edited by J. Jorge Klor de Alva et al. Studies on Culture and Society, vol. 2, 273–293. Albany: Institute for Mesoamerican Studies, University of Albany, and State University of New York, 1988.

Phelan, John L. *El reino milenario de los franciscanos en el Nuevo Mundo.* México: UNAM, Instituto de Investigaciones Históricas, 1972.

Prem, Hanns J. "Calendar Traditions in the Writings of Sahagún." In *The Work of Bernardino de Sahagún, Pioneer Ethnographer of Sixteenth-Century Aztec Mexico,* edited by J. Jorge Klor de Alva et al. Studies on Culture and Society, vol. 2, 135–149. Albany: Institute for Mesoamerican Studies, University of Albany, and State University of New York, 1988.

"Proceso contra fray Pedro de San Sebastián, provincial de la orden de San Francisco." Archivo General de la Nación, Inquisición, vol. 20, doc. 12, citado por Georges Baudot, *La pugna franciscana por México.*

México: Consejo Nacional para la Cultura y las Artes y Alianza Popular Mexicana, 1990.

Proceso inquisitorial del cacique de Tetzcoco. Edición de Luis González Obregón. México: Publicaciones de la Comisión Organizadora del Archivo General y Público de la Nación. 1910.

Puga, Vasco de. *Provisiones, cédulas, instrucciones para el gobierno de la Nueva España.* Edición facsimilar de la impresa en México por Pedro Ocharte en 1563. Madrid: Ediciones de Cultura Hispánica, 1945 (Colección de Incunables Americanos, siglo XVI).

Quiñones Keber, Eloise. "Reading Images: The Sahaguntine Illustrations." In *The Work of Bernardino de Sahagún. Pioneer Ethnographer of Sixteenth-Century Aztec Mexico,* edited by J. Jorge Klor de Alva et al. Studies on Culture and Society, vol. 2, 199–210. Albany: Institute for Mesoamerican Studies, University of Albany, and State University of New York, 1988.

———. "Deity Images and Texts in the 'Primeros Memoriales' and the 'Florentine Codex.'" In *The Work of Bernardino de Sahagún, Pioneer Ethnographer of Sixteenth-Century Aztec Mexico,* edited by J. Jorge Klor de Alva et al. Studies on Culture and Society, vol. 2. 255–272. Albany: Institute for Mesoamerican Studies, University of Albany, and State University of New York, 1988.

———. "Appendix. The Sahaguntine Corpus: A Bibliographic Index of Extant Documents." In *The Work of Bernardino de Sahagún, Pioneer Ethnographer of Sixteenth-Century Aztec Mexico,* edited by J. Jorge Klor de Alva et al. Studies on Culture and Society, vol. 2. 341–345. Albany: Institute for Mesoamerican Studies, University of Albany, and State University of New York, 1988.

Ramírez, José Fernando. "Códices mejicanos de Fr. Bernardino de Sahagún." *Boletín de la Real Academia de la Historia* (Madrid) 6 (1885): 85–124.

———. "Apuntes para la cronología de Sahagún." *Anales del Museo Nacional* (México) 1a. época, 7 (1903): 137–152.

———. "Códice mexicano de fray Bernardino de Sahagún." *Anales del Museo Nacional* (México) 2a. época, 1 (1903): 1–34.

Ricard, Robert. *La conquista espiritual de México. Ensayo sobre el apostolado y los métodos misioneros de las órdenes mendicantes en la Nueva España de 1523–1572.* Traducción de Angel Ma. Garibay. México: Editorial Jus-Editorial Polis, 1945.

Robertson, Donald. *Mexican Manuscript Painting of the Early Colonial Period: The Metropolitan Schools.* New Haven, Conn.: Yale University Press, 1959.

———. "The Sixteenth-Century Mexican Encyclopedia of Fray Bernardino de Sahagún." *Cahiers d'Histoire Mondiale* (Paris) 9, no. 3 (1966): 617–628.

———. "The Treatment of Architecture in the *Florentine Codex* of Sahagún." In *Sixteenth-Century Mexico: The Work of Sahagún,* edited by Munro S. Edmonson, 151–164. Albuquerque: School of American Research and University of New Mexico Press, 1974.

Rosell, Cayetano. "*Historia universal de las cosas de la Nueva España* por el M.R.P. Bernardino de Sahagún." *Boletín de la Real Academia de la Historia* (Madrid) 2 (1883): 181–185.

San Antonio, Juan de. O. F. M. *Biblioteca universal franciscana.* 3 vols. Madrid: Tipografía de la Casa de la Madre Agueda, 1732–1733.

Seler, Eduard. "Vorschlag, die aztekischer Manuscripten Sahagún's Herausgegeben mit Übersetzung." In *Actas del IX Congreso Internacional de Americanistas,* I, 116–117. Huelva, España: 1892.

———. "Zauberei und Zauberer in alten Mexico." In *Museum für Völkerkunde,* VI, Heft 2–4, 29–57. Berlin: 1899.

Sierra, Justo. *Evolución política del pueblo mexicano.* México: Fondo de Cultura Económica, 1950.

Solana, Marcial. *Historia de la filosofía española.* Vol. 2. Madrid: Espasa, 1941.

Suarez de Peralta, Juan. *Tratado del descubrimiento de las Indias (noticias históricas de Nueva España.* Compuesto en 1589. Federico Gómez de Orozco, editor. México: Secretaría de Educación Pública, 1949.

Sullivan, Thelma D. "Nahuatl Proverbs, Conundrums, and Metaphors Collected by Sahagún." *Estudios de Cultura Náhuatl* (México: UNAM, Instituto de Investigaciones Históricas) 14 (1963): 43–177.

———. "Tlatoani and Tlatocayotl in the Sahagún Manuscripts." *Estudios de Cultura Náhuatl* (México: UNAM, Instituto de Investigaciones Históricas) 14 (1980): 225–238.

———. "A Scattering of Jades: The Words of Aztec Elders." In *Symbol and Meaning Beyond the Closed Community: Essays in Mesoamerican Ideas,* edited by Gary H. Gossen, 9–17. Studies on Culture and Society. Albany: Institute for Mesoamerican Studies, University of Albany, and State University of New York, 1986.

Temprano, Juan Carlos, ed. Historia de las cosas de la Nueva España *de Bernardino de Sahagún.* 2 vols. Madrid: Historia 16, 1990 (Crónicas de América 55).

Toro, Alfonso. "Manuscritos en lengua mexicana existentes en la Biblioteca Nacional de México." *Ethnos: Revista dedicada al estudio y mejoría de la población indígena de México* (México), 2a. época, 1, no. 1 (1923): 72–77.

————. "Importancia etnográfica y lingüística de las obras de fray Bernardino de Sahagún." *Anales del Museo Nacional de Arqueología, Historia y Etnografía* (México), 4a. época, 2 (1924): 1–18.
————. "Importancia etnográfica y lingüística de las obras de fray Ber-
nardino de Sahagún." En *Annaes do XX Congresso Internacional de
Americanistas* (Rio de Janeiro, 20 a 30 de agosto de 1922), II, 2a. parte,
263–277. Rio de Janeiro: Imprenta Nacional, 1928.
Torquemada, fray Juan de. *Monarquía indiana.* Edición coordinada por
Miguel León-Portilla. Vol. 1–6 texto, vol. 7 estudios e índices. Méxi-
co: UNAM, Instituto de Investigaciones Históricas, 1975–1983.
Torre, Ernesto de la. *Fray Pedro de Gante.* México: Seminario de Cultura
Mexicana, 1973.
Vetancourt, Agustín de. *Teatro mexicano. Descripción breve de los sucesos
ejemplares, históricos y religiosos del Nuevo Mundo de las Indias. Crónica
de la provincia del Santo Evangelio de México, menologio franciscano.*
Edición facsimilar de la de México, 1697–1698. México: Porrúa, 1971.
Villoro, Luis. *Sahagún or the Limits of the Discovery of the Other.* Colllege
Park: University of Maryland, 1999 (1992 Lecture Series, Working
Papers No. 2).
Viñaza, Conde de la. *Bibliografía española de lenguas indígenas de América.*
Estudio preliminar de Carmelo Sáenz de Santa María. Edición fac-
similar de la de 1892. Madrid: Ediciones Atlas, 1977.
Zantwijk, Rudolf van. "La cosmovisión de los informantes indígenas
interrogados por Sahagún en Tepepulco (primera mitad del siglo
XVI)." In *The Indians of Mexico in Pre-Columbian and Modern Times.* In-
ternational Colloquium, edited by M. Jansen and Th. J. J. Leyenaar,
135–169. Leiden: Rijksmuseum voor Volkerkunde, 1982.
————, ed. *De Azteken: Kroniek van een verdwenen cultuur* (by Bernardino
de Sahagún). Amsterdam: Meuleuhoff, 1991.
Zimmermann, Gunter. "Fray Bernardino de Sahagún's Enzyklopädie
der aztekischen Kultur: Hintergrunde, Entstehung, Charakterisier-
ung der Bücher 9 und 10, Metaphorik." *Baessler Archiv, Beiträge zur
Völkerkunde* (Neue Folge) 23, no. 2 (1975): 347–364.
Zulaica Gárate, Román. *Los franciscanos y la imprenta en México en el siglo
XVI.* Estudio bio-bibliográfico. México: Pedro Robredo, 1939.

INDEX

Bandelier, Fanny R., 17
Barbarians, 136
Barberini, Francesco (Cardinal), 125
Bassacio, Arnald, 96
Baudot, Georges, 19, 214, 216, 250
Beltrami, Jules-César, 36
Beltrán de Guzmán, Nuño, 40, 82, 84, 86, 87, 89, 107
Belvís of Monroy, 47, 109
Benavente Motolinía, Toribio de, 47–48, 73, 77, 83, 100, 107, 140, 200–201, 202, 256
Benedictines, 32
Berrocal, Our Lady of, 46–47
Bestiary, 179
Beverages, 161
Bible, 44, 210. *See also* New Testament; Scriptures
Biondelli, Bernardino, 14, 36, 247
Book of the Days, 178
Book of the Conquest, 221, 248, 251, 252
Bosch de Souza, María Guadalupe, 17
Brief Compendium, 17, 199–200, 204
Brief declaration (text), 208
Brinton, Daniel G., 14
Briviesca, Critóbal de, 203
Browne, Walden, 9–10
Buildings, 136, 161
Bustamante García, Jesús, 18
Bustamante, Carlos María, 13, 234, 235

Calendar, 179, 182, 200, 230, 232; computations, 149; Gregorian, 231; Nahua, 16, 183
Calepino, Ambrosio, 135
Calpan, 104, 107
Camino del cielo, 231
Campeche, 132
Cancino, Juan, 249
Cantares, 196. *See also* Songs

Canticles, 138. *See also Psalmodia christiana*
Carnality. *See* Sins
Carochi, Horacio, 12
Casas, Bartolomé de las, 42, 74
Castillo, Victor Manuel, 17
Castro, Florencio Vicente, 22
Celestial phenomena, 149, 205. *See also* Heavenly bodies
Ceremonies, 148
Cervantes de Salazar, Francisco, 227
Ceynos, Francisco, 88
Characters, 135. *See also* Writing system
Charles V, 39, 40, 41, 86, 141, 251
Chavero, Alfredo, 13
Chiapas, 100
Chichimecs, origins, 160, 161, 162
Chimalpahin Cuauhtlehuanitzin, Domingo de San Antón Muñón, 12, 26, 225, 256
China, 253
Chirinos, Peralmíndez, 79
Chocaman (town), 108, 109
Cholula, 104, 108, 109, 110, 136
Christian Psalmody. *See Psalmodia christiana*
Christianity, 80, 93, 107, 109, 132, 134, 145, 159, 208, 247, 251, 252, 253; primitive, 108, 232
Chroniclers, 142, 225, 255
Cicero, 136
Ciudad Real, Antonio de, 230
Ciudad Rodrigo, Antonio de, 26, 69, 72
Clapion, Juan, 47
Clark, Charles Upson, 125
Clash of beliefs, 172–73. *See also* Indians, and friars
Clavijero, Francisco Xavier, 12
Cline, Howard F., 18, 214, 215, 218, 235
Cline, Susan L., 235

University of Mexico, 122, 227
Utensils, 159
Utopias, 88

Valencia, Martín de, 46, 60, 81,
109, 232, 251
Valeriano, Antonio (Sahagún's
assistant), 144, 173
Vegerano, Alonso (Sahagún's as-
sistant), 144, 173
Velasco, Blanca (wife of Viceroy
Manrique), 248
Velasco, Luis de (viceroy), 146
Velázquez Diego (governor of
Cuba), 141
Vélez, Andrés, 249
Veracruz (Mexico), 141
Vetancourt, Agustín de, 12
Villoro, Luis, 17
Virgil, 136
Vision of the Vanquished, 129,
246, 259
Vives, Juan Luis, 44
Vocabulary, 135, 136, 183; trilingual,
230, 245, 246. See also Linguistics
Volcanic activity, Sahagún on, 111

Weapons, 160, 161
Welch, William, 125
Western Indies, 253
Words, 134, 135, 272. See also
Linguistics
Writing system, 135, 144, 179

Writings, Sahagún's: categoriza-
tion, 176; cessation of support,
198, 253; clean copy, 183, 196,
208, 211, 214, 215, 252; columns,
233, 234; dispersed, 199, 202,
254; edited, 165–66; friars' complaints, 206; idolatry, 217; judgment, 197, 201; lost manuscript
("from 1569"), 171; Nahuatl,
138, 147, 148, 215; organization,
139, 168, 169–70, 171, 174–75,
182; religious themes, 208;
returned, 204; royal orders,
210–11, 216, 217, 219, 225; summary of, 200; transcriptions,
146; translations, 115, 204, 205,
209, 210

Xaltocan, 113
Ximénez de Cisneros, Francisco,
39, 43, 44, 48
Xochicalco, 136

Yucatán, 132

Zantwijk, Rudolph Van, 19
Zorita, Alonso, 113
Zuazo, Alonso, 79
Zumárraga, Juan de (archbishop
of Mexico), 70, 83, 84, 85, 95,
100, 107; letter to Charles V, 86;
questionnaire, 89

Made in the USA
Middletown, DE
04 September 2020